Fundamentals of Business Organizations for Paralegals

ASPEN PUBLISHERS

Fundamentals of Business Organizations for Paralegals

Third Edition

Deborah E. Bouchoux, Esq.

Georgetown University
Member, California (inactive) and District of Columbia bars

Wolters Kluwer
Law & Business

AUSTIN   BOSTON   CHICAGO   NEW YORK   THE NETHERLANDS

Aspen Publishers
Attn: Permissions Department
76 Ninth Avenue, 7th Floor
New York, NY 10011-5201

To contact Customer Care, e-mail customer.care@aspenpublishers.com, call 1-800-234-1660, fax 1-800-901-9075, or mail correspondence to:

Aspen Publishers
Attn: Order Department
PO Box 990
Frederick, MD 21705

Printed in the United States of America.

1 2 3 4 5 6 7 8 9 0

ISBN 978-0-7355-7912-5

Library of Congress Cataloging-in-Publication Data

Bouchoux, Deborah E., 1950-
   Fundamentals of Business organizations for paralegals / Deborah E. Bouchoux. — 3rd ed.
   p. cm.
   Includes index.
   ISBN 978-0-7355-7912-5
   1. Business enterprises — Law and legislation — United States. 2. Legal assistants — United States — Handbooks, manuals, etc. I. Title.

KF1355.B68 2009
346.73'065 — dc22

                                                                    2009017550

About Wolters Kluwer Law & Business

Wolters Kluwer Law & Business is a leading provider of research information and workflow solutions in key specialty areas. The strengths of the individual brands of Aspen Publishers, CCH, Kluwer Law International and Loislaw are aligned within Wolters Kluwer Law & Business to provide comprehensive, in-depth solutions and expert-authored content for the legal, professional and education markets.

CCH was founded in 1913 and has served more than four generations of business professionals and their clients. The CCH products in the Wolters Kluwer Law & Business group are highly regarded electronic and print resources for legal, securities, antitrust and trade regulation, government contracting, banking, pension, payroll, employment and labor, and healthcare reimbursement and compliance professionals.

Aspen Publishers is a leading information provider for attorneys, business professionals and law students. Written by preeminent authorities, Aspen products offer analytical and practical information in a range of specialty practice areas from securities law and intellectual property to mergers and acquisitions and pension/benefits. Aspen's trusted legal education resources provide professors and students with high-quality, up-to-date and effective resources for successful instruction and study in all areas of the law.

Kluwer Law International supplies the global business community with comprehensive English-language international legal information. Legal practitioners, corporate counsel and business executives around the world rely on the Kluwer Law International journals, loose-leafs, books and electronic products for authoritative information in many areas of international legal practice.

Loislaw is a premier provider of digitized legal content to small law firm practitioners of various specializations. Loislaw provides attorneys with the ability to quickly and efficiently find the necessary legal information they need, when and where they need it, by facilitating access to primary law as well as state-specific law, records, forms and treatises.

Wolters Kluwer Law & Business, a unit of Wolters Kluwer, is headquartered in New York and Riverwoods, Illinois. Wolters Kluwer is a leading multinational publisher and information services company.

To my colleague, mentor, and friend,
Frederick G. Tellam

Summary of Contents

Contents

Introduction to Business Organizations and Agency Law

2

◆ ◆ ◆

Sole Proprietorships

3

◆ ◆ ◆

General Partnerships

4
◆ ◆ ◆

Limited Partnerships

5
◆ ◆ ◆

Limited Liability Partnerships

6
◆ ◆ ◆

Limited Liability Companies

7

◆ ◆ ◆

Introduction to Corporations

8
◆ ◆ ◆

Formation of Corporations

9

◆ ◆ ◆

Corporate Financial Structure

10
◆ ◆ ◆

Corporate Management

11
◆ ◆ ◆

Corporate Dividends

12
◆ ◆ ◆

Changes in the Corporate Structure and Corporate Combinations

14
◆ ◆ ◆

Termination of Corporate Existence

15

◆ ◆ ◆

Corporate Variations

Contents

Preface

Concepts relating to business organizations surround us every day. The evening news broadcasts often begin with a report on stock prices, the recent corporate accounting or compensation scandals, or the latest corporate mergers. The ups and downs of major companies such as Microsoft and General Motors are analyzed in depth. Commercials promote brokerage companies that facilitate stock purchases. Newspapers often devote a separate section to business and financial news. Nevertheless, many of us have only a vague notion of the import and effect of the news of business organizations that we hear about every day. Some individuals are intimidated by the financial sections of newspapers and periodicals, assuming that only those with degrees in business or finance are capable of understanding the business news.

This text is intended to provide readers with a fundamental understanding of the various types of business organizations that operate in the United States. Learning about the advantages and disadvantages of different forms of business entities will provide you with the knowledge necessary to understand the business concepts that surround us. Equally important, understanding the various ways in which business is conducted in this country will enhance your ability to perform as a paralegal. According to a 2008 survey by the National Association of Legal Assistants, except for litigation, corporate work represents the largest specialty practice area for paralegals, with 32 percent of paralegals engaged in some corporate work.

Although the study of business organizations is undoubtedly most useful for paralegals intending to work in the corporate field, the concepts discussed in this text cross over to many other practice fields. For example, litigation paralegals will need to know whether partners in a partnership may be personally sued for partnership obligations, whether members in a limited liability company are liable for the company's debts, and under which circumstances corporate directors may be sued for negligence in managing their corporations. Paralegals working with general practitioners will need to know how to form the business organizations described in this text, draft resolutions, and prepare minutes for corporate meetings.

Each of the varieties of business organizations is discussed thoroughly. The nature of the entity, its advantages and disadvantages, the relative ease with which the entity may be formed, its dissolution, and its tax consequences are all addressed. Each chapter includes a discussion of the pertinent topic, a section devoted to the possible tasks to be performed by paralegals relating to that business enterprise, a brief summary of a judicial opinion illustrating a topic discussed in the chapter, references to Internet resources enabling you to locate additional materials of interest, a brief summary of the key features covered in the chapter, a list of key terms in the chapter, discussion questions challenging you to apply the concepts discussed in the chapter to fact patterns, and questions requiring you to locate information accessing commonly used business-related Internet sites.

The text begins with an introduction to the various business entities and then progresses from the simplest, the sole proprietorship, through partnerships, to the most complex, the business corporation. The newest forms of business entities, the limited liability partnership and limited liability company, are also discussed. Chapters include sample forms to illustrate the principles discussed and key terms highlighting the terms discussed. Appendices provide additional forms, and a glossary is included for easy reference to the many and often difficult terms used in the law of business organizations.

This third edition of the text includes the following new features:

- New case summaries illustrating core principles in each chapter
- Discussion of the newly revised Uniform Limited Liability Company Act of 2006
- Treatment of the financial crisis of 2008
- Recent amendments to the Model Business Corporations Act
- Enhanced discussion of the 2001 Uniform Limited Partnership Act and limited liability limited partnerships
- New discussion on entity domestications (changing the state of organization) and conversions (changing the form of a business entity)
- Discussion of new and emerging trends in corporate governance, shareholder activism, and corporate reform, including the trend toward electing directors by majority rather than plurality vote
- Updated forms

When you begin reading this text, you might be unfamiliar with most of the business enterprises and concepts discussed. As you move forward in class and through the chapters and discussion questions, you will readily be able to measure your progress. When you complete this text and your class, you will have gained a thorough introduction to business organizations as well as familiarity with the terms and concepts required by paralegals in the business or corporate fields and those that we hear and read about each and every day.

Deborah E. Bouchoux
Spring 2009

Acknowledgments

I would like to express my sincere appreciation to the many individuals who contributed greatly to the development of this text. As always, my first thoughts and gratitude go to Susan M. Sullivan, Program Director of the Paralegal Program at the University of San Diego, who gave me my first teaching job and opened a door to a challenging and exciting field. Sue has been a valued friend as well as a respected colleague.

A special thank you to my family: my husband, Donald, and our children Meaghan, twins Elizabeth and Patrick, and Robert, for their patience and understanding while I completed this text and its third edition.

Many thanks also to the various reviewers who evaluated the manuscript on behalf of the publisher. I have also received continuing evaluation from my students throughout my twenty-year career as a paralegal educator. My students' comments and insights regarding methods of teaching, productive assignments, and effective class discussion have been a great help.

I wish to thank the following states whose forms are reprinted in the text: California, Connecticut, Delaware, Florida, Nevada, New York, and Washington.

Finally, a special thank you to the individuals at Aspen Publishers who generously provided guidance and support throughout the development of this text, including Carol McGeehan, Publisher; Melody Davies, Editorial Director; Betsy Kenny, Developmental Editor; David Herzig, Executive Legal Editor; Kaesmene Harrison Banks, Senior Editor; and Teresa F. Horton, Copyeditor.

Fundamentals of
Business
Organizations
for
Paralegals

1

◆ ◆ ◆

Introduction to Business Organizations and Agency Law

◆ ◆ ◆

A. Introduction

This text will discuss the nine most common ways of doing business in this country. While each type of business structure will be described in detail in the chapters to come, a brief overview follows. Other enterprises, such as joint ventures and nonprofit corporations, will also be discussed in later chapters.

1. Sole Proprietorship

In a **sole proprietorship**, one individual owns all of the business assets and is the sole decision-maker. The sole proprietor has unlimited **personal liability** assets for business obligations, meaning that liability for business debts extends beyond business assets to the sole proprietor's personal assets, such as savings accounts, furniture, and other personal belongings.

2. General Partnership

In a **general partnership**, two or more persons co-own all of the business assets and share decision-making, profits, and losses. All general partners have unlimited personal liability for the business obligations.

3. Limited Partnership

A **limited partnership** is managed by one or more general partners, all of whom have unlimited personal liability for business obligations, and one or more

Sole proprietorship
Business owned and operated by one person

Personal liability
Liability extending beyond business assets to personal

General partnership
A voluntary association of two or more persons to carry on a business for profit

Limited partnership
Business created under a state statute in which some partners have unlimited personal liability and others have no liability beyond the amount contributed to the business

limited partners, who do not manage the business and have no liability beyond the amount contributed to the business.

4. Limited Liability Partnership

Limited liability partnership
Business entity providing limited liability for its partners

This new form of business enterprise alters a basic principle of partnership law: Partners are not liable for the torts or wrongful acts of their co-partners. In nearly all states, the partners are not personally liable either for the torts of their partners or contractual obligations incurred by the entity or other partners. These entities are ideally suited for professionals, such as doctors, lawyers, and accountants.

5. Limited Liability Company

Limited liability company
Business entity providing limited liability for its members

Another new form of business structure is the **limited liability company**. In all states, this business entity provides limited liability for its members whether obligations arise in tort or contract. These entities may be managed by their members or by designated managers.

6. Business Corporation

Business corporation
Legal entity existing under the authority of the state legislature

A **business** (or *for-profit*) **corporation** is an entity created under state statute. This legal entity may own property, enter into contracts, and sue and be sued. Because the business corporation is a "person," it is subject to taxation. In what is referred to as *double taxation*, its owners, called *shareholders*, also pay tax on distributions made to them, although the tax rates have been reduced under a 2003 tax bill passed by Congress.

Shareholders are protected from personal liability, and their loss is limited to their investment in the corporation. Although the shareholders own the corporation, the corporation is managed by its board of directors, who typically appoint officers to carry out the directors' policies and goals.

7. Professional Corporation

Professional corporation
Corporation formed by professionals

Professionals such as doctors, lawyers, and accountants may incorporate to obtain certain tax and other benefits available to business corporations. Nevertheless, these professionals remain personally liable for their own negligence and the negligence of those they supervise.

8. S Corporation

S corporation
Corporation that passes all income to its shareholders, who pay tax on income

Certain small business corporations are provided relief against double taxation. Called an **S corporation** after the original subchapter of the Internal Revenue Code providing such relief, the corporation itself does not pay taxes, and all income earned is passed through to the shareholders. All shareholders (who must not number more than 100) must agree to the election of S status, and only eligible corporations may apply for this status. A typical business corporation is referred to as a *C corporation* to distinguish it from an S corporation.

9. Close Corporation

Close corporations are generally corporations owned by small numbers of family members and friends, who are active in operating the business. Only certain types of corporations can qualify to be treated as close corporations. The shareholders in a close corporation are allowed more flexibility in operating the corporation and usually function without adhering to all of the formalities required of other business corporations.

Close corporation
Small corporation whose shareholders are active in managing the business and that operates informally

---

PRACTICE TIP

It can be difficult to understand the various types of business structures and their features. Consider keeping a "cheat sheet" or index card near your desk on which you describe the most prominent features of each form of entity. After you refer to this several times, you will likely have no difficulty remembering the differences between a general partnership, a limited partnership, and a limited liability partnership. Alternatively, access the site "My Corporation" at *http://mycorporation.intuit.com* and select "Comparison Chart," or refer to the inside cover of this text for a chart comparing and contrasting business structures.

B. Considerations in Selection of Business Enterprise

Although a sole proprietorship or other business entity may be ideal for one individual, it may be inadvisable for another. Determining which form of business structure is the most appropriate for a client involves evaluation of a number of factors. The attorney you work with will counsel the client to consider the following factors:

- **Ease of Formation**. The ease with which a business can be formed should be carefully considered. For example, a sole proprietorship is easy and inexpensive to form, whereas a corporation requires compliance with state statutes and can be expensive to form.
- **Management**. Some individuals prefer to manage their business themselves, and others prefer to partner with colleagues to manage the enterprise.
- **Liability**. The liability an individual faces is one of the most critical factors to consider in selecting a form of business enterprise. Some enterprises shield the individuals involved from any personal liability, whereas others expose the business owner to greater risk.
- **Continuity of Existence**. Some enterprises, such as corporations, are capable of existing perpetually. Others, such as sole proprietorships, do not have such continuity of existence. Thus, consideration should be given to the intended duration of the enterprise.

- **Transferability**. Clients must consider how easy it is to "get into" and "get out of" the business enterprise. It may be difficult to withdraw from a partnership, but it is usually easy to sell stock and transfer out of a corporation. If clients foresee a need to liquidate their investment in a business for cash, they should consider how easy or difficult it will be to transfer into and out of the enterprise.
- **Profits and Losses**. A sole proprietor retains all business profits, but she is also solely liable for all losses. Partners share profits and losses with each other, but some losses suffered by a partner might arise due to another partner's actions. Clients should evaluate the allocation of profits and losses when considering business enterprises.
- **Taxation**. Clients should always consider applicable tax requirements. For some, the individual tax rates may be best; for others, the corporate tax rates may yield the best advantages. Many entities afford single or pass-through taxation; corporations are burdened by double taxation.

C. How Business Is Conducted in This Country

Many individuals perceive that business in the United States is conducted by huge corporations that affect every aspect of financial growth and development. Most would be surprised to discover that sole proprietorships (businesses conducted by one person) dominate the business landscape.

According to the *Statistical Abstract of the United States* 483 (128th ed. 2009), more than 70 percent of business in this country is conducted by sole proprietors. Moreover, more than 90 percent of all workers in the United States work in businesses employing fewer than 100 people. Nevertheless, business corporations account for a disproportionately high share of revenue. In 2005, business receipts showed the following approximate amounts:

- Sole proprietorships: $1.2 trillion
- Partnerships: $3.7 trillion
- Business corporations: $24 trillion

See Figure 1-1 for a chart showing where individual employees worked in 2004.

D. Agency in Business Organizations

Agent
One who acts for or represents another

Principal
The person for whom an agent acts

Understanding the concepts of agency is necessary to understand the way business enterprises operate. In brief, an **agent** is someone who agrees to act for or represent another, called the **principal**. Because businesses usually act through third parties, it is important to determine whether these third parties have the authority to obligate or bind the business and its partners or members.

Agency relationships arise in a variety of settings. When an employee of a store sells goods, he does so as the agent of the store owner, the principal. When a partner in a partnership signs a contract, she may bind the partnership under the principles of agency law. When the president of a corporation signs a lease,

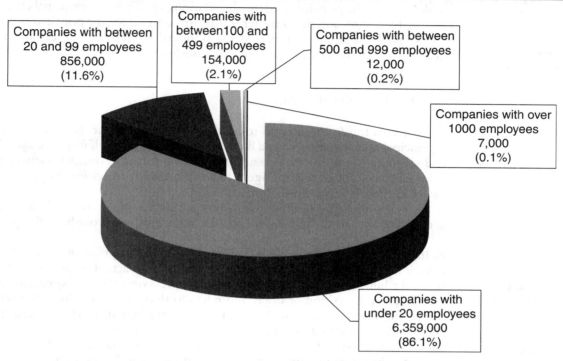

FIGURE 1-1

Companies Indexed by Numbers of Employees (2004) (In thousands)

Companies with between 20 and 99 employees 856,000 (11.6%)

Companies with between100 and 499 employees 154,000 (2.1%)

Companies with between 500 and 999 employees 12,000 (0.2%)

Companies with over 1000 employees 7,000 (0.1%)

Companies with under 20 employees 6,359,000 (86.1%)

Source: *Statistical Abstract of the United States* 496 (127th ed. 2008)

he binds the corporation under agency principles. Agency relationships permeate almost all forms of business enterprise. Thus, a thorough understanding of some of the basic principles of agency law is critical to understanding the various forms of business enterprise to be discussed in this book.

1. *Formation of Agency Relationship*

There are two primary ways in which an agency relationship can be created:

Agreement. Most agency relationships are created by mutual agreement: One party agrees to act for the other, either orally or in writing. For example, if a home owner decides to sell her home and lists it with a real estate agency, the parties will likely set forth their relationship and duties in a written agreement. An agreement by which one party agrees to act for the other is an **express agency**, whether it is written or oral.

Agency relationships can also be implied. For example, individuals who work in small retail shops seldom have written agreements detailing their duties. Yet the acts they perform on behalf of their employers (ordering goods, accepting returns,

Express agency
An agency agreement, written or oral

selling goods) bind their employers, the principals. These are examples of **implied agency**; there is no formal agreement, yet their words, conduct, or prior dealings show the existence of their agency relationship.

Estoppel. Sometimes an agency relationship arises because it would be inequitable to allow the principal to deny the relationship. Thus, if a principal creates the reasonable impression that another is authorized to act for the principal, an agency by estoppel has been created, and the principal is precluded or estopped from denying the existence of the agency relationship.

2. *Authority of Agents*

Often a third party desires to hold a principal liable for the acts of an agent. A principal may attempt to avoid liability by distancing herself from the agent's acts and claiming the agent had no authority to act for the principal. Generally, the third party will allege that the agent had the authority to act for the principal and thus the agent's acts bind the principal.

An agent has the ability to bind the principal in three ways: by being granted actual authority to do an act, by apparent authority, or through ratification.

Actual Authority. Generally, a person may properly appoint another to perform any act he could perform. Thus, a principal may grant actual authority to an agent to act for him. This actual authority can be express or implied. **Express authority** may be given in writing or orally and refers to those acts the principal specifically directs the agent to perform. An agent also has **implied authority** to perform acts customarily performed by an agent or those acts that are reasonably necessary to allow the agent to perform her duties. For example, a manager hired by a restaurant has not only the express authority to do acts directed by the restaurant's owner, but has the implied authority to do any acts reasonably necessary to operate the restaurant, such as hiring and firing employees, ordering supplies, and giving free meals to unhappy customers.

Apparent Authority. Apparent authority arises when by his conduct, a principal causes a third person reasonably to believe the agent has the authority to act for the principal. Assume that an employee always accompanies her employer, the owner of a dress shop, to New York City to the annual fashion shows to order new fashions for the shop. If one year only the employee attends and orders the new stock, the store owner would be bound to pay for the employee's orders because the store owner's previous conduct reasonably led others to believe the employee had the authority to make orders. The store owner will be precluded or estopped from asserting that the employee, her agent, lacked authority to make orders and is thus bound by the agent's conduct.

As discussed below, the principal may always ratify previous action by the agent and thereby become obligated by the agent's actions, whether authorized or not.

Ratified Authority. Even if an agent has neither express nor implied authority to perform an act, the principal can nevertheless *ratify* or accept the agent's act and thereby become obligated by the agent's actions. For example, assume Candy has

---

Implied agency
An agency relationship in which there is no express agreement, but the parties' words, conduct, or prior dealings show the existence of their agency relationship

Agency by estoppel
An agency arising from acts that lead others to believe an agency relationship exists

Express authority
Actual authority granted by one to another, in writing or orally

Implied authority
Power to perform acts customarily performed by agents

Apparent authority
Authority that arises through words or conduct of principal leading others to believe agent has authority to act for principal

Ratification
Acceptance of an act

retained a real estate agent to sell her house. If the real estate agent has been instructed to present no offer to Candy for her house under $200,000, and yet presents an offer to Candy for $190,000, which Candy accepts, Candy has ratified this unauthorized act by her agent. Ratification thus occurs when the principal accepts the agent's act even though the agent had no authority to do the act, or the act exceeded the scope of the agent's authority.

3. Duties of Agents and Principals

An agency relationship creates *fiduciary duties* between the principal and the agent. The principal places trust and confidence in the agent, and the agent owes the utmost duty of good faith, candor, and fair dealing to the principal. Other duties also arise from the agency relationship.

Fiduciary duties
Duty to act in utmost good faith and fair dealing

Agent's Duties.   Generally an agent owes four duties to her principal:

- **Performance**. An agent must perform the work or duties required by the principal, whether set forth in a written agreement or implied from the nature of the agency relationship. The agent must perform these duties with reasonable diligence and due care.
- **Notification**. An agent must disclose all information relating to the agency to her principal. An agent selling a house for home owners may not decide for herself, "This offer is so low I won't bother telling the owners about it." In agency law, it is presumed the principal knows all that the agent knows.
- **Loyalty**. The agent must act solely for the benefit of the principal and may not engage in any transaction that would be detrimental to the principal or that would conflict with the principal's interest. Thus, an attorney may not represent both a husband and wife in a divorce proceeding unless each party consents.
- **Accounting**. An agent must account to the principal for all money or property paid out or received on the principal's behalf. The principal's funds must be maintained separately from the agent's; the funds may not be commingled.

Principal's Duties.   Principals owe three duties to their agents:

- **Compensation**. Principals must pay agents for their services. If no fixed compensation is agreed upon, the agent is entitled to compensation in a reasonable and customary amount.
- **Reimbursement and Indemnification**. The principal must reimburse the agent for costs and expenses incurred on the principal's behalf. For example, employers routinely reimburse employees for their travel expenses incurred on behalf of the employer. The principal is also generally required to indemnify or compensate the agent for liability incurred by the agent while performing duties for the principal. The agent will not be indemnified for reckless or willful misconduct, but the agent will be indemnified for acts directed or authorized by the principal.

- **Cooperation**. The principal must not hinder the agent in the performance of her duties. This duty to cooperate includes a duty to provide the agent with what she will need to perform duties, such as a credit card, an office, necessary equipment, and so forth.

4. Liability for Agent's Torts

An agent is liable for her own torts or civil wrongs. Such torts might include assault, battery, negligence, fraud, or malpractice. The question often arises whether the principal is liable for torts committed by the agent. The general rule is that a principal is liable for the torts of his agent committed in the course and scope of employment. However, if the agent is on a "frolic" or "detour," or performing a personal endeavor, the principal is not liable. Thus, a trucking company may be liable for accidents caused by its drivers while they are performing their duties for their employer-principal. On the other hand, if a driver leaves his designated route to visit a friend and in the course of this visit causes an accident, the employer-principal will likely not be held liable because the employee-agent was engaged in activities on his own behalf.

Respondeat superior
Liability imposed on employers for acts of employees

This liability theory is called *respondeat superior* (literally, "let the master answer") and results in liability being imposed on the employer-principal even though she did not actually commit the wrong. This doctrine imposes **vicarious liability** on the employer-principal, meaning that liability is imposed without regard to actual fault.

Vicarious liability
Liability imposed on one for another's acts, without regard to actual fault

Employer-principals may also be liable for failure to supervise an employee properly, for improper selection of an employee (as is the case when an employer hires an obviously unqualified employee), or for wrongful retention of an employee (as is the case when the employer does not terminate employment although grounds for termination exist, such as acts of violence and threats by the employee).

5. Termination of Agency

Agency relationships may be terminated when the stated time period expires if the agreement provides a period of duration (such as a six-month listing period for a real estate agent), when the purposes of the agency have been accomplished, by mutual agreement, by death or bankruptcy of either party, or by either party by reasonable notice to the other. Upon termination of the agency relationship, the agent no longer has any authority to bind the principal.

6. Agency in Business Relationships

This overview of the relationship, duties, and obligations of agents and principals is fundamental to an understanding of many forms of business enterprise. For example, you will see in Chapter Two that a sole proprietor is vicariously liable for the acts of her employees. In Chapter Three, you will see that any partner in a general partnership has the ability to sign contracts, hire employees, and perform other acts; and these acts bind the other partners and the partnership. You will learn that directors and officers are agents of a corporation and thus owe fiduciary duties to the corporation.

E. Role of Paralegal

Before a business is formed, the role of a paralegal will likely be limited to researching various types of business entities, gathering forms and fee schedules from secretaries of state so that forms will be ready for preparation once the client and attorney determine the appropriate form of entity for the client, collecting tax forms, and interviewing clients to gather some initial information from them as to their business needs and goals.

Case Illustration
Agent's Duty of Disclosure

Case Name: *Sierra Pacific Industries v. Carver*, 163 Cal. Rptr. 764 (Ct. App. 1980)

Facts: An owner of real estate entered into an agreement with a real estate agent to list real estate. The agent sold the real estate to his daughter and son-in-law without informing the seller of the agent's relationship to the buyers. When the seller discovered this fact, it sued the agent for fraud.

Holding: The seller need not pay any commission. An agent has a fiduciary duty to his principal to disclose all material information that is relevant to the subject matter of the agency. An agent must refrain from dual representation in a sales transaction unless both parties consent after full disclosure. In this case, the agent breached his duty of disclosure.

Key Features
of Agency Relationships

◆ Formation of agency occurs through agreement (which may be express or implied) or estoppel.
◆ Agents have actual authority or apparent authority to act for their principals. Principals may always ratify the unauthorized acts of their agents.
◆ Agents and principals owe fiduciary duties to each other.
◆ Agents are liable for their own torts, and principals are liable for an agent's torts and acts committed in the course and scope of the agency.

Internet Resources

State statutes: www.law.cornell.edu
www.findlaw.com

Tax information: www.irs.gov

General information: www.sba.gov (Web site of the U.S. Small Business Administration offers excellent information on starting a business)

www.nass.org (Web site of the National Association of Secretaries of State allows direct linking to each state's secretary of state home page for easy access to forms and general information on business entities; select "About NASS," then "Our Members," and then "Contact Roster")

www.megalaw.com (Web site of MegaLaw, a general legal site that provides access to a wide array of legal sources, including federal and state statutes, and links to numerous helpful resources)

www.hoovers.com (Web site offering addresses, phone numbers, and brief capsules on hundreds of companies doing business in the United States)

Forms: www.allaboutforms.com
www.siccode.com/form.php
www.megalaw.com

Key Terms

Sole proprietorship
Principal
Personal liability
Express agency
General partnership
Implied agency
Limited liability partnership
Ratification
Registered limited liability partnership
Agency by estoppel
Limited liability company

Express authority
Business corporation
Implied authority
Professional corporation
Apparent authority
S corporation
Fiduciary duties
Close corporation
Respondeat superior
Agent
Vicarious liability

Discussion Questions

1. ABC Inc., the owner of an apartment building, has hired Ava to manage the building. Although the owner wishes to charge $700 per month for rental of each unit, Ava is charging $750 per month and retaining the extra funds. Has Ava breached any duties to her principal? Discuss.

2. Assume the same set of facts as given in Question 1. Assume that although the owner has instructed Ava to investigate the backgrounds of prospective tenants to ensure they can pay the rent and will be good tenants, Ava has begun dispensing with these background checks so that she can rent as many units as possible. Has Ava breached any duties to her principal? Discuss.

3. Assume the same set of facts as given in Question 1. Assume that Ava purchased new lights for the common areas at the premises to ensure that all walkways are well lighted. ABC Inc. and Ava have no agreement as to which party should pay for such items. Will Ava be reimbursed for this expenditure? Discuss.

4. Andrea is an agent for Tess, an actress. Tess has had trouble getting roles recently and has just discovered that Andrea has been steering acting roles to her niece, who is also an actress. Has Andrea breached any duties to Tess? Discuss.

5. We Will Move You Inc., a corporation, has hired several employees to drive its moving vans. In the course of a move, one of the drivers leaves the designated moving route to buy lunch and causes an accident. Will the corporation be liable for this accident? Discuss. What if one of the movers left the designated moving route to visit an old fraternity friend? Discuss.

Net Worth

1. Access the Web site for Hoover's and locate information about McDonald's Corporation. In how many countries does the corporation operate? What companies are identified as its top three competitors?

2. Access the Web site for the SBA. Access "Start Your Business," "Choose a Structure," and "Forms of Ownership." What is the first advantage given for a sole proprietorship? What is the first disadvantage given for a sole proprietorship?

3. Access the Web site for the National Association of Secretaries of State.
   a. Who is the current Secretary of State for Florida?
   b. Locate the Web site for the Colorado Secretary of State. Select "Business Center" and review the Glossary. What is the definition given for a limited liability company?

2

◆ ◆ ◆

Sole Proprietorships

◆ ◆ ◆

A. Characteristics of Sole Proprietorships

Many people dream of owning their own business. For most of these entrepreneurs, the sole proprietorship is an ideal way of pursuing this dream. The **sole proprietorship** is an unincorporated business owned and operated by one person, who is generally called the **sole proprietor** (or the *individual proprietor*). Almost any kind of business can be conducted as a sole proprietorship: a retail toy shop, a restaurant, or a law office. The key feature of a sole proprietorship is that it is managed and owned by one person. This person may hire managers and employees to assist her in running the business, but the business is characterized by a sole decision-maker.

    In a family-run business it may be difficult to determine whether the business is a partnership or a sole proprietorship. If family members share decision-making, the business is likely a general partnership. If only one person makes decisions, then the business is likely a sole proprietorship. It does not matter what the parties call their enterprise; courts are free to examine the business and determine its true nature.

    Sole proprietorships are governed exclusively by state and local laws (except for federal laws relating to taxes, civil rights, and so forth). Most sole proprietorships are governed solely by state or local laws, and no permission is required from the state to form a sole proprietorship.

Sole proprietorship
A business owned and operated by one person

Sole proprietor
Owner of a sole proprietorship

B. Advantages of Sole Proprietorships

There are several advantages in operating as a sole proprietorship, including the following:

- **Ease of Formation.** The sole proprietorship is easily and inexpensively formed and operated.

13

- **Managerial Discretion.** The sole proprietor is free to make all decisions regarding the business. The sole proprietor may select the name of the business, establish its location, hire employees, and decide what products and services will be offered. The owner is not vulnerable to the negligence of a partner and may sell the business without securing approval from anyone.
- **Retention of Profits.** The sole proprietor may keep all profits generated by the business.
- **Pass-Through Tax Status.** The sole proprietorship's income is passed through to the sole proprietor, who pays taxes at her appropriate individual rate. The business itself pays no tax.

C. Disadvantages of Sole Proprietorships

There are some disadvantages in operating a business as a sole proprietor, including the following:

- **Unlimited Personal Liability.** The chief disadvantage of a sole proprietorship is that the sole proprietor is personally liable for the debts and obligations of the business. For example, if rent is owed to a landlord or money is owed to a supplier, these creditors are not limited to seizing money in the business accounts. The sole proprietor's liability extends beyond what has been invested in the business to her personal assets. Those assets may include money in bank accounts, art collections, and furniture. Although state statutes allow some exemptions (for example, certain jewelry and heirlooms may not be seized by creditors in most states, and homestead exemptions may exist to protect one's personal residence), the front door of the sole proprietor's house is virtually wide open and the contents therein available for picking by business creditors. Moreover, the sole proprietor is liable not only for business debts, but also for the torts or civil wrongs committed by employees in the course and scope of their employment. To protect against the disadvantage of unlimited **personal liability**, the sole proprietor may seek to obtain insurance; however, insurance is not available for all risks. The sole proprietor may also try to negotiate agreements with third parties whereby they agree not to seize his personal assets.
- **Lack of Continuity.** Because the sole proprietorship is so closely affiliated with the sole proprietor, the sole proprietorship generally terminates upon the death of the sole proprietor. If the business assets descend to an heir who continues to operate the business, a new sole proprietorship has been created.
- **Difficulties in Raising Capital.** If a partnership needs to raise additional **capital**, or money, there may be several partners who contribute the needed funds. Corporations raise money by selling stock. The sole proprietor, however, is limited in the methods of obtaining additional funds. The sole proprietor is limited to her own personal funds or may attempt to borrow money. If the sole proprietor has no money and a bank or other lender refuses to lend funds, the sole proprietorship may well collapse.

Personal liability
Liability extending beyond what is invested in a business to an individual's personal assets (also called *unlimited liability*)

Capital
Money used to form and operate a business

FIGURE 2-1
Sole Proprietorships

Advantages	*Disadvantages*
Easy to form and maintain	Unlimited personal liability
Inexpensive to form	Limited ways to raise capital
Owner is sole decision-maker	Lack of continuity
Management is informal and flexible	Possible lack of expertise in
All profits retained by owner	management
Pass-through tax status	

- **Management Vulnerabilities.** The sole proprietor has the flexibility of making all business decisions, but this may be a disadvantage as well. As the business grows, special expertise may be needed. A partnership may admit new partners, and a corporation may rely on its board of directors to provide this business expertise. The sole proprietor, as the sole decision-maker, however, may need to expend funds to hire outside consultants and advisors. (See Figure 2-1 for a chart comparing the advantages and disadvantages of sole proprietorships.)

D. Formation of Sole Proprietorships

One of the greatest advantages of a sole proprietorship is the lack of formalities in forming and organizing this enterprise. Most of the requirements involved in creating the sole proprietorship are common to almost any business.

1. Licensing Considerations

If the sole proprietor will be engaged in a business that has licensing requirements, he will need to comply with these. For example, a real estate or insurance agent must pass a test to become licensed, and a restaurant that serves alcohol requires a liquor license. To determine whether the business is one that requires a license, review your state's statutes and administrative codes, or contact any association that may govern the profession, such as a department of realtors. Sole proprietors may conduct business in other localities or states as well, so long as those states' requirements are followed.

2. Name Considerations

Many sole proprietors choose to operate their business under a name other than their own. For example, Kevin Harris might operate his auto repair shop as

Fictitious name
Name that must be registered with state or local officials because it does not disclose the surname of the business owner

Fictitious business name statement
Record filed with public officials to identify the owner of a business operating under a name other than the owner's surname

DBA
Doing business as; another name for a fictitious business name statement

"Car Care." Such a name is called an *assumed name, trade name,* or **fictitious name**. Generally, if a sole proprietor intends to operate under a fictitious name, the name must be registered with the local or state authority, usually in the county in which the business will be conducted. An example of a **fictitious business name statement** is shown in Figure 2-2. The fictitious business name statement allows consumers to determine the actual owner of a business if litigation must be brought against the owner. The statement is sometimes called a **DBA** (meaning "doing business as"), because it identifies that the true owner is doing business as or under another name.

Although standards vary from state to state, the general rule in determining whether the fictitious business name statement must be filed is as follows: If the business name includes the sole proprietor's last name and does not imply that others are involved (by using terms such as "and Company" or "Associates"), no statement need be filed. Thus, "Tammy's Crafts" is fictitious, whereas "Smith's Repairs" is not. Filing the statement is inexpensive and easy; thus, when there is any doubt, the fictitious business name statement should be filed. Failure to file the statement may result in a fine or refusal to allow the sole proprietor to initiate litigation (although most states allow the sole proprietor to cure the defect by filing the statement in order to litigate). The statement is usually valid for a few years and can be renewed. Some states, including California, also require that the name be published in a newspaper to provide wider public notice.

Finally, the sole proprietor may not operate under a name likely to cause confusion with another enterprise. The state or local agency that accepts the fictitious name statement may check to see if the name is available in that locality. For a more thorough check (for example, for a business that intends to operate in several jurisdictions or nationwide), the sole proprietor should have searches of business names conducted throughout the nation. This will ensure that the name is available nationwide and that it does not infringe the name of another party. Two companies that specialize in such comprehensive name searches are the following:

CT Corsearch	*Thomson CompuMark*
345 Hudson Street	500 Victory Road
New York, NY 10014	North Quincy, MA 02171
(800) 732-7241	(800) 692-8833
www.ctcorsearch.com	http://compumark.thomson.com

Some searching may also be done of registered trademarks through the database of the U.S. Patent and Trademark Office at www.uspto.gov.

3. Business and Sales Tax Permits and Other Formalities

Some jurisdictions require that the sole proprietor obtain a basic license to do business. Additionally, if the sole proprietor will be selling goods, arrangements must be made to pay sales tax to the appropriate authority, such as the municipality or state. A sole proprietor who hires employees must apply for an employer

---

FIGURE 2-2

Florida Fictitious Business Name Statement

APPLICATION FOR REGISTRATION OF FICTITIOUS NAME
Note: Acknowledgements/certificates will be sent to the address in Section 1 only.

Section 1

1. _____
   Fictitious Name to be Registered (see instructions if name includes "Corp" or "Inc")

   _____

   _____
   Mailing Address of Business

   _____ _____ _____
   City   State   Zip Code

3. Florida County of principal place of business: _____

   _____
   (see instructions if more than one county)

   This space for office use only

Section 2

A. Owner(s) of Fictitious Name If Individual(s): (Use an attachment if necessary):

1. _____   2. _____
   Last   First   M.I.   Last   First   M.I.

   _____   _____
   Address   Address

   _____ _____ _____   _____ _____ _____
   City   State   Zip Code   City   State   Zip Code

B. Owner(s) of Fictitious Name If other than an individual: (Use attachment if necessary):

1. _____   2. _____
   Entity Name   Entity Name

   _____   _____
   Address   Address

   _____ _____ _____   _____ _____ _____
   City   State   Zip Code   City   State   Zip Code

   Florida Registration Number _____   Florida Registration Number _____

   FEI Number: _____   FEI Number: _____
   ☐ Applied for   ☐ Not Applicable   ☐ Applied for   ☐ Not Applicable

Section 3

I (we) the undersigned, being the sole (all the) party(ies) owning interest in the above fictitious name, certify that the information indicated on this form is true and accurate. In accordance with Section 865.09, F.S., I (we) understand that the signature(s) below shall have the same legal effect as if made under oath. (At Least One Signature Required)

_____   _____
Signature of Owner   Date   Signature of Owner   Date

Phone Number: _____   Phone Number: _____

Section 4

FOR CANCELLATION COMPLETE SECTION 4 ONLY:
FOR FICTITIOUS NAME OR OWNERSHIP CHANGE COMPLETE SECTIONS 1 THROUGH 4:

I (we) the undersigned, hereby cancel the fictitious name _____

_____, which was registered on _____ and was assigned

registration number _____

_____   _____
Signature of Owner   Date   Signature of Owner   Date

Mark the applicable boxes   ☐ Certificate of Status — $10   ☐ Certified Copy — $30
NON-REFUNDABLE PROCESSING FEE: $50

Single   CR4E001 (11/03)

identification number to withhold federal income tax, using Form SS-4, available from the Internal Revenue Service (IRS) at (800) 829-1040 or at www.irs.gov. Arrangements will also need to be made to contribute to Social Security and worker's compensation funds.

PRACTICE TIP

After your first experience helping to form a sole proprietorship, prepare a file folder with your notes, and record useful phone numbers, contacts, and Web sites. The next time you need to form a sole proprietorship or file a fictitious business name statement, your own form files will provide an easy-to-follow blueprint.

E. Taxation of Sole Proprietorships

The sole proprietorship itself does not pay tax. Income derived from the business is simply added to any other income the sole proprietor makes from any other source and the sole proprietor pays tax on this entire amount according to the IRS tax brackets or schedules (see Figure 2-3). Thus, if a sole proprietor earns $50,000 from the sole proprietorship, earns $20,000 in royalties for writing magazine articles, and wins $10,000 in Las Vegas, the sole proprietor must pay tax on $80,000. The income earned from the business is reported by the sole proprietor on a form called Schedule C, which is attached to the sole proprietor's individual tax return (Form 1040). The sole proprietor may declare and deduct various business expenses, such as advertising costs, insurance, and interest paid, and may use these to offset income. The sole proprietor pays tax on all net income, even money retained for anticipated business needs.

F. Role of Paralegal

Paralegals are involved in the following tasks:

- Determining whether the business is one requiring a license;
- Reviewing state statutes to determine requirements for fictitious business names and preparing and filing a fictitious business name statement, if needed (see Figure 2-2);
- Considering whether a full name search should be conducted for the business name; and
- Obtaining appropriate tax forms and business permits.

FIGURE 2-3
Federal Taxation for Individuals (2008)

Taxable Income
(Taxpayer Filing Singly)

Taxable Income: Over	But not over	Tax	Tax +%	On amount over
$ 0	$8,025	$ 0.00	10	$ 0
8,025	32,550	802.50	15	8,025
32,550	78,850	4,481.25	25	32,550
78,850	164,550	16,056.25	28	78,850
164,550	357,700	40,052.25	33	164,550
357,700		103,791.75	35	357,700

Taxable Income
(Married Taxpayers Filing Jointly)

Taxable Income: Over	But not over	Tax	Tax +%	On amount over
$ 0	$16,050	$ 0.00	10	$ 0
16,050	65,100	1,605.00	15	16,050
65,100	131,450	8,962.50	25	65,100
131,450	200,300	25,550.00	28	131,450
200,300	357,700	44,828.00	33	200,300
357,700		96,770.00	35	357,700

Case Illustration
When Fictitious Business Name Statement Must Be Filed

Case: *Williams v. Nuckolls*, 644 S.W.2d 670 (Mo. Ct. App. 1982)

Facts: The plaintiff paid the defendant for an automobile. The bill of sale identified the seller as "Mel Nuckolls Auto Sales" and stated that the sale was "as is." The day after the sale, the plaintiff was involved in an automobile accident when the car's brakes failed. The plaintiff alleged, among other things, that the defendant should have filed a fictitious business name statement.

Holding: There was no violation of the fictitious business name statement law when the individual, Mel Nuckolls, conducted business under the name "Mel Nuckolls Auto Sales." The inclusion of the sole proprietor's surname in the business name was sufficient such that no fictitious business name needed to be filed.

Key Features
of Sole Proprietorships

- ◆ Business is owned and managed by one person.
- ◆ Sole proprietor retains all profits and bears all losses.
- ◆ Sole proprietor's personal assets can be reached to satisfy business obligations ("personal liability").
- ◆ Business is easily and inexpensively formed.
- ◆ All income earned (and loss incurred) is passed through to sole proprietor, who pays tax according to appropriate individual tax bracket.

Internet Resources

State statutes:	www.law.cornell.edu www.megalaw.com
Tax forms:	www.irs.gov
Trademark searching:	www.uspto.gov
General information:	www.nass.org (for links to each state's secretary of state and general business information) www.sba.gov (Web site of Small Business Administration, offering the Small Business Startup Guide and other excellent publications) www.toolkit.cch.com (site offering a wealth of information on starting and operating a business)

Key Terms

Sole proprietorship	Fictitious name
Sole proprietor	DBA
Personal liability	Fictitious business name statement
Capital	

Discussion Questions

1. Identify whether the following business names are likely fictitious names such that fictitious business name statements should be filed:
O'Brien Auto Repairs
Pat's Auto Repairs
O'Brien & Sons Auto Repairs
James Sanders: Your Tech Support
Tech Support Services of Richmond
Ellie's Catering Services
Shaw & Associates

2. Janice Woods is a sole proprietor conducting business as an event planner. On many occasions, her husband attends events with her to help transport supplies, run errands, and so forth. Do Janice's husband's activities render the business a partnership? Discuss.

3. Assume the same facts as in Question 3. What if Janice's husband decided to lease new office spaces and placed a security deposit for those premises? Would your answer change? Discuss.

4. Assume the same facts as in Question 2. If Janice's husband causes an automobile accident on his way to one of the events at which he will be helping Janice, which individuals will likely face liability for this accident?

5. Assume the same facts as in Question 2. Janice owes $20,000 to one of her suppliers. Janice has $10,000 in her business accounts. From what sources may the supplier recover the money owed? Is there anything Janice could have done to protect herself? Discuss.

6. A law firm client, William Nichols, has considerable wealth that he has saved over the years. He is now considering forming a sole proprietorship to offer financial consulting services. Discuss the most significant disadvantage to William in operating as a sole proprietorship.

Net Worth

1. Access the SBA Web site. Select "Small Business Planner," then "Start Your Business." Locate information on the disadvantages of operating as a sole proprietorship. Why may a sole proprietorship have a difficult time attracting high-caliber employees?
2. Locate Texas's Business and Commerce Code.
   a. What is the duration of an assumed name certificate in Texas?
   b. What penalty might a defendant incur if a defendant in a civil action failed to file an assumed name certificate?
3. Access the Web site for the Alameda County, California, county clerk and recorder. Locate information about the business "Flowers by Josie." When was the fictitious business name statement filed and when will it expire?
4. Access the Web site for the IRS and locate the individual 1040 tax table. If you are single and earn $48,000, what taxes will you pay?

3

♦ ♦ ♦

General Partnerships

♦ ♦ ♦

A. Introduction

A **general partnership** is a voluntary association of two or more persons who agree to carry on business together for profit. The "persons" may be natural persons or other entities, such as partnerships or corporations. The agreement may be either written or oral, although a written agreement is clearly preferable because it provides certainty in the event of a dispute among partners. General partnerships are easy and inexpensive to form and there is little state regulation. The partners share decision-making and management of the business. Partners, however, suffer the disadvantage of **personal liability**, meaning that their personal assets can be reached by creditors. Partners are agents of each other and the partnership; thus, one partner can bind the partnership and other partners by her acts, possibly resulting in ruinous personal liability for an act other partners may not have known of or approved. These partnerships are often called "general" partnerships to distinguish them from limited partnerships (discussed in Chapter Four).

Partnerships are governed by their state statutes, most of which are based on the **Uniform Partnership Act (UPA)**, approved in 1914 by the National Conference of Commissioners on Uniform State Laws (the "Conference"). In 1992, the Conference adopted a **Revised Uniform Partnership Act (RUPA)** and amendments were made to the RUPA throughout the 1990s. Although the Conference refers to the revised act as the "Uniform Partnership Act (1997)," for ease of reference, this text refers to the original 1914 act as the UPA and the revised 1997 act as the RUPA. At the time of this writing, 36 states and the District of Columbia have adopted the RUPA, and the remainder of the states (except Louisiana, which follows its own state statutes) follow the UPA. It is expected that eventually all states will adopt the RUPA. See Figure 3-1 for identification of which states follow each act.

The UPA and RUPA act as a "safety net" for partnerships. Generally, partners may agree to manage their partnership any way they see fit so long as they do not

General partnership
A voluntary association of two or more persons to carry on a business for profit

Personal liability
Liability for business debt, which extends beyond what is invested in a business to include an individual's personal assets

UPA
Uniform Partnership Act, model for partnership legislation in about one fourth of the states

RUPA
Revised Uniform Partnership Act, model for partnership legislation in about three fourths of the states

FIGURE 3-1
Table of Jurisdictions Following UPA and RUPA

UPA	*RUPA*
Georgia	Alabama
Indiana	Alaska
Massachusetts	Arizona
Michigan	Arkansas
Missouri	California
New Hampshire	Colorado
New York	Connecticut
North Carolina	Delaware
Pennsylvania	District of Columbia
Rhode Island	Florida
South Carolina	Hawaii
Utah	Idaho
Wisconsin	Illinois
	Iowa
	Kansas
	Kentucky
	Maine
	Maryland
	Minnesota
	Mississippi
	Montana
	Nebraska
	Nevada
	New Jersey
	New Mexico
	North Dakota
	Ohio
	Oklahoma
	Oregon
	South Dakota
	Tennessee
	Texas
	Vermont
	Virginia
	Washington
	West Virginia
	Wyoming

engage in unlawful acts. Often, however, a dispute may arise on some issue on which the partners' agreement is silent. In such cases, the UPA or RUPA will govern the issue. The text of both the UPA and the RUPA can be found at the Conference's Web site at www.nccusl.org.

The RUPA retains most of the basic features of the UPA, but it does include some significant changes, primarily those governing breakups of partnerships. Under the UPA, a partnership is dissolved and must wrap up or wind up its business whenever any one of the partners departs for any reason. The RUPA attempts to provide more stability and continuity to partnerships by providing that only certain departures trigger a dissolution. Most dissociations or departures of partners result merely in a buyout of the departing partner's interest. The RUPA also provides that a partnership is a separate entity and thus property may be acquired in the partnership's name and the partnership may sue and be sued in its own name. Finally, the RUPA allows a general partnership to convert to a limited partnership and vice versa or to merge with other partnerships to form a new entity.

B. Partnership Property

1. Contributions to the Partnership

Partners may contribute cash, property, or services to the partnership. Once contributed, and unless a partner specifies otherwise, the property (for example, office furniture or a car) then becomes the property of the partnership, and the contributing partner cannot retrieve the property. If property or services are contributed, the partners should agree on their stated value. If they cannot agree, an expert should be retained to appraise the contribution. During the partnership's existence, when the partnership acquires property with partnership funds, it is presumed that the property is owned by the partnership itself, not by the individual partners.

2. Property Rights of the Partnership and of Partners

Under UPA § 24, there are three types of property rights claimed by a partnership or its partners.

Specific Partnership Property. Specific property acquired by the partnership, such as cars or computers, is owned by the partnership itself, rather than by the individual partners, who therefore cannot transfer or assign any interest in this property and whose individual creditors cannot seize it.

Partnership Profits. A partner has an "**interest in the partnership**," meaning a share of partnership profit (and loss). The right to profit is a personal property right, and a partner may transfer or assign this right to another and it can be seized by a partner's creditor. For example, if Dean owes spousal support to his ex-wife, he may have the partnership write a check to his ex-wife each month from his share of partnership profits rather than having the partnership write a check to him and

Interest in the partnership
A partner's right to profits (or share of losses)

then Dean having to write a personal check to his ex-wife for the spousal support. Under RUPA § 502, the only transferable interest of a partner is his or her share of partnership profits.

Management Rights.   Partners have the right to participate in management of the partnership, usually through voting at partnership meetings. A partner may not assign or transfer this right to another. Such a transfer to an unknown third party would violate the voluntary nature of a partnership.

C. Advantages of General Partnerships

Partnerships offer a variety of advantages to their partners:

- **Ease of Formation.** A general partnership can be easily formed. Often no filings need be made with any state or local agency and no written agreement is required (although it is always better to have a written agreement to govern the partnership). Thus, general partnerships are simple and relatively inexpensive to form.
- **Flexible Management.** General partnerships offer their partners the ability to share management. A partner will have others to rely on to provide expertise and advice. Partnerships can appoint certain partners to manage the business or partners may co-manage the business.
- **Ease of Raising Capital.** Partnerships may raise capital by requiring additional contributions from their members or by admitting new partners. By contrast, a sole proprietor has no one else to rely on for capital contributions. Other partners may also help bear the burden if losses are sustained by the partnership.
- **Pass-Through Taxation.** Partnerships do not pay federal income tax. Income earned is passed through to the individual partners, who declare and pay tax on their respective share of partnership profits.

D. Disadvantages of General Partnerships

General partnerships have three primary disadvantages:

Joint and several liability
Principle that each partner and the partnership are liable to pay all of a debt or obligation

- **Unlimited Personal Liability.** The chief disadvantage of doing business in a general partnership is that each partner has unlimited personal liability for debts and obligations of the partnership. Thus, partners' personal assets (such as their savings accounts or art collections) are vulnerable to seizure by partnership creditors, assuming no statutory exemptions exist protecting certain assets. Moreover, the liability that partners face for partnership obligations is joint and several. **Joint and several liability** means that each partner is entirely liable for all obligations. A creditor can sue all partners for a wrongful act or may pick and choose among the partners as to which ones will be sued. With regard to obligations to third parties, each partner is 100 percent liable. Innocent third-party creditors are highly protected, and it is up to partners later on to sort out the true allocation of the damages among themselves. Thus, if a wealthy partner is "targeted," he must pay the entire sum owed to a creditor for a partnership debt although his interest in the partnership may be only 10 percent. This partner may later seek appropriate reimbursement from his co-partners.

Like sole proprietors, partners may attempt to protect themselves against unlimited personal liability by obtaining insurance or by attempting to secure agreements from others that they will not look to a partner's personal assets to satisfy partnership debts. Additional protection is afforded under the **marshaling of assets** principle, which requires creditors to first exhaust all partnership assets before they can attack the personal assets of any partner. For example, if a creditor is owed $80,000 and the partnership has $70,000 in assets, the creditor must first seize the $70,000. Only then may the creditor attack the individual partners and hold them personally liable for the remaining $10,000 owed. RUPA § 307(d) specifically confirms that creditors must first exhaust partnership assets before attacking the personal assets of an individual partner.

Marshaling of assets
Partnership theory requiring creditors to first exhaust partnership assets before pursuing partners' individual assets

Under 1996 amendments to the UPA, a traditional partnership may choose to operate as a limited liability partnership, the effect of which is to eliminate a partner's personal liability for any partnership obligation. Limited liability partnerships are discussed in Chapter Five.

- **Lack of Continuity.** Under the UPA, a partnership cannot survive the death or withdrawal of a partner (unless the partners have specified otherwise in their partnership agreement). This lack of continuity is an unattractive feature of a general partnership and provides less stability than does a corporation, which can exist perpetually. The RUPA attempts to reduce the harsh effect of the UPA by providing that partnerships no longer dissolve every time a partner departs.
- **Difficulty in Transferring Partnership Interest**. As discussed previously, the only transferable property a partner has is his share of the partnership's profits. Because a partnership is a voluntary arrangement, one partner may not simply transfer all of his partnership rights to another; the other partners have not agreed to do business with a newcomer. Admission of a new partner requires consent from the other partners.

E. Formation of General Partnerships

Formation of a general partnership is easily accomplished because the essence of a general partnership is a voluntary agreement to conduct business for profit. Thus, once the parties have agreed to form the entity, few formalities remain. The **partnership agreement** may be written or oral, or the partnership may arise from their course of conduct, showing that they co-manage their business and share profits. Thus, if Karen and Greg sit down over coffee and decide to open a computer consulting business and if their agreement has sufficient certainty to create a contract, a partnership has been created even though no formal document has been prepared.

Partnership agreement
An agreement by two or more persons to do business together as a partnership; may be oral or written

The partnership may operate under a fictitious name. Generally, if all of the partners' surnames are included in the business name, then it is not a fictitious name. If the partnership operates under a fictitious name, it must file a fictitious business name statement. In many jurisdictions, the same fictitious business name statement is used for partnerships as for sole proprietorships (see Figure 2-2).

If the business is subject to licensing requirements, the partnership must comply with those requirements. Similarly, if the business is to sell goods, the partnership must obtain a sales tax permit and must comply with laws relating to Social Security, withholding taxes, and workers' compensation.

In most instances, a general partnership may operate in a state other than the one in which it was formed without filing any documents or notices other than those relating to licensing and the partnership name (namely, a fictitious business name statement).

F. Operation of General Partnerships

1. Duties and Rights of Partners

Partners owe each other fiduciary duties and thus must deal with each other in good faith. While partners may eliminate or vary many UPA or RUPA provisions by their agreement, under RUPA § 103(b), they may not eliminate their duties of good faith, loyalty, and fair dealing, or unreasonably reduce the duty of due care each partner owes to other partners and to the partnership. Moreover, their agreement may not unreasonably restrict a partner's right of access to books and records.

Each partner is an agent of the partnership for business purposes, and partners bind the partnership by their acts in the ordinary course of partnership business (unless the partner has no authority to so act and the person with whom the partner is dealing knows the partner lacks authority). This is referred to as **general agency**, which, simply put, means that each partner has the authority to sign contracts, execute documents, and make purchases that will bind the partnership.

Thus, if Partner A purchases baking supplies for a catering partnership, the partnership must pay the bill when it arrives, even though the other partners might not have granted authority to Partner A to so act. A court will protect the innocent third party, the supplier, and the partners must later sort out the allocation of liability due to Partner A's breach of fiduciary duty (and probable breach of the partnership agreement).

Due to the risk inherent in this partnership principle that partners are agents of the partnership and thus their acts bind the partnership, RUPA § 303 allows partnerships to file an optional **Statement of Authority** with state officials to provide public notice of which partners have authority to perform certain acts. A partner may file a **Statement of Denial** to deny information given in the Statement of Authority.

2. Management of the Partnership

Unless the partners decide otherwise, all partners have equal rights in the management of the partnership business. Thus, if the parties have not agreed on a formula for voting, each partner has one vote in management matters,

General agency
The authority of a partner to act for and bind the partnership and other partners

Statement of Authority
Document filed with secretary of state providing notice of partners who are authorized to act for partnership

Statement of Denial
Document filed with secretary of state denying information in Statement of Authority

regardless of her initial and later capital contributions to the partnership. UPA § 18(e); RUPA § 401(f). Moreover, unless the partners agree otherwise, decision-making in the partnership is by majority vote. For example, if Luis contributed $6,000 to a partnership, Greg contributed $3,000, and Jill contributed $1,000 and they have not agreed on a formula for voting, they will each have one vote on partnership matters, even though Luis's contribution is significantly more than that of the other partners. There are, however, some matters that are considered so extraordinary that they require unanimous approval under UPA § 9, including performing any act that would make it impossible to carry on the partnership business, disposing of the goodwill of the business, and submitting a partnership claim to arbitration. The RUPA position is that any act not in the ordinary course of the partnership's business must be authorized by all partners, unless the partners have agreed otherwise. RUPA § 301(2).

3. Compensation, Profits, and Accounting

The general rule is that partners do not receive a regular and fixed salary from the partnership. Rather, they are paid from partnership profits, which will vary from time to time. Nevertheless, if the partners desire, they may always agree to pay regular salaries. According to UPA § 18(a) and RUPA § 401(b), however, unless the partners agree otherwise, each partner is entitled to an equal share of the partnership profits (and is chargeable with a share of losses in the same proportion as profits), regardless of capital contributions to the partnership. Thus, in a three-person partnership that has profits of $150,000, each partner would receive $50,000, regardless of contribution (assuming there was no agreement otherwise). To avoid these default provisions of the UPA and the RUPA, most partnership agreements provide for the sharing of profits and losses in proportion to the amount contributed to the partnership by each partner. Nevertheless, partners are free to devise any arrangement they desire regarding the sharing of profits and losses. For example, if one partner has special expertise that is needed by the partnership, she may be given a greater than ordinary share of profits and may not be required to bear any losses.

Partners are entitled to be reimbursed for expenses incurred on behalf of the partnership, and partners are entitled to inspect and copy the partnership books and records to determine whether distributions are correct.

G.   The Partnership Agreement

Although a written partnership agreement is not required by law, it is better practice to have a formal written partnership agreement that fully sets forth the partners' rights, duties, and liabilities. Moreover, a written agreement lends certainty to operation of the partnership business and provides a way to resolve future disputes. The agreement may provide any terms the partners desire with regard to the partnership so long as the terms are not illegal. Thus, the parties may agree to distribute profits and losses as they like and to manage the business in any desired way. In the absence of any agreement, however, the UPA or the RUPA acts as the default statute and provides missing partnership terms. A form of partnership agreement is found at

Appendix B. Although the content of a partnership agreement may vary widely, the following are some typical provisions found in partnership agreements:

- **Name of Partnership.** The partnership may operate under the names of its partners or under a fictitious name, so long as the appropriate filing is made.
- **Names and Addresses of Partners.** Partners' names and addresses should be listed so that communications can be provided to them.
- **Recitals.** Most partnership agreements recite the parties' intent to form a partnership.
- **Purpose.** The parties may state their specific business purpose; however, this statement should not be so limited that it restricts the partnership's growth. Many partnerships set forth their purpose and then add the words "and any other acts incidental thereto or as may be agreed upon by the partners" to accommodate changes in business strategy.
- **Address.** The principal place of the partnership's business is set forth so that partners and others can communicate with the partnership.
- **Term.** There are several alternatives the partners can select for the term of the partnership:

  1. The partners may select a definite term by stating, for instance, "This partnership shall come into existence on May 1, 2006, and shall terminate on May 1, 2010." A partnership without a specific term is called a **partnership at will**.
  2. The partners may agree that the partnership will terminate upon their mutual agreement.
  3. The partners may provide that the partnership will terminate once its purposes (for example, building a housing project) have been accomplished.
  4. The partners may agree that the partnership will terminate upon notice of withdrawal of any partner. In this case, consideration should be given to whether the withdrawing member is entitled to receive a return of her contribution and profits before the partnership's stated term expires.

- **Financial Provisions.** Various provisions relating to financial items should be provided, including the following:

  1. The initial contributions of the partners should be specified. If services or property are contributed, they should be described and assigned a monetary value.
  2. The agreement should indicate under what circumstances additional capital might need to be contributed. Each partner's expected additional contributions should be clearly stated. Similarly, withdrawals of capital prior to the termination of the partnership should be discussed. Many agreements provide that no withdrawal of capital is allowed prior to dissolution of the partnership. This is an effective way to discourage partners from withdrawing from the partnership before its agreed-upon term.
  3. If loans or advances to the partnership are permissible, this should be set forth.
  4. If some profit will be retained for emergencies, this should be set forth.

Recitals
Introductory clauses in agreements setting forth basis for agreement

Partnership at will
A partnership with no specific term

- **Profits and Losses.** The agreement should clearly specify each partner's share of profits and losses. There are several alternatives:

  1. Profits and losses may be shared equally by the partners.
  2. Profits may be shared (and losses borne) in accordance with any contributions to the partnership. Thus, if Partner A contributed 54 percent of the business capital and Partner B contributed 46 percent, Partner A would be entitled to 54 percent of any profits and Partner B would receive 46 percent of any profits. This is the most common scheme for division of profits and losses in partnerships.
  3. Certain profits may be guaranteed for a partner, and he or she may bear no losses or a disproportionately low share of losses.
  4. The agreement should specify that losses caused by reckless conduct or fraud must be borne by the partner committing such acts.
  5. If salaries are desired, they should be set forth in this section.
  6. The agreement should provide that partners will be reimbursed for obligations and expenses incurred in the ordinary course of the partnership business.

- **Management and Control.** There are several alternatives for managing and controlling a partnership:

  1. The partners may agree to manage the partnership equally, with each partner having an equal vote.
  2. The partnership may be managed by partners who vote in accordance with their contributions. In our example, Partner A would have 54 percent of the votes to cast on any issue. This is the most common approach in smaller partnerships.
  3. Decisions can be made by simple majority vote or by a greater than majority vote. Certain matters, such as borrowing money or selling significant assets, may require unanimous approval.
  4. One partner may be appointed as a managing partner with the right to make all ordinary daily business decisions. Any limitations on this partner's authority should be set forth. Designating a managing partner is a common approach in larger partnerships.
  5. Various committees may be established for certain functions. For example, a larger partnership may have a compensation committee and an audit committee. If committees are established, their duties should be described.

- **Admission of New Partners and Withdrawal of Partners.** The manner in which new partners will be admitted should be set forth. If the partners do not agree otherwise, unanimous consent will be required. Any matters relating to withdrawal of a partner should also be set forth, particularly whether the withdrawing partner will be repaid his contribution upon withdrawal. If partners may be expelled, the reasons for and methods of expulsion should be clearly provided.
- **Dissolution.** This section of the agreement should specify any actions that will cause a dissolution of the partnership and the process of winding up its

affairs. The partners should identify any acts that may cause a dissolution, such as unanimous agreement or expiration of the partnership term. The agreement should identify a partner who will liquidate or wind up the business by completing contracts, collecting assets, and paying creditors. Both the UPA and the RUPA require that partnership assets must first be applied to pay any creditors. Only after creditors are fully satisfied may partners receive any distributions.

- **Miscellaneous Provisions.** Many other provisions may be included in a partnership agreement.

Non-compete clause
Clause in agreement restricting signatory from competing with another during and after parties' relationship terminates

1. The partners may wish to provide that any withdrawing partner cannot engage in any activity competitive with the partnership business for some period of time. Known as **non-compete clauses**, these provisions ensure that a withdrawing partner will not take customer lists and knowledge acquired within the partnership and use it for his benefit to the detriment of former partners. Generally, non-compete clauses are enforceable so long as they are reasonable in length of time, scope, and geographic area. State laws vary, however, so a thorough review of pertinent statutes is required. For example, California forbids the use of non-compete clauses entirely unless they are bargained for in connection with the sale of a business.
2. The agreement should include a method for resolving disputes, perhaps by submitting disputes to arbitration.
3. The location of and rights of inspection of partnership books and records should be set forth.
4. Other "standard" provisions (such as how notice of meetings will be given, that the agreement will be governed by the laws of a certain state, that no amendment can be made to the agreement unless in writing and signed by all partners, and so forth) are also included.

- **Signature and Date.** The agreement should be signed and dated by all partners. If a partner is a corporation, the agreement should be signed by the appropriate corporate officer.

PRACTICE TIP

Make a point of reviewing partnership agreements and collecting sample agreements and sample clauses from agreements you find in your office, in form books, from colleagues, and from the Internet. Make your own form files. Become the "go to" person in your office for partnership agreements. Always be on the lookout for new clauses and provisions, and continually improve the agreements you draft by including these new, improved provisions.

H. Transferability of Partnership Interest

Although partners may assign their profits in the partnership, they may not, without the consent of the other partners, substitute another partner for themselves. Transfer of profits does not carry with it the right to be a partner. In fact, RUPA § 503(d) expressly provides that upon transfer, the transferor retains all rights and duties of a partner (such as the right to participate in management and personal liability for partnership obligations) other than the right to receive the distributions transferred to the transferee. The transferor partner retains partnership rights and duties until he or she is dissociated or withdraws. New partners may be admitted only upon the consent of all existing partners (or less than unanimous consent, if provided by the partnership agreement). New partners should sign the agreement. They will not be personally liable for any obligations arising before their admission to the partnership and will have personal liability only for obligations incurred after their admission.

Under the UPA, if there is no definite term of the partnership agreement, the withdrawal of one partner causes a dissolution. Because this is such a drastic rule, the agreement should provide a procedure for the withdrawal of partners so that no dissolution is caused. For example, the agreement may allow a partner to withdraw upon 30 days' notice, state that the remaining partners may continue the business after a partner's departure, and specify whether and how the withdrawing partner will be paid the value of her interest. If a withdrawing partner has breached the partnership agreement (for instance, by withdrawing before the term specified in the agreement), she may be liable for damages caused by this breach, usually called a **wrongful dissolution**.

> **Wrongful dissolution**
> Departure from a partnership in breach of partnership agreement

I. Dissolution and Winding Up

1. UPA Approach

Under the UPA, dissolution of the partnership triggers a winding up, namely, a wrapping up of the business affairs of a partnership. A variety of events cause a dissolution, including the following: the ending of the term of a partnership; the withdrawal at will of any partner (if there is no definite term or purpose of the partnership); unanimous agreement of all partners; and the death, expulsion, or bankruptcy of a partner. Thus, any time a partner leaves the partnership, the partnership is dissolved and must wind up its affairs. If the partnership agreement contains terms, however, that allow the partnership to continue doing business after the death, withdrawal, expulsion, or bankruptcy of a partner, the partnership may continue; it need not wind up. Nevertheless, under the UPA, unless the partners have provided for such continuity in their agreement, the partnership will dissolve and then wind up every time a partner leaves.

A partner may also apply to a court for a decree of dissolution when, among other events, the partnership business can only be carried on at a loss or a partner is shown to be of unsound mind or becomes incapable of performing partnership obligations.

2. RUPA Approach

To ameliorate the harsh effects of the UPA approach requiring a dissolution and winding up of a partnership every time a partner leaves the enterprise, the

RUPA provides that in almost all cases, a partnership may buy out the interest of a partner who leaves the partnership (such departure being referred to as a **disso-ciation**), and the partnership will continue its business.

The RUPA provides that only the following departures trigger a dissolution and winding up:

- In a partnership at will, when a partnership receives notice of a partner's express will to depart (although if none of the partners wants the partnership wound up, and if all partners consent, the partnership may continue); and
- In a partnership for a definite term or purpose, and within 90 days after a wrongful dissociation occurs (namely, a withdrawal in breach of agreement) or when a dissociation occurs due to death, expulsion, or bankruptcy, and at least half the remaining partners express their will to wind up the partnership business. For example, if a term partnership has eight partners and one of the partners dies, the partnership will be dissolved only if four of the remaining seven partners affirmatively vote in favor of dissolution within 90 days after the death.

Thus, in sum, generally, a dissociation from a term partnership does not affect the existence of the partnership, because it continues *unless* a majority affirmatively vote to dissolve or disband.

In any other instance (for example, death of a partner in an at-will partnership), no dissolution is caused, and the effect of the dissociation is only that the departing partner is bought out. Thus, under the RUPA, the partnership, as a separate entity, continues despite the dissociation of its members. The RUPA allows the partnership to file a **Statement of Dissociation** with its state agency identifying a dissociated partner. Third parties are bound by this notice 90 days after it is filed. Thus, the partnership is not liable for the dissociating partner's acts after that period (if no statement is filed, they are liable for a departing partner's acts for two years). Under the RUPA, even if the partnership is dissolved, at any time before winding up is completed all of the partners (including any dissociating partner who is not a wrongfully dissociating partner) can agree to continue doing business and thereby avoid termination of the partnership.

3. Winding Up

A partnership that dissolves must wind up its business by completing its contracts, collecting its assets, paying its creditors in full, and then distributing any remaining assets to the business partners according to the partners' agreement (or, if no agreement, in equal shares). If creditors cannot be paid in full, partners must make the appropriate personal contributions to pay these debts.

J.   Taxation of Partnerships

A partnership is not a tax-paying entity. All profits or losses are **passed through** to the partners, who report their respective income (whether or not distributed) or losses on a separate form called Schedule K-1, which is attached to their individual Form 1040 tax returns. Thus, the taxation of partners is much like the taxation of sole proprietors.

Although the partnership itself does not pay federal taxes, it does file an information return, Form 1065, to report income, gains, and losses. The information return is used to ensure that the individual partners correctly report their share of partnership income and losses.

Because there may be certain advantages to paying tax at corporate rates (primarily the fact that, generally, income that is not distributed by corporations is not taxed to the owners), the Internal Revenue Service now allows partnerships to **"check the box"** on a designated IRS form (Form 8832) and elect to be taxed as a corporation, if desired. If no election is affirmatively made, the default provision is that the entity will automatically be treated as having the typical pass-through taxation of a partnership.

Check the box
Method by which businesses elect how they wish to be taxed, namely, as a corporation

K. Joint Ventures

A **joint venture** is a form or variety of partnership; however, rather than being formed to carry out an ongoing business, it is formed by two or more persons to carry out a single enterprise for profit. Upon completion of the single undertaking, the joint venture dissolves. For example, an agreement by two people to build a single residential house is a joint venture, whereas an agreement to engage in the ongoing construction of residential housing creates a partnership. Joint ventures are governed by partnership principles. Thus, their members, called joint venturers, owe fiduciary duties to each other, their agreement may be either written or oral, no state formalities are required to form the venture, the joint venturers will share profits and losses according to their agreement (and in the event there is no agreement on this issue, profits and losses are typically shared equally), the joint venturers have unlimited joint and several personal liability for the venture's debts and obligations, and the joint venture is treated as a partnership for tax purposes.

Joint venture
A type of partnership formed to carry out a single enterprise

L. Role of Paralegal

Paralegals play an integral role in the formation and operation of general partnerships, including performing the following tasks:

- Researching requirements for fictitious business names;
- Preparing and filing the fictitious business name statement (see Figure 2-2);
- Obtaining appropriate forms, including those for tax identification numbers and income tax payments;
- Consulting with clients to determine appropriate terms for partnership agreement (see Figure 3-2 for a questionnaire and checklist to use in drafting the agreement);
- Drafting the partnership agreement; and

- Working with clients to provide any notices required under partnership agreements (for example, notices of meeting, notices of dissociation, and Statements of Authority).

Case Illustration
Joint and Several Liability of Partners

Case: *Gildon v. Simon Property Group, Inc.*, 145 P.3d 1196 (Wash. 2006)

Facts: The plaintiff was injured in a slip and fall inside a shopping mall owned by Northgate Mall Partnership, a general partnership. Plaintiff sued Simon Property Group, which was the general partner of the partnership but did not name the partnership itself. The defendant general partner claimed, among other things, that it was a "small" general partner. The trial court dismissed the plaintiff's action and the Court of Appeals reversed.

Holding: The Washington Supreme Court affirmed. Under the RUPA (adopted in Washington), partners are jointly and severally liable for all partnership obligations without regard to whether they are "mere" or small partners. Although partners are allowed to modify many statutory provisions in their partnership agreements, partners are not permitted to modify the principle of joint and several liability. In this case, the plaintiff alleged that the defendant general partner was directly liable to her for its acts. Because a defendant is always liable for its own acts and torts, the plaintiff was not required to name the partnership itself.

Key Features
of General Partnerships

- ◆ Partnerships are formed by agreement, either oral or written.
- ◆ All partners share rights to manage the partnership.
- ◆ Partners share profits and losses according to their agreement; if no agreement, profits and losses are shared equally, regardless of contributions to the partnership.
- ◆ Partners have unlimited personal liability for partnership obligations.
- ◆ Partners' liability is joint and several, meaning that any partner is completely liable for any debt.

- ◆ Partnerships are easily and inexpensively formed.
- ◆ Partners owe each other fiduciary duties and are agents of the partnership.
- ◆ Under the UPA, nearly any withdrawal by a partner causes a dissolution of the partnership.
- ◆ Under the RUPA, withdrawal of a partner may not necessarily trigger a winding up; in many instances, a departing partner will be bought out.
- ◆ Partnerships file information tax returns but do not pay federal taxes; all income, whether distributed or not, is passed through to the partners, who pay tax at appropriate individual rates.

FIGURE 3-2

Partnership Checklist and Questionnaire

1. Proposed Name of Partnership _____
   Alternative Names[s] _____
2. Names and Addresses of all Partners
   a. _____   b. _____
   _____   _____
   _____   _____
   c. _____   d. _____
   _____   _____
   _____   _____
3. Address of Partnership _____
   _____
4. Purpose of Partnership _____
   _____
5. Duration of Partnership _____
6. Capital Contributions of Partners
   a. _____   b. _____
   c. _____   d. _____
7. Distribution of Profits and Losses
   a. _____   b. _____
   c. _____   d. _____
8. Management of Partnership/Voting/Decisions that Require Unanimous Approval
   _____
   _____
   _____
9. Designation of Managing Partner _____
10. Rights to Admit New Partners _____
    _____
11. Rights of Partners to Withdraw _____
    _____
12. Events that Will Cause Dissolution and Winding Up _____
    _____
    _____
13. Manner of Resolving Disputes (namely, litigation or arbitration) _____
14. Fiscal Year and Method of Accounting _____
15. Banking Information _____
16. Other _____
    _____
    _____
    _____

Internet Resources	

Tax forms: www.irs.gov

State forms and information: www.nass.org

Text of UPA and RUPA: www.nccusl.org

General information: www.tannedfeet.com
www.about.com
www.megalaw.com

Partnership agreement forms: www.ilrg.com
www.lectlaw.com
www.allboutforms.com

Key Terms

Personal liability
UPA
RUPA
General partnership
Fictitious business name statement
General agency
Statement of Authority
Statement of Denial
Recitals
Partnership at will
Non-compete clause

Interest in the partnership
Joint and several liability
Marshaling of assets
Partnership agreement
Wrongful dissolution
Dissociation
Statement of Dissociation
Pass-through tax status
Check the box
Joint venture

Discussion Questions

Fact Scenario. Phil, Brian, and Greg have formed a general partnership to provide auto detailing services. Although they have a written partnership agreement, it does not discuss division of profits or losses or how the partnership will be operated. It does provide that the partnership will last for three years. Phil contributed $20,000 to the partnership, Brian contributed $45,000 to the business, and Greg contributed $35,000 to the business.

1. Last year the partnership made a profit of $200,000. How will this be divided among the partners? Why? If the partnership sustained a loss of $200,000, how would this be allocated? Why?

2. The partnership has decided that it should raise an additional $10,000. What share of this sum must each partner contribute?

3. Without the other partners' knowledge, Greg has purchased a significant amount of supplies for the business. Who is liable to pay for these supplies? Why? Discuss fully.

4. Brian has decided to leave the partnership after only one year. Discuss the effect of his withdrawal from the partnership under both the UPA and the RUPA.

5. The partnership owes $15,000 to its landlord and has $10,000 in its bank accounts. Who is liable for payment of the money owed to the landlord? Discuss.

6. Greg has decided to transfer his partnership interest to Cynthia. What rights, if any, does Cynthia have in the partnership?

7. Assume that at the end of its term, the partnership is dissolving. It owes $5,000 for taxes and $4,000 to Brian for wages Brian paid to certain employees. The partnership has $20,000 in its accounts. Discuss how the debts will be paid and any assets distributed under both the UPA and the RUPA.

8. What is the advantage to the partnership of filing a Statement of Dissociation after a partner leaves the partnership?

Net Worth

1. Access the Web site for the Secretary of State of New Hampshire and review the Application for Certificate of Authority for Foreign Partnership.
   a. What fee is required to file this document?
   b. What information is required in Section 4 of the document?
2. Access the Web site for the Secretary of State of California. What is the fee to file a Statement of Partnership Authority?
3. Access the Web site of the National Conference of Commissioners on Uniform State Laws. Select "Final Acts and Legislation" and then "Partnership Act."
   a. Select "Summary" and review the information relating to dissolution of partnerships. What is the most significant change in the 1994 Act over the 1914 Act?
   b. Select "Illinois" and review Section 101. What is the definition of "partnership at will"?

4

♦ ♦ ♦

Limited Partnerships

♦ ♦ ♦

A. Introduction to Limited Partnerships

Unlike sole proprietorships and general partnerships, which are formed with either no or minimal government involvement, limited partnerships are creatures of statute and may be formed only by compliance with state law, namely, by the filing of a certificate of limited partnership with the appropriate state official. A **limited partnership** is a partnership formed by two or more persons, pursuant to a statute, having as its members one or more general partners and one or more limited partners. The partners may be natural persons or entities, such as other partnerships or corporations.

Limited partnership
Business entity created in accord with state statutes that provides limited liability to some of its members, called limited partners

The primary advantage of a limited partnership is that it affords limited liability to the limited partners, so that their maximum potential loss is their investment in the enterprise. In exchange for this protection, limited partners forgo any management of the partnership; all management and control is provided by the general partners, who retain unlimited, personal, and joint and several liability for their acts. Limited partnerships enjoy pass-through tax treatment, meaning that the limited partnership itself does not pay taxes. All taxable income is passed through to the partners, who pay taxes according to their respective tax brackets.

Limited partnerships are governed by each state's statutes, which are modeled after the Uniform Limited Partnership Act, drafted by the National Conference of Commissioners on Uniform State Laws and approved in 1916, and the **Revised Uniform Limited Partnership Act (RULPA)**, approved in the mid-1970s and later amended in 1985. All states except Louisiana, which has its own separate statutes governing limited partnerships, adopted the RULPA, although there are variations from state to state. The RULPA itself was revised in 2001, although at the time of the writing of this text, only 14 states have fully adopted it. As time progresses, additional states may begin adopting the 2001 Act because it affords significant full-shield protection from personal liability for both general and limited partners.

RULPA
Revised Uniform Limited Partnership Act; the model for limited partnership legislation in most states

The 2001 Act is discussed in Section J of this chapter. Because the RULPA is at present the dominant law governing limited partnerships, and the one followed by the majority of American jurisdictions, focus in this edition of the text remains on the RULPA.

As with general partnerships, the parties in a limited partnership are free to provide the terms and conditions under which their entity operates; if no agreement is reached, however, the RULPA acts as a default statute and provides those terms and conditions. The various uniform acts governing limited partnerships are found at www.nccusl.org.

Limited partnerships are not quite as popular now as they once were because new entities (limited liability partnerships and limited liability companies, discussed in Chapters Five and Six, respectively) allow protection from personal liability and yet still allow their participants to engage in management, whereas a **limited partner's** limited liability protection is dependent on refraining from management of the entity. As evidence of the waning popularity of limited partnerships, in 2007, only six limited partnerships were formed in the State of Georgia under the ULPA. In contrast, nearly 60,000 limited liability companies were formed.

B. Rights and Duties of Partners

1. General Partners

Because limited partners may not participate in the control of the limited partnership, every limited partnership must have at least one **general partner** who is fully responsible for managing the business. The management rights and responsibilities of general partners in a limited partnership are the same as those of general partners in a general partnership. Thus, general partners owe fiduciary duties to the limited partners and to the limited partnership. They are agents of the partnership who can bind the partnership for obligations. The limited partnership agreement provides their specific duties and responsibilities; if the agreement fails to provide such terms, management and control is shared equally among general partners, just as in a general partnership. General partners have personal and joint and several liability for the limited partnership's debts and obligations, meaning that their personal assets can be reached by creditors if partnership assets are insufficient to satisfy such debts.

Under the new 2001 Act, several states allow a limited partnership to file a registration statement with the secretary of state, which results in the general partner(s) having limited liability. This variety of partnership is called a **limited liability limited partnership** and is discussed in Section J of this chapter.

2. Limited Partners

Limited partners, occasionally called "silent partners," are passive investors in a limited partnership. A limited partner invests his money in the limited partnership and knows that this represents the maximum loss he will face. In fact, limited partnerships developed to afford wealthy individuals an opportunity to invest in a business and yet not expose all of their other assets to personal liability. Because

Limited partner
A member of a limited partnership who does not participate in controlling the business and whose liability is limited to amount invested in the business

General partner
Member in a limited (or general) partnership who controls the business and has unlimited personal liability

Limited liability limited partnership
A limited partnership providing protection from limited liability to its general partners; recognized fully in 14 states

limited partners do not manage the business, they have no personal liability for partnership debts and obligations. Their partnership interests are generally readily transferable.

A limited partner may lose limited liability status by acting as a general partner. Although limited partners have the right to be provided copies of the partnership tax returns and to review corporate books and records and to be informed of the partnership's affairs, they may not "control" the business. Under RULPA § 303(a), if a limited partner participates in the control of the business, she is liable to those persons who transacted business with the entity reasonably believing that the limited partner was a general partner.

Numerous cases have attempted to define what acts constitute "control." There is no bright line test, but RULPA § 303(b) provides that the limited partner may engage in the following activities, among others, without being subject to personal liability:

1. Being a contractor, agent, or employee of the limited partnership.
2. Consulting with and advising a general partner with respect to the business.
3. Requesting or attending a partners' meeting.
4. Proposing one or more of the following matters:
   - The dissolution and winding up of the business.
   - The sale or transfer of all or substantially all of the partnership's assets.
   - The admission or removal of a general or limited partner.
   - An amendment to the partnership certificate or agreement.

The RULPA also specifies that activities undertaken by limited partners that are not specifically enumerated in the preceding list, often referred to as the "safe harbor" list, do not necessarily constitute an act of control by a limited partner that would subject him to personal liability.

Additionally, a limited partner's last name may not be used in the name of the limited partnership (unless it is also the name of a general partner or the business operated under that name before the partner's admission). A limited partner who knowingly allows her surname to be used in the partnership name will be liable to creditors who do not know she is a limited partner. Thus, if a limited partner's surname is "Smith," that name should not be used in the business name.

These prohibitions against a limited partner "controlling" the business or having her surname used in the business name seem to be based on what third parties are likely to believe. If a third party sees an individual engaged in managing a business or notes that person's surname in the business name, he is likely to believe that person is a general partner with unlimited personal liability.

C. Advantages of Limited Partnerships

- **Attracting Capital.** A limited partnership is an ideal way of attracting capital for an enterprise. Wealthy individuals can invest money in the enterprise knowing in advance their maximum exposure is limited to the amount of their contributions. Moreover, if additional capital is needed, new limited partners may be easily admitted to the partnership, and yet the general partners will not surrender any of their ability to manage and control the business.

- **Limited Liability.** As noted earlier, individuals may invest in a limited partnership. So long as they do not control the business or knowingly allow their surnames to be used in the business name, they will not be liable for any amount beyond their contributions to the partnership, which contributions may be cash, property, services, or a promise to contribute cash, property, or services in the future.

- **Easy Transferability of Interest.** Limited partners can easily transfer their interests to others. The assignee will become a new limited partner if such is allowed by the limited partnership agreement or if all other partners agree. Moreover, generally, a limited partner has the right to withdraw from the partnership and demand a return of contributions upon giving six months' written notice to each general partner.

- **Continuity of Existence.** Limited partnerships do not necessarily dissolve upon the withdrawal of a general partner so long as there is at least one other general partner and the parties' agreement permits the business to be continued by the remaining general partner. Additionally, because limited partners do not control the business, their withdrawal generally does not cause a dissolution.

- **Pass-Through Taxation.** Like general partnerships, limited partnerships do not pay federal income tax. Profits earned are allocated to the individual partners, who pay according to their appropriate tax brackets.

D. Disadvantages of Limited Partnerships

- **Lack of Control by Limited Partners.** Although the key advantage to being a limited partner is limited liability, it comes at a price. Limited partners cannot control the business or they risk loss of their limited liability status. Thus, for individuals who prefer to manage their investments and affairs, a limited partnership is not an ideal choice. Additionally, because the general partner has full authority to manage the business, the limited partners must have complete confidence in this individual.

- **Unlimited Liability for General Partner.** General partners assume all of the responsibility for managing the enterprise and have unlimited personal and joint and several liability for its debts and obligations. If a corporation is used as a general partner, the corporation manages the business through its directors and officers, and the corporate entity has limited liability. Creditors of the limited partnership can reach only the assets in the limited partnership's accounts and those in the corporate general partner's accounts. No individuals have any personal liability; thus, many limited partnerships rely on corporate general partners to achieve such protection from unlimited liability. For example, the general partner is identified as ABC Inc., and documents are signed by ABC's appropriate officer, probably its president.

- **Formalities and Expenses of Organization.** A limited partnership is often said to be a "creature of statute," meaning it cannot be formed without substantial compliance with statutory formalities. Various documents must be filed with any state in which the limited partnership operates. Annual reporting requirements may be imposed as well. Thus, filing fees and legal fees are often involved, and the paperwork is far more complex than that for general partnerships.

E. Formation of Limited Partnerships

1. Contents of the Limited Partnership Certificate

To form a limited partnership, a **limited partnership certificate** must be prepared, signed, and filed with the secretary of state (or equivalent official) in the state of the partnership's organization. Under RULPA § 201 the following items must be included:

- **Name.** The name of the limited partnership may not be the same as or deceptively similar to those of other businesses. Moreover, the name must include, without abbreviation, the words "limited partnership," although most states allow abbreviations such as "L.P." Finally, the name of the entity may not include a limited partner's surname unless a general partner shares that surname or the partnership operated under that name prior to the limited partner's admission to the entity. Many states allow a name to be reserved for use of the proposed limited partnership prior to its actual formation.

- **Office and Registered Agent.** The limited partnership must provide an address for an office in the state to which documents and notices can be sent. Equally important, an **agent for service of process** must be identified. The agent is either an individual residing in the state or a company in the state that is authorized to receive service of process (litigation summonses and complaints) for the entity. Any individual who wishes to file suit against the limited partnership will then serve the summons and complaint upon the registered agent. In many states one can now search online for the name and address of the registered agent.

- **Names and Addresses of General Partners.** The names and business addresses of the general partner(s) must be provided. Because the limited partners do not participate in the control of the business, they should be able to conduct some investigation, or **due diligence**, into the background of the general partner. Identification of the general partner in this public document affords such an investigative opportunity.

- **Dissolution Date.** The latest date for dissolution of the limited partnership is given to provide notice to limited partners so they will know when final distributions may be made.

- **Other Matters.** The certificate may include other items, such as events triggering dissolution, information regarding additional contributions, and the like; however, because the certificate is a public document, most general partners comply narrowly with the state requirements and do not include other matters, because changes to these items would necessitate later amendments to the certificate. (See Figure 4-1 for a form of certificate of limited partnership.)

Limited partnership certificate
The document filed with a state that creates a limited partnership

Agent for service of process
The person or entity that receives service of process on behalf of a business entity

Due diligence
Investigation conducted prior to entering an agreement or consummating a transaction

---

FIGURE 4-1

Delaware Certificate of Limited Partnership

STATE OF DELAWARE
CERTIFICATE OF LIMITED PARTNERSHIP

- **The Undersigned,** desiring to form a limited partnership pursuant to the Delaware Revised Uniform Limited Partnership Act, 6 Delaware Code, Chapter 17, do hereby certify as follows:

- **First:** The name of the limited partnership is _____
_____ .

- **Second:** The address of its registered office in the State of Delaware is _____
_____ in the city of _____ .
Zip code _____ . The name of the Registered Agent at such address is
_____ .

- **Third:** The name and mailing address of each general partner is as follows:

  _____
  | |
  | |
  | |
  | |
  _____

- **In Witness Whereof,** the undersigned has executed this Certificate of Limited Partnership as of _____ day of _____ , A.D. _____ .

By:_____
　　　　　General Partner

Name: _____
　　　　　(type or print name)

> ## PRACTICE TIP
>
> Keep a copy of active clients' certificates of limited partnership in a file folder near your desk. Legal documents (contracts, promissory notes, and so forth) must recite the limited partnership's correct name and be signed by a general partner. Keeping the certificate handy will help you double-check spelling, abbreviations, and punctuation in limited partnership names and the correct presentation of general partners' names without needing to review voluminous files.

2.   Filing the Certificate of Limited Partnership

In most states, the form of the certificate of limited partnership is provided by the state. Almost all states provide downloadable forms on their Web sites (see Appendix A). The certificate must be signed by all general partners. It is then sent to the secretary of state with the appropriate fee for filing. A limited partnership is formed at the time of the filing of the certificate with the secretary of state. A few states require that the certificate also be filed in the county in which the entity will principally conduct its business. Carefully review your state statutes to ensure compliance with statutory requirements.

3.   Amending the Certificate of Limited Partnership

In the event of significant changes in the limited partnership, a certificate of amendment must be prepared and filed with the secretary of state. RULPA § 202(b) provides that an amendment must be filed within 30 days after any of the following events:

- Admission of a new general partner;
- Withdrawal of a general partner; or
- The continuation of the business after the withdrawal of a general partner.

Moreover, in the event a general partner becomes aware that the certificate contains a false statement or that any other fact set forth in the original certificate has changed (such as a change in registered agent), the general partner must promptly amend the certificate.

4.   Foreign Limited Partnerships

A limited partnership can be formed in one state and expand its operations and conduct business in another state so long as it files the appropriate application or certificate in the other state. To protect its citizens, every state has the authority to regulate business within its borders. A limited partnership formed in one state and doing business in another is referred to as a **foreign limited partnership** in the

Foreign limited partnership
A limited partnership doing business in a state other than the one in which it was formed

Domestic limited partnership
A limited partnership doing business in its state of formation

Doing business
Activities enumerated by a state that require an entity to qualify before entering the state to transact business

second state (and a **domestic limited partnership** in its home state). Many activities, such as merely bringing or defending a lawsuit or engaging in an isolated transaction, are not considered "**doing business**" such that an application must be filed in the foreign state. Carefully review your state statutes to determine what activities require the foreign limited partnership to apply. Under RULPA § 907, failing to file the application when required will preclude the limited partnership from maintaining any lawsuit in that state until the defect or omission is cured.

In many respects, the application in a foreign jurisdiction mimics the original certificate of limited partnership, and an agent for service of process in the foreign jurisdiction must be identified. Generally, the application forms are available for downloading from each state's secretary of state Web site (see Appendix A).

F. Limited Partnership Agreement

Limited partnership agreement
Agreement among partners in a limited partnership, usually written but may be oral

According to RULPA § 101(9), a **limited partnership agreement** is any valid agreement among partners, whether written or oral, governing the affairs and conduct of the partnership. Although an oral agreement is permissible, a written agreement should always be prepared because it will provide guidance for the management of the entity. The checklist for general partnerships provided in Figure 3-2 may be used as a guide in drafting a limited partnership agreement.

A limited partnership agreement is very similar to a general partnership agreement (see Appendix B). Thus, the name of the partnership, its purpose, duration, address, need for additional contributions, identification of all partners and their initial contributions, and so forth should all be included. Following are some special items to be considered:

- **Profits and Losses.** As with general partnerships, agreements for limited partnerships usually provide that profits and losses will be shared in proportion to the partners' respective contributions to the limited partnership. If a written agreement fails to provide for allocation of profits and losses, RULPA § 503 provides that profits and losses will be allocated on the basis of the contributions made by the partners. This is quite different from the general partnership principle that in the absence of an agreement, profits and losses are divided equally regardless of contribution.
- **Rights and Duties of General Partner.** Because limited partners do not control the business, the general partner's duties and responsibilities should be described in great detail so limited partners are fully aware of the general partner's management obligations.
- **Admission of New General and Limited Partners.** Under RULPA §§ 401 and 301(b), additional general and limited partners may be admitted as provided by the written agreement of the partners or, in the absence of an agreement, with the written consent of *all* partners. Thus, if desired, the parties may allow admission of any new partner upon a simple majority vote (or as otherwise agreed).
- **Withdrawal of Limited Partners.** RULPA § 603 provides that if a limited partnership agreement does not specify the events that allow a limited partner to withdraw, a limited partner may withdraw from the partnership

upon giving six months' notice to each general partner. Upon withdrawal, the limited partner is entitled to receive any distributions to which she is entitled. Because limited partners are merely passive investors, much like shareholders in a corporation, their continued membership in the entity is not critical to operation of the partnership business; thus, they may freely withdraw from a limited partnership (whether voluntarily or by death) without causing a dissolution.

G. Transferability of Limited Partnership Interests

A limited or general partner's interest in the partnership (meaning her rights to profits) is assignable in whole or in part. No permission for such a transfer is required from any partner. Thus, a limited or general partner may easily transfer her interest in the partnership to another. The assignment, however, does not automatically entitle the assignee to become a member of the partnership. The assignee will become a limited partner with attendant partnership rights only if the assignor gives that right in accordance with the terms of the limited partnership agreement *or*, in the absence of an agreement, all other partners consent.

Generally, unless the limited partnership agreement provides otherwise, a partner (whether general or limited) ceases to be a partner upon assignment of all of her partnership interest. Such an action by a general partner is an **event of withdrawal** that triggers dissolution and winding up unless the partnership agreement allows the business to continue or all partners, within 90 days, agree in writing to continue the business.

Any partner's interest in the limited partnership (and right to distributions) may also be seized by a creditor.

Partnership interest
A partner's share of partnership profits (and losses)

Event of withdrawal
Action by general partner that usually causes dissolution of limited partnership

H. Dissolution and Winding Up of Limited Partnerships

There are two types of dissolution of a limited partnership: nonjudicial (a dissolution occurring without involvement of a court) and judicial (a dissolution involving court action).

As to **nonjudicial dissolution**, under RULPA § 801, a limited partnership is dissolved and its business must be wound up upon the following:

Nonjudicial dissolution
Dissolution of an entity without court involvement

- Expiration of the time specified in the limited partnership certificate;
- The occurrence of any events specified in a written partnership agreement;
- Written consent of all partners; or
- An event of withdrawal of a general partner (meaning an assignment of all of the general partner's interest to another; expulsion, death, or bankruptcy of a general partner; or voluntary withdrawal by the general partner). Nevertheless, there will be no dissolution if there is another general partner to carry on the business and the agreement permits the business to be carried on *or* if within 90 days after the withdrawal, all partners agree in writing to continue the partnership business.

Judicial dissolution
Dissolution of an entity ordered by a court

As to **judicial dissolution**, any partner may apply to a court to dissolve the limited partnership when it is no longer reasonably practicable to carry on the business in conformity with the partnership agreement. RULPA § 802.

Upon dissolution, winding up will occur: assets will be collected; obligations will be completed; and creditors will be paid, following which partners and former partners will receive any outstanding distributions. Partners then receive a return of their contributions and, finally, a distribution of their profits.

When the limited partnership is dissolved, it should cancel its certificate of limited partnership in its state of organization and cancel or withdraw any applications in any foreign states in which it is doing business.

I. Taxation of Limited Partnerships

Taxation of a limited partnership is nearly identical to taxation of a general partnership. All of the income earned by the limited partnership, whether distributed or not, is passed through to the partners, who declare their share on their own individual tax returns (using Schedule K-1). The limited partnership does not pay federal tax but it files an information tax return with the Internal Revenue Service using Form 1065 (just as does a general partnership). Like general partnerships, if desired, the limited partnership may "check the box" on tax Form 8833 and elect to be taxed as a corporation (see Chapter Three). Limited partnerships may be required to pay various taxes in the state of their organization and any foreign jurisdictions in which they do business.

J. The 2001 Uniform Partnership Act and Limited Liability Limited Partnerships

2001 Act
Revised version of uniform limited partnership act, fully adopted in 14 states, providing significant protection from liability for all partners

As mentioned above, in 2001 the National Conference of Commissions on Uniform State Laws completed a full revision of the current uniform acts governing limited partnerships. The Uniform Limited Partnership Act of 2001 (**2001 Act**) has been fully adopted in the following 14 states: Arkansas, California, Florida, Hawaii, Idaho, Illinois, Iowa, Kentucky, Maine, Minnesota, Nevada, New Mexico, North Dakota, and Virginia. Although only these 14 states have fully adopted the 2001 Act, a number of other states (including Delaware and South Dakota) recognize LLLPs. Their statutes allow limited partnerships to elect LLLP status and thereby limit the liability of general partners in a limited partnership. The 2001 Act does not change the basic structure of limited partnerships but provides greater flexibility and protection to two types of limited partnerships: sophisticated groups seeking strong and centralized management (usually commercial limited partnerships) and family limited partnerships (limited partnerships entered into by family members to achieve estate and tax planning benefits).

The 2001 Act is a stand-alone act, meaning it is not dependent on either the UPA or RULPA. Its full text is available at the Conference's Web site at www.nccusl.org. Its significant provisions are as follows:

- **Full Liability Shield for General Partners.** One of the significant disadvantages for a general partner in a limited partnership under the RULPA is complete personal liability for any obligations of the limited partnership. The 2001 Act allows a limited partnership to state in its certificate whether it is a limited liability limited partnership. 2001 Act § 201(a)(4). If such an election is made, the general partners will be fully shielded from any personal liability, whether it arises in tort or contract, and limited partnership obligations must be satisfied solely by the limited partnership itself.

- **Full Liability Shield for Limited Partners.** Whereas the RULPA position is that a limited partner is shielded from personal liability only if he does not control the limited partnership, the 2001 Act provides that a limited partner is not personally liable for any obligation of the limited partnership even if the limited partner participates in the management and control of the business. 2001 Act § 303. This full shield applies whether or not the limited partnership has elected to be a limited liability limited partnership.
- **Use of Limited Partner's Name.** The 2001 Act allows the use of any partner's name (even that of a limited partner) in the limited partnership's name. 2001 Act § 108(a).
- **Annual Report.** The 2001 Act requires a limited partnership to file an annual report with the secretary of state providing basic information about the limited partnership. 2001 Act § 210.
- **Dissolutions.** The 2001 Act provides that a limited partnership may be continued after a general partner's withdrawal upon a majority vote of all partners (under the RULPA, a unanimous vote is needed). 2001 Act § 801.

Note that several states have recognized limited liability limited partnerships without adopting the 2001 Act in full. Their statutes allow limited partnerships to elect LLLP status and thereby limit the liability of all partners in the limited liability limited partnership.

K. Role of Paralegal

Because limited partnerships may be formed only in substantial compliance with appropriate state statutes, the organization and operation of limited partnerships offer unique opportunities for paralegals to play a key role in the creation and maintenance of limited partnerships, including the following tasks:

- Checking name availability for the entity and any required signals (such as "limited partnership" or "L.P.");
- Drafting and filing the certificate of limited partnership (see Figure 4-1);
- Drafting the limited partnership agreement (see the checklist and questionnaire provided as Figure 3-2 and the partnership agreement at Appendix B);
- Filing applications to do business in foreign jurisdictions, if desired; and
- Monitoring changes in the limited partnership, filing amendments to the certificate when necessary, and canceling certificates, if needed.

Case Illustration
Limited Partners May Not Control Partnership

Case: *Gonzales v. Chalpin*, 552 N.Y.S.2d 419 (App. Div.), *aff'd*, 565
           N.E.2d 1253 (N.Y. 1990)

Facts: The plaintiff was hired by the defendants as superintendent of
           their apartment building and to perform extensive repairs. After
           the plaintiff was fired, he sued the defendant limited partnership
           and the individual limited partner, Edward Chalpin. The trial
           court ruled in favor of the plaintiff and the defendants appealed.

Holding: The judgment against the defendants, including limited partner
           Chalpin, was affirmed. Chalpin performed an extensive role in
           running the affairs of the limited partnership (including signing
           checks for the partnership). If a limited partner plays an active
           role in partnership affairs, he becomes liable as a general partner.

Key Features
of Limited Partnerships

◆ Limited partnerships must have at least one general partner and one
   limited partner.
◆ The general partner in a limited partnership functions identically to and
   assumes the same risks as a general partner in a general partnership,
   namely, personal liability.
◆ Limited partners do not have personal liability for the entity's obligations
   (so long as they do not control the business); their liability is limited to
   their investment in the business.
◆ Formation of limited partnerships requires filing a Certificate of Limited
   Partnership with the appropriate state agency.
◆ Limited partners may freely enter and exit the partnership.
◆ Limited partnership agreements may be oral or written; if no written
   agreement on profits and losses exists, they are allocated on the basis
   of contributions made by partners.
◆ Limited partnerships offer pass-through taxation, meaning that the entity
   does not pay tax; all income is passed through to the partners, who pay at
   their appropriate individual tax rates.
◆ Under the 2001 Act, limited partners may manage and control the limited partnership's business without incurring personal liability, and if the
   limited partnership elects to be a limited liability limited partnership,
   the general partner will also be fully shielded from personal liability.

Internet Resources	
Tax forms:	www.irs.gov
State forms and information:	www.nass.org
Text of RULPA and 2001 Act:	www.nccusl.org
General information:	www.findlaw.com
	www.about.com
	www.megalaw.com
Limited partnership agreements:	www.ilrg.com
	www.lectlaw.com
	www.allboutforms.com

Key Terms

Limited partnership
RULPA
Limited liability limited partnership
Limited partnership certificate
Due diligence
Domestic limited partnership
Foreign limited partnership
Doing business

Limited partner
General partner
Limited partnership agreement
Partnership interest
Nonjudicial dissolution
Judicial dissolution
Event of withdrawal
2001 Act

Discussion Questions

Fact Scenario.   Mike Dalton, Tom Peters, and Amy Latham have formed Dalton & Peters, L.P., an Alabama limited partnership, under the RULPA. Dalton and Peters are the general partners and Latham is the limited partner. Although the partnership has a written agreement, it does not discuss certain issues, including sharing of profits and losses and withdrawals of general partners. Dalton contributed $40,000 to the partnership, Peters contributed $35,000 to the partnership, and Latham contributed $25,000 to the partnership. Use the RULPA to answer the following questions.

1. The limited partnership certificate was filed but due to a typo identified the last date upon which the partnership was to dissolve as June 1, 2110, rather than as June 1, 2010. What is the effect of this error?

2. Which of the following activities are permissible for Latham?

- Contributing a trademark to the partnership rather than cash.
- Decorating the partnership offices (pursuant to a contract between the limited partnership and Latham).

- Guaranteeing a loan made by Bank of America to the limited partnership.
- Suggesting the dissolution of the limited partnership.
- Proposing a meeting to discuss removing Peters as a general partner.
- Inspecting the partnership's tax returns.
- Leasing a new office for the location of the partnership's business.

3. The partnership made $200,000 in profits this year. How will they be divided among the partners? How would these profits be divided if the partnership were a general partnership?

4. Dalton has just withdrawn from the limited partnership. What is the effect on the limited partnership of this withdrawal?

5. The limited partnership has decided to admit Amy Latham's husband, Doug Latham, as a new general partner. May the limited partnership's name be Peters & Latham, L.P.? Discuss.

6. The limited partnership has begun doing business in Mississippi without having first registered to do business there. What is the effect of this failure to transact business without registration?

7. The partnership has decided to dissolve and wind up. It has assets of $150,000 and owes $50,000 to the Bank of America. How will its assets be distributed upon winding up?

8. The partnership has decided to convert to a limited liability limited partnership. What effect will this have on the partners' liability for partnership obligations?

Net Worth

1. Access the Web site of the Secretary of State of Delaware.
   a. What is the filing fee to file a Certificate of Limited Partnership in Delaware?
   b. What is the fee to reserve a name for a limited partnership in Delaware?
2. Access the Web site of the Secretary of State of North Carolina. What is the fee to cancel a Certificate of Limited Partnership?
3. Access the Web site of the Secretary of State of Illinois and review the records for the LP/LLLP/LLP Database — Certificate of Existence.
   a. Who is the agent for service of process for Alden Gardens L.P.?
   b. When was Franklin Park Associates L.P. originally filed? What is its period of duration?
4. Access the Web site of the Secretary of State of Georgia. How many limited partnerships were formed under the ULPA in Georgia in 2006?
5. Access the Web site of the National Conference of Commissioners on Uniform State Laws. Select "Final Acts & Legislation." Review the Limited Partnership Act ("Final Act 2001") for Arizona. What does Section 404(c) provide?

5

♦ ♦ ♦

Limited Liability Partnerships

♦ ♦ ♦

A. Introduction

Limited liability partnerships (LLPs), often called *registered limited liability partnerships*, are a fairly new form of business enterprise that combine some of the best features of partnerships (flexible management and pass-through taxation) and corporations (limited liability). LLPs arose out of the failures of various savings and loan institutions in the 1980s, which left investors without solvent defendants to sue. Those investors then sued the attorneys and accountants who had provided legal and accounting advice to the institutions. Because these law and accounting firms operated as general partnerships, partners in one office found themselves subject to unlimited personal, joint and several liability for advice given by their partners in another office, who were perhaps thousands of miles away. To remedy this situation, limited liability partnerships were created as a way to shield partners from liability for the wrongful acts of their co-partners.

The LLP is now recognized in all United States jurisdictions. An LLP is very similar to a general partnership. In fact, an LLP is simply a "standard" general partnership that files a statement electing LLP status with the state. However, one critical feature of general partnership law is changed: There is no *unlimited* personal liability. American jurisdictions, however, are divided as to the extent to which personal liability can be avoided in an LLP. There are two approaches:

- **Partial Shield States.** In three states, a partner in an LLP does not have personal liability obligations for the wrongful or negligent acts or omissions (torts) of his or her partners but does retain personal liability for other partnership obligations, namely those arising from contract; for example, lease obligations or bank loans of the LLP.
- **Full Shield States.** In 48 jurisdictions (and under the RUPA), a partner is not personally liable for either the wrongful or negligent acts or omissions of other partners or for commercial, contractual, or other obligations of the

Limited liability partnership
Partnership providing protection against liability for wrongful conduct of other partners (also called *registered limited liability partnership*)

Partial shield states
States in which partners in an LLP retain liability for contractual obligations

Full shield states
States in which partners in an LLP are fully protected from personal liability, whether arising in tort or contract (also called *bulletproof* states)

partnership, making the LLP partner much like a shareholder in a corporation with regard to liability. Full shield states are sometimes called *bulletproof* states because the liability of the partners is impenetrable or bulletproof. As each year passes, more and more states adopt full shield status.

LLPs as a form of partnership are thus governed nearly exclusively by partnership laws and principles. In 1997 the RUPA was expressly amended to add a new article to recognize limited liability partnerships. LLPs are thus governed by state statutes and the agreement of their members. In the absence of agreement, the state statutes (many of which are based on the RUPA) control and serve as default statutes to fill in the gaps. In all states, LLPs are subject to state registration requirements and, in some states, to mandatory insurance requirements. The text of Article 10 of the RUPA, which governs LLPs, can be found at www.nccusl.org.

Although the LLP is ideal for professionals, such as those practicing law or accounting, and was created with those professionals in mind, in most states any other partnership may convert to an LLP or a business may form as an LLP so long as its business is lawful. A few states, however, including California, Nevada, New York, and Oregon, limit LLPs solely to the practice of specified professions, such as law and accounting. The LLP form is not available in those states for other businesses, such as real estate development, consulting, or marketing. In fact, professional service firms dominate the types of businesses that register as LLPs. For example, all of the "Big Four" accounting firms operate as LLPs, and most major law firms in the United States operate as LLPs. The popularity of the LLP is so widespread that formation of limited partnerships has significantly decreased.

B. Advantages of LLPs

The greatest advantage of an LLP is that in all states partners in an LLP are protected against unlimited personal liability for the negligent acts and misconduct of their co-partners, unless:

- A partner supervised or directed the partner who engaged in the wrongful act;
- A partner was directly involved in the act giving rise to liability; or
- A partner had knowledge or notice of the act of liability and failed to take reasonable steps to prevent or cure it (the rule in some states).

Partners in LLPs always retain personal liability for their own negligence or misconduct, and the LLP itself is fully liable for the negligent acts and omissions of any of its partners. For example, if Mark is a partner in an LLP that practices law and he commits an act of malpractice, Mark will retain personal liability for his negligence, but Mark's co-partners will not have any personal liability (assuming they did not direct or supervise Mark's act). The LLP itself will also be liable for Mark's negligence. Of course, LLP partners also retain personal liability when they have agreed to do so, for example, if they agree to personally guarantee repayment of a loan made to the LLP itself.

1. *Partial Shield States*

In the three partial shield states, the protection against unlimited liability does not apply to all acts of one's partners; it applies only to wrongful acts and omissions, such as negligence. Thus, in those states, a partner in an LLP remains personally liable for other debts and obligations incurred by a partner or the partnership, such as money borrowed, contractual commitments, rent, and other such debts and obligations. Using our example concerning Mark, although Mark's co-partners do not have personal liability for Mark's act of malpractice, in the partial shield states they would be subject to personal liability for new office equipment purchased by Mark. The LLP itself will have liability for both the act of malpractice and the contractual obligation.

2. *Full Shield States*

In the 48 jurisdictions that follow the full shield or bulletproof approach (which is also the approach of RUPA § 306(c)), a partner in an LLP is not, solely by reason of being a partner, personally liable for any obligation of the LLP, whether the obligation arises in tort, contract, or otherwise. Even in full shield states, however, partners in LLPs retain liability for their own wrongful acts and those of others under their supervision. The LLP itself will have liability for obligations arising out of either tort or contract.

Full shield states have steadily gained in popularity, and many states (for example, Illinois, Michigan, Ohio, and Texas) that once were partial shield states have amended their statutes to afford full shield or bulletproof status to LLPs. Most experts expect this trend to continue over the years.

Section 306(c) of the RUPA clearly states that "an obligation of a partnership incurred while the partnership is a limited liability partnership, *whether arising in contract, tort, or otherwise*, is solely the obligation of the partnership" (emphasis added). Many states have adopted this exact language, making it clear that partners in an LLP have no liability for act of the partnership or their co-partners, whether those acts arise in tort or contract.

Some states, however, have statutory provisions that are less clear. For example, Tennessee's statute provides that a partner in an LLP is not liable for "debts, obligations and liabilities of or chargeable to the partnership or another partner, whether in tort, contract, or otherwise, *arising from omissions, negligence, wrongful acts, misconduct or malpractice* committed while the partnership is a registered limited liability partnership . . . ." Tenn. Code Ann. § 61-1-306 (emphasis added). Thus, although the statute originally states that LLP partners are not liable for obligations in tort or contract, language immediately following suggests that liability is limited only if the obligation arises from negligence, wrongful acts, or misconduct. Language in other states, such as Kentucky, Michigan, New Hampshire, and West Virginia, is similarly ambiguous. Presumably, case law in these states will clarify these issues. In any event, a plaintiff suing an LLP in one of those states may be able to "draft around" the statutory language to allege that the shield doesn't fully protect the LLP's partners.

See Figure 5-1 for a chart identifying full shield and partial shield states.

FIGURE 5-1
Full Shield and Partial Shield States

Full Shield Jurisdictions		Partial Shield States
Alabama	Montana	Louisiana
Alaska	Nebraska	South Carolina*
Arizona	Nevada	Utah
Arkansas	New Hampshire**	
California*	New Jersey	
Colorado	New Mexico*	
Connecticut*	New York	
Delaware	North Carolina	
District of Columbia	North Dakota	
Florida	Ohio	
Georgia	Oklahoma*	
Hawaii	Oregon	
Idaho	Pennsylvania	
Illinois	Rhode Island*	
Indiana	South Dakota	
Iowa	Tennessee**	
Kansas	Texas*	
Kentucky**	Vermont	
Maine	Virginia	
Maryland	Washington*	
Massachusetts*	West Virginia* **	
Michigan**	Wisconsin	
Minnesota	Wyoming	
Mississippi		
Missouri		

*State includes some form of insurance or financial responsibility requirement.

**See note in text regarding extent of liability shield.

EXAMPLES

1. **Full Shield.** Gina is an attorney with a large LLP law firm in New York, a full shield state. Her partner, Sam, forgot to file an appeal brief, and her partner, Tim, recently signed a long-term lease for office space. Gina will not have any personal liability for either Sam's malpractice or for any liability under the lease signed by Tim.

2. **Partial Shield.** Sarah is an accountant in an LLP firm operating in South Carolina, a partial shield state. Her partner Randy failed to perform an

accounting audit for a client and her partner Mike recently signed a contract to buy real estate in Charleston. Sarah will not have any personal liability for Randy's accounting malpractice but will have personal liability for the real estate contract signed by Mike.

Other advantages of a general partnership, such as the sharing of management duties and responsibilities and the ability to raise capital by admitting new partners, exist in the LLP as well. Moreover, at least for many professionals who are accustomed to practicing in a partnership, the LLP is a comfortable and familiar business structure because it is in fact a partnership (although the LLP has abolished the principle of unlimited personal liability that attaches to general partners for torts). Finally, LLPs afford the pass-through tax status of partnerships.

C. Disadvantages of LLPs

Following are some of the disadvantages of LLPs:

- LLPs can only be formed in strict compliance with state statutes, and therefore they are somewhat complicated and may be expensive to form.
- Some states require LLPs to have certain liability insurance in place, imposing an administrative and financial burden on many LLPs.
- Because in three states LLPs have only partial shield protection, operating an LLP on a nationwide basis may result in different levels of liability in different states. Some states have enacted statutes to cover this issue. For example, Cal. Corp. Code § 16958 provides that the laws of the jurisdiction under which a foreign limited liability partnership is organized shall govern its organization and internal affairs and the liability of its partners.
- In several states, LLPs have a term of existence of one year, after which they must be renewed. Thus, LLPs lack continuity in those states.
- As mentioned earlier, several states allow LLPs to be formed only for the practice of law, medicine, accounting, and so forth. In those states, the LLP structure is then not available for other types of business, such as real estate development.
- Some states base their LLP organization or filing fees on the number of partners in the LLP. For example, in Texas, the filing fee to form an LLP is $200 per partner. Thus, a law firm with 100 partners would pay $20,000 to organize as an LLP, a filing fee that is extraordinarily high. Other states (such as Illinois) place upper limits on the filing fee, so that the fee is $100 per partner, but no more than $5,000 for an entire firm.
- Many states require LLPs to file annual reports or renewal forms, imposing a paperwork and financial burden.
- Because LLPs impose liability on partners for those whom they supervise, some experts have questioned whether LLPs thus encourage senior partners to avoid supervising junior partners.

D. Formation of LLPs

The formation of an LLP is somewhat similar to the formation of a limited partnership. States have application forms of varying extensiveness, and filing fees are imposed. In Delaware, the Statement of Qualification need contain only the following six elements:

1. The name of the LLP (which must include the words "limited liability partnership," "registered limited liability partnership," or abbreviations of those words, to provide notice to the public that the entity shields its partners from liability for misconduct of other partners);
2. The address of the LLP's principal office in the state and name and address of its agent for service of process;
3. The number of partners the LLP will have;
4. The effective date of the statement;
5. An application statement reading, "The partnership elects to be a limited liability partnership"; and
6. Signature of an authorized partner.

See Figure 5-2 for a sample application form. This application must be renewed on an annual basis in some states. Failure to renew the application can result in a revocation of authority to conduct business as an LLP in the state (although most states allow the LLP to be reinstated once it cures any default).

Just as a new business may form as an LLP, an existing general or limited partnership may convert to an LLP. In many instances, law, accounting, and medical practices that once existed as general partnerships have converted to the LLP form. All signs, letterheads, business cards, and other written materials must carry a signal (such as "LLP") to indicate the entity has adopted the LLP form.

An LLP formed in one state may do business in another state as an LLP. The procedure for operating in another state is much the same as that for a limited partnership: An application must be completed and filed with the other state asking it to recognize the LLP as a foreign limited liability partnership. An agent for service of process in the foreign state must be designated. Review state statutes to determine what constitutes "doing business" in the state so that the LLP applies in the foreign jurisdiction only when necessary. For example, merely holding meetings or engaging in an isolated transaction in another state are generally not considered "doing business" such as would require a business to register with a state as a foreign LLP before it commences those activities. (See Chapter Thirteen for a further discussion on "doing business" in other states.)

Due to the statutory variations in LLP coverage, some issues remain unsettled. For example, if an LLP is formed in a full shield state and begins doing business in a partial shield state in which a partner in an LLP breaches a contract, are all partners jointly and severally liable as they would be in the partial shield state, or is no liability imposed on the partners for this breach of contract because the home state is a full shield state? Unfortunately, there is no clear answer to this question. At a minimum, the LLP should consider forming in a full shield state and then inserting provisions into all of its contracts providing that the law of that jurisdiction will apply in any action relating to the contract, thus affording a

FIGURE 5-2

Nevada Application for Registration — Limited Liability Partnership

ROSS MILLER
Secretary of State
206 North Carson Street
Carson City, Nevada 89701-4299
(775) 684 5708
Website: www.nvsos.gov

Certificate of Registration
Limited-Liability Partnership
(PURSUANT TO NRS CHAPTER 87)

USE BLACK INK ONLY - DO NOT HIGHLIGHT   ABOVE SPACE IS FOR OFFICE USE ONLY

1. Name of Limited-Liability Partnership: (see instructions)	
2. Street Address of Principal Office:	Street Address City State Zip Code

3. Registered Agent for Service of Process: (check only one box)	☐ Commercial Registered Agent:
	                Name
	 ☐ Noncommercial Registered Agent **OR** ☐ Office or Position with Entity
	     (name and address below) (name and address below)
	
	 Name of Noncommercial Registered Agent OR Name of Title of Office or Other Position with Entity
	
	 Street Address City Nevada Zip Code
	 Mailing Address (if different from street address) City Nevada Zip Code

4. Name and Business Address of Each Managing Partner in this State: (attach additional pages if more than 3)	1)
	    Name
	
	 Business Address City Nevada Zip Code
	 2)
	    Name
	
	 Business Address City Nevada Zip Code
	 3)
	    Name
	
	 Business Address City Nevada Zip Code

5. Name and Signature of Authorized Managing Partner(s): (see instructions)	The partnership, hereafter, will be a registered limited-liability partnership: X _____ Name Managing Partner Signature X _____ Name Managing Partner Signature X _____ Name Managing Partner Signature
6. Certificate of Acceptance of Appointment of Registered Agent:	I hereby accept appointment as Registered Agent for the above named Entity. X _____ Authorized Signature of Registered Agent or On Behalf of Registered Agent Entity Date

This form must be accompanied by appropriate fees.

Nevada Secretary of State NRS 87 DLLP Registration
Revised on 7-1-08

credible argument that the full shield law governs no matter where the breach occurs. As states continue the trend of converting from partial shield status to full shield status, this issue will decrease in importance.

PRACTICE TIP

Create your own "form book." Collect all of the LLP forms provided by your state's secretary of state and keep them handy in a file folder. Tape the filing fee schedule on the left side of the folder. Include the citations to your state's LLP statutes. You will then be ready to respond to most questions about LLPs in your state and to prepare most organizational and renewal documents. Also, print the instructions for each form. These instructions often provide valuable information about how and where to file documents, how to calculate filing fees, how to calculate insurance amounts or cash reserves (if required) in your state, and so forth.

E. Operation of LLPs

The operation of an LLP is nearly identical to that of a general partnership. The fiduciary duties owed by partners to each other apply. Each partner in the LLP is an agent of the LLP and can thus bind the partnership by entering into contracts, hiring employees, and so forth. The partners who co-manage the business will likely have a written LLP agreement very similar to that for a general partnership (although oral agreements are permissible). The agreement will indicate each partner's contributions, include the formula for profits and losses, discuss admission and withdrawal of partners, and specify the conditions that will cause dissolution of the partnership. The general partnership agreement provided in Appendix B can be easily modified for an LLP. Just as with general partnerships, in the absence of an agreement, profits, losses, management, and control of the LLP will be shared equally regardless of capital contributions, and partners may dissociate without necessarily causing a dissolution and winding up. For example, if Dave contributes $10,000 to an LLP, Julio contributes $6,000, and Hillary contributes $4,000 and they do not agree on the division of profits, profits of $100,000 will be divided into three equal parts rather than being allocated according to their contributions. Similar to a general partnership, to protect creditors, interim distributions may not be made unless the LLP is solvent.

Perhaps the most significant difference between the operation of a general partnership and an LLP is that some states require the LLP to maintain liability insurance. This insurance is designed to protect injured parties who previously would have been able to sue numerous partners for acts of negligence. Under LLP law, only the LLP itself and the partner committing the wrongful act have liability for a wrongful act, so an injured party is limited to the partnership's assets and those of the malfeasing partner. The LLP is thus required in some states to carry a certain amount of insurance (or to set aside funds to satisfy possible judgments against the LLP or its partners). For example, in Texas, the insurance or reserved capital amount is $100,000; in Connecticut, the amount is $250,000 if the LLP engages in providing professional services (such as legal services). Most states, however, do not impose insurance or financial responsibility requirements, and some states have recently repealed their insurance requirements, reasoning that insurance is not required under the RUPA and that other similar business entities are not required to maintain such insurance. (See Figure 5-1 for identification of states requiring insurance.)

F.   Transferability of Interest and Admission of New Partners

Identical to general partnership law, a partner in an LLP may assign her profits to another but cannot fully substitute another in her place because this would violate the voluntary nature of a partnership. A new partner with full rights to participate in the LLP may be admitted upon the consent of all existing partners or as provided in the LLP agreement.

In most cases, the agreement provides that the withdrawal of one partner will not cause a dissolution, and a method will be provided in the agreement for dissociation of a partner and a buy-out of her interest.

G.   Dissolution and Liquidation of LLPs

Dissolution of LLPs is similar to that of general partnerships. The partnership agreement will likely discuss the events that will cause dissolution of the LLP. If the partnership agreement is silent on these issues, the RUPA will provide the terms and conditions for dissociation and dissolution. Recall from Chapter Three that under the RUPA not every dissociation of a partner triggers a dissolution and winding up. If no dissolution is caused, the LLP will buy out the dissociating partner's interest.

Before the LLP dissolves, it must liquidate or wind up by collecting any debts due it, satisfying any obligations, liquidating assets, and then distributing the proceeds to creditors and, last, to the partners. A certificate of withdrawal should be filed in the state of formation and in any state in which the LLP has been operating.

H.   Taxation of LLPs

The income earned by the LLP (whether distributed or not) is passed through to the individual partners, who pay taxes at whatever rate is appropriate to them. The LLP itself does not pay federal income taxes, but it must file the information tax return required of all partnerships. The tax forms used by general partnerships and general partners (discussed in Chapter Three) are also used for LLPs and their partners. Just like general and limited partnerships, LLPs may choose to "check the box" and elect to be taxed as a corporation (see Chapter Three).

I. Growth and Trends in LLPs

LLPs have seen unprecedented growth in the little more than 20 years they have been in existence. Because lawsuits are significant threats for professionals such as doctors, lawyers, and accountants, the LLP has been of particular interest to professionals. The increase in LLP registrations in the mid-1990s far exceeded those for corporations and other forms of partnerships. The majority of LLPs are professional firms. In fact, law firms make up the largest single group formed as LLPs, followed by medical firms and then accounting firms. Some states limit LLPs solely to the practice of certain professions; other types of businesses (for example, real estate development companies and marketing consulting firms) must operate in some other business form (often as limited liability companies, discussed in Chapter Six).

J. Role of Paralegal

Paralegals will be engaged in the following tasks:

- Reviewing state statutes regarding requirements for naming the LLP and any signals required for the name;
- Conducting research to determine whether the state affords full shield or partial shield protection and whether there are any insurance requirements in the state;
- Drafting and filing the application to conduct business as an LLP (see Figure 5-2);
- Drafting the LLP agreement (an existing form of the general partnership agreement can be easily modified for use by an LLP; see Appendix B);
- Filing applications in any state in which the LLP wishes to conduct business as a foreign LLP;
- Filing any required annual reports;
- Withdrawing applications in states in which the LLP ceases to do business; and
- Reviewing LLP written materials to ensure they comply with state requirements as to the name designation.

Case Illustration
Limited Liability of LLP Partners

Case: *Verizon Yellow Pages Co. v. Sims & Sims P.C.*, 15 Mass. L. Rptr. 734 (Super. Ct. 2003)

Facts: In a suit for a business debt, the plaintiff sought to disqualify an attorney, John Cannavo, from representing one of the defendants, which was a limited liability partnership. Cannavo was a partner in the limited liability partnership and would be a necessary witness at trial.

Holding: The motion to disqualify was granted. Cannavo has no right to represent the limited liability partnership *pro se* (on his own behalf). His rights are distinct from those of the limited liability partnership because only it would be liable for any judgment rendered in the case. Should the plaintiff be successful it could collect up to the limit of the partnership's assets and would never be able to reach Cannavo's personal assets. Moreover, Cannavo will be a necessary witness in the trial of this matter and thus cannot act as counsel under Massachusetts rules of professional conduct.

Key Features
of LLPs

◆ Partners in LLPs have no personal liability in any state for negligent acts of their co-partners.
◆ In almost all states, called full shield states, LLP partners have no personal liability either for negligent acts of their co-partners or for contractual obligations of the LLP or of their co-partners.
◆ In all states, partners in LLPs retain liability for their own negligent acts and those they direct or supervise. The LLP itself is also liable for such acts.
◆ LLPs are formed by filing an application with the state of formation.
◆ Identical to general partnerships, the LLP agreement may be oral or written; in the absence of an agreement, profits, losses, management, and control are shared equally regardless of capital contribution.
◆ LLPs have the pass-through taxation of general partnerships.
◆ LLPs continue the modern trend of business structures that allow their members to manage the enterprise and yet be shielded from personal liability.

Internet Resources

State statutes: www.law.cornell.edu
www.findlaw.com

Tax forms: www.irs.gov

Text of RUPA:	www.nccusl.org
State forms:	www.nass.org
General information:	www.findlaw.com
	www.toolkit.cch.com
	www.megalaw.com
Forms of agreements:	www.allaboutforms.com
	www.siccode.com/form.php

Key Terms

Limited liability partnership
Partial shield states
Full shield states

Discussion Questions

Fact Scenario.   Young & Diaz, LLP, is a law firm with offices in several states. Use the RUPA to answer these questions.

1. The LLP would like to open a new office in Arizona, a state in which it has not conducted business, and would also like to open a bank account in Nevada, a state in which it has not conducted business. What must the LLP do?

2. Cal, one of the LLP partners in Alaska, committed an act of legal malpractice. Discuss the liability for the partnership, Cal, and all other partners for this act.

3. Without any authority, Frances, one of the LLP partners in Utah, obligated the partnership to lease new cars for various partners. Discuss the liability for the partnership, Frances, and the partners in Delaware and in Utah for this act.

4. Why would some states require the LLP to obtain liability insurance?

5. Kyle, one of the senior partners in the firm, is the supervisor of Kim, one of the new attorneys in the firm's Chicago office. Kyle has been ill recently and has been unable to meet with Kim. Kim recently committed an act of legal malpractice. Describe the liability of the LLP, Kyle, Kim, and all other LLP partners for this act.

6. The LLP has no specific term. Tim, one of the partners in the California office, has unexpectedly died. What is the effect of Tim's death on the LLP?

7. The partnership has no agreement regarding the division of profits and losses. How will profits be divided this year? Discuss.

8. The LLP neglected to file its annual report this year. What is the effect of this failure? Is there anything the LLP can do to "save" itself?

Net Worth

1. Access the Web site of the Delaware Secretary of State.
    a. What is the fee in Delaware if a partnership with 10 partners wishes to apply to become a Delaware LLP?
    b. What is the fee to file an annual report in Delaware for an LLP?
2. Access the Web site of the Illinois Secretary of State. What is the fee to file a Renewal Statement for an Illinois LLP with 60 partners?
3. Access Rhode Island's statutes. If a law firm has eight partners, what liability insurance must it maintain?
4. Access the Web site of the law firm Mayer Brown. Under what business structure does the firm operate?

6

◆ ◆ ◆

Limited Liability Companies

◆ ◆ ◆

A. Introduction

Like limited liability partnerships, limited liability companies are a fairly new form of business organization recognized in all United States jurisdictions. Limited liability companies continue the trend seen in limited liability partnerships of combining the most attractive features of partnerships and corporations in a new enterprise.

The **limited liability company (LLC)** derives its first benefit from corporation law: Its **members** are protected from personal liability for the company's acts and the acts of other members, whether arising in tort or contract. Its second benefit comes from partnership law: All money earned by the company is passed through directly to the members, who pay tax on the money at their individual rates. The company itself does not pay tax on earnings, thus avoiding the burden of double taxation.

LLCs are governed by their applicable state statutes. Because the LLC is relatively new, there is little case law interpreting LLC statutes, and the statutes vary widely from state to state. Due to these variations in state laws, the National Conference of Commissioners on Uniform State Laws drafted the **Uniform Limited Liability Company Act (ULLCA)**. By the time the ULLCA was finally released in 1996, most states had already adopted their own LLC legislation; thus, few states adopted the ULLCA. The ULLCA was revised again in 2006, and as of the date of this text, it has only been adopted in Idaho and Iowa. It borrows heavily from both partnership and corporate law, reflecting the nature of the LLC as a hybrid entity combining the best features of partnerships with the best features of corporations. The text of the ULLCA is available at the Conference's Web site at www.nccusl.org.

LLCs may conduct business in states other than the state of their formation, assuming they comply with the applicable state statutes of those jurisdictions. For example, professionals (including doctors and lawyers) may not adopt the LLC form in California.

Limited liability company
Entity providing full protection for its members from all personal liability, whether arising in tort or contract

Members
Participants in a limited liability company

ULLCA
Uniform Limited Liability Company Act, a uniform act governing operation and management of LLCs

Although LLCs are similar to limited liability partnerships (LLPs), discussed in Chapter Five, they differ in five primary ways:

1. LLPs are a species of partnership and are governed primarily by partnership principles; LLCs are an entirely new form of business enterprise.
2. Only full shield states offer full protection from liability for LLP partners for wrongful acts of co-partners and contractual obligations, whereas a hallmark of LLC statutes is full protection from personal liability for all LLC members whether the liability arises in tort or contract.
3. All states but Wyoming permit a one-person LLC; LLPs, however, because they are a form of partnership, must always have at least two partners.
4. LLPs, as a variety of partnership, must be formed for a profit-making purpose. LLCs, however, may be formed for nonprofit purposes.
5. Generally, the traditional professions (such as law, accounting, and medicine) comprise the majority of LLPs, whereas businesses in the "emerging" professions (computer consulting, marketing, and management services) tend to adopt the LLC form.

B. Advantages of Limited Liability Companies

1. Limited Liability and Full Management

The LLC provides complete protection to its members from personal liability. Although limited partners have limited liability, that limited liability hinges upon the limited partners' passivity with regard to management of the business. In an LLC, by contrast, the members may be active in management and yet retain their limited liability, offering tremendous advantages to investors who wish to be active in the management of their money and yet not expose their other assets to liability. The liability of a member of an LLC is limited to the investment contributed by that member, although the LLC itself, of course, has liability for the wrongful acts of its members, and LLC members always retain personal liability for their own wrongful acts and those performed under their supervision and control. Thus, if one of the members of a professional LLC commits an act of legal malpractice, he and the LLC have liability for the act, but the other LLC members do not.

2. Flexible Management

The LLC may be managed by its members, which is the most common approach, or the members may decide to appoint or elect managers to operate and manage the business. These appointed managers need not be members of the LLC. The ability to have a member-managed LLC or manager-managed LLC provides great operating flexibility.

3. One-Person LLCs

At present, all jurisdictions except Wyoming permit one-member LLCs. Thus, sole proprietors in the vast majority of states may form an LLC, which allows them to protect their assets from personal liability. Moreover, if the business grows, an LLC can easily accommodate the admission of new members. Thus, for a sole proprietor with significant personal assets, the LLC is an attractive form of business enterprise because it offers full protection against personal liability for obligations of the business, yet affords opportunity for sole decision-making, management, and control.

4. Pass-Through Tax Status

One of the key advantages of an LLC is that it is taxed as a partnership. All of the income earned by the LLC, whether distributed or not, is immediately passed through to the members, who then declare their respective portion of the profits on their individual federal tax returns and pay taxes at their appropriate rates. This pass-through tax status offers advantages over a corporation, whose income is taxed twice: once when earned by the corporation and again when received by the corporate owners, the shareholders, as dividends.

Although one type of corporation, the S corporation, offers pass-through tax status (see Chapter Fifteen), it is subject to a number of restrictions. For example, the number of shareholders in an S corporation is limited to 100 individuals, and, by law, nonresident aliens are not permitted to be shareholders. The LLC is not subject to these restrictions.

C. Disadvantages of LLCs

Although there are some disadvantages of doing business as an LLC, the advantages far outweigh any disadvantages. The primary disadvantages of LLCs are as follows:

- While a member of an LLC may transfer his financial interest in the LLC to another, the transferee will not become a member of the LLC unless the operating agreement so provides or *all* other LLC members consent. (Note that some states permit the assignee to become a member upon a majority vote.) This limitation may serve to restrict growth within an LLC.
- Because the LLC is a relatively new form of business, little case law interpreting LLCs exists.
- Formation of an LLC can be slightly complicated and expensive due to the various forms and documents required.
- A few states limit the LLC to a single term, generally 30 years. This is a minority approach; however, paralegals will need to review the pertinent state statutes to determine whether such a limitation exists. Most states allow an LLC to exist perpetually but require the filing of annual reports.
- Although each state recognizes LLCs, and an LLC may thus conduct business in numerous states, the variations among state statutes may make it somewhat complicated for a business to operate nationwide as an LLC.

D. Formation of LLCs

The formation of an LLC closely parallels the formation of a corporation. The document that creates the LLC, usually called the articles of organization (or certificate of organization), must be filed with the appropriate state authorities. Moreover, the LLC must be governed by an agreement, usually called the operating agreement.

1. Articles of Organization

Articles of organization
Document filed with the state that creates an LLC

An LLC is created by the filing of a document, called the **articles of organization**, with the appropriate state agency, usually the secretary of state. Each state has its own statutory requirements for the contents of the articles of organization. Following are the usual elements required in the articles of organization:

1. The name of the company, including any required abbreviations or signals;
2. The address of the initial designated office;
3. The name and street address of the initial agent, who will receive service of process;
4. The name and address of each organizer;
5. Whether the company is to exist perpetually; and
6. A statement regarding how the entity is to be managed (for example, whether it will be managed by one person or all members).

The articles must be signed and then filed with the secretary of state with the requisite filing fee. See Figure 6-1 for the form to create a California LLC. Creation of the LLC results in a new legal entity separate and distinct from its members, who thus have no personal liability for the LLC's debts and obligations (unless they agree to assume such liability).

2. Operating Agreement

Operating agreement
Agreement governing the operation of an LLC

The document containing the provisions for the operation and governance of the LLC is usually called an **operating agreement**. In a few states it must be a written agreement; most states and the ULLCA permit an oral agreement. The operating agreement for an LLC is very similar to a partnership agreement. The LLC operating agreement must, however, be tailored to meet the specific requirements of the LLC statutes in the state of formation. The operating agreement is a private document; it is not filed with any state agency.

The operating agreement may be flexibly written; and, although it may not unreasonably restrict a member's right to information or records, or in most states, unreasonably eliminate the duties of good faith, fair dealing, and loyalty owed by and to LLC members, or unreasonably reduce their duty of due care, members are

FIGURE 6-1
California LLC Articles of Organization

LLC-1   File # _____

State of California
Secretary of State

LIMITED LIABILITY COMPANY
ARTICLES OF ORGANIZATION

A $70.00 filing fee must accompany this form.

IMPORTANT – Read instructions before completing this form.   This Space For Filing Use Only

ENTITY NAME (End the name with the words "Limited Liability Company," or the abbreviations "LLC" or "L.L.C." The words "Limited" and "Company" may be abbreviated to "Ltd." and "Co.," respectively.)

1. NAME OF LIMITED LIABILITY COMPANY

PURPOSE (The following statement is required by statute and should not be altered.)

2. THE PURPOSE OF THE LIMITED LIABILITY COMPANY IS TO ENGAGE IN ANY LAWFUL ACT OR ACTIVITY FOR WHICH A LIMITED LIABILITY COMPANY MAY BE ORGANIZED UNDER THE BEVERLY-KILLEA LIMITED LIABILITY COMPANY ACT.

INITIAL AGENT FOR SERVICE OF PROCESS (If the agent is an individual, the agent must reside in California and both Items 3 and 4 must be completed. If the agent is a corporation, the agent must have on file with the California Secretary of State a certificate pursuant to Corporations Code section 1505 and Item 3 must be completed (leave Item 4 blank).

3. NAME OF INITIAL AGENT FOR SERVICE OF PROCESS

4. IF AN INDIVIDUAL, ADDRESS OF INITIAL AGENT FOR SERVICE OF PROCESS IN CALIFORNIA   CITY   STATE   ZIP CODE

                                                                                    CA

MANAGEMENT (Check only one)

5. THE LIMITED LIABILITY COMPANY WILL BE MANAGED BY:

☐ ONE MANAGER

☐ MORE THAN ONE MANAGER

☐ ALL LIMITED LIABILITY COMPANY MEMBER(S)

ADDITIONAL INFORMATION

6. ADDITIONAL INFORMATION SET FORTH ON THE ATTACHED PAGES, IF ANY, IS INCORPORATED HEREIN BY THIS REFERENCE AND MADE A PART OF THIS CERTIFICATE.

EXECUTION

7. I DECLARE I AM THE PERSON WHO EXECUTED THIS INSTRUMENT, WHICH EXECUTION IS MY ACT AND DEED.

_____   _____
DATE   SIGNATURE OF ORGANIZER

                                 _____
                                 TYPE OR PRINT NAME OF ORGANIZER

LLC-1 (REV 04/2007)   APPROVED BY SECRETARY OF STATE

free to regulate the affairs of the LLC as they wish. The operating agreement should include at minimum the following provisions:

1. **Name of the LLC.** Like any business name, the LLC's name may not be deceptively similar to that of another business such that there would be a likelihood of confusion in the marketplace. Thus, a search should be conducted to ensure that the name is available, and a check should be made of the state statutes to determine what signal must be used in the business name. Most states (and the ULLCA) require that the name include "limited liability company" or "limited company" or an abbreviation thereof, such as "LLC" or "LC." The full name of the LLC (together with its identifying signal indicating adoption of the LLC form) should appear on all correspondence and written documents of the LLC to provide notice to the public that the entity is operating as an LLC. Most states allow the business to reserve a name during its formation period by filing an application to reserve the name for some period of time, often 90 days.

2. **Names and Addresses of Members.** The names and addresses of all members should be set forth so that notices and information can be communicated to them.

3. **Recitals.** A recitation should be made confirming the intent of the members to form an LLC.

4. **Purpose.** The purpose of the LLC should be stated broadly enough so that the LLC can expand and grow without requiring amendment of the operating agreement. In most states, a general clause is acceptable stating that the purpose of the LLC is to engage in any business lawful in the state.

5. **Address.** The principal place of business of the LLC should be provided so that members can easily communicate with the LLC.

6. **Term.** A review of the pertinent state statutes is required to ensure that the LLC complies with any restrictions as to the duration of the LLC. Most states and the ULLCA provide that if no specific term is set forth, the LLC will have perpetual existence.

7. **Financial Provisions.** The initial contributions by members to the LLC should be described. Contributions may be in the form of cash, services, or property. Typically, profits and losses will be shared according to the respective interests contributed by the members, although the parties are free to make other arrangements. With regard to additional contributions, the general rule is that they will be made in proportion to the initial capital contributions. This section of the operating agreement should also discuss distributions of assets. Under the ULLCA, if the agreement is silent, distributions by the LLC before its dissolution must be in equal shares.

8. **Operation of the LLC.** One of the distinct advantages of an LLC is that it may be a **member-managed LLC** without subjecting those members to unlimited liability. If the operating agreement is silent, each member will have an equal right to manage the LLC business. Member-managed LLCs thus operate similarly to general partnerships in that every member is able to conduct business on behalf of the LLC. Because an LLC with

Member-managed LLC
An LLC managed by its members

a large number of members will find it difficult to be governed by all members, larger LLCs often elect a managing committee or board of managers, much the way a corporation is managed by its board of directors rather than its individual shareholders. Such an LLC is referred to as a **manager-managed LLC.** A manager need not be a member of the LLC.

Manager-managed LLC
An LLC managed by appointed managers rather than by its members

If managers are to be elected, the operating agreement should indicate how often elections will be held, the term of office for each manager, and the duties of the managers. If restrictions are to be imposed on managers, they should be clearly stated. For example, the operating agreement may restrict the managers from borrowing money in excess of a certain amount.

Generally, members of an LLC have the same fiduciary duties to the LLC and its members that general partners have, namely, a duty to act in good faith and in the best interests of the LLC. Managers will not be personally liable for decisions affecting the LLC unless they have breached a certain duty, violated a law, or acted in bad faith with conscious disregard of the best interests of the LLC. Thus, managers will not be liable for some mere error in business judgment. The recently revised ULLCA § 110 allows an operating agreement to vary some of these duties. For example, the ULLCA now provides that an operating agreement may eliminate the duty of loyalty or alter the duty of due care so long as such is not "manifestly unreasonable."

9. **Meetings and Voting.** The operating agreement should provide how often regular meetings will be held, where they will be held, and the procedures for sending notices of and conducting the meetings. Most ordinary business decisions are made by majority vote of the members (if the LLC is member-managed) or the managers (if the LLC is managed by a board of managers). Extraordinary matters, such as amending the operating agreement, admitting new members, or dissolving the LLC, often require unanimous approval of all members.

10. **Admission of New Members and Dissociation of Members.** According to ULLCA § 401(d), unless the operating agreement provides otherwise, admission of a new member to the LLC requires unanimous agreement. This requirement may impose a natural restriction on the size of the LLC due to the difficulty of achieving unanimous agreement on nearly anything once a group reaches a certain size.

A member may withdraw or dissociate according to terms specified in the operating agreement or articles of organization. If no specific provisions are provided, a member may withdraw from the LLC upon notice to the LLC. Nevertheless, if the withdrawal is a breach of the operating agreement or occurs prior to the time set forth in the operating agreement for the term of the LLC, the dissociation is wrongful, and the withdrawing member may be liable for any damages caused.

11. **Transferability of Interests.** A member's financial interest in an LLC is personal property. ULLCA § 502 provides that an LLC member may freely transfer his or her right to distributions, but remember that the transferee will become a member of the LLC only if the operating agreement so provides or all other members consent. If such consent cannot

be obtained, the assignee will have the right to the assignor's financial interest in the LLC but will have no management rights.

12. **Dissolution.** The agreement should specify the events that will trigger a dissolution of the LLC. Many operating agreements provide that any of the following events will cause a dissolution:

   (a) Upon expiration of the period fixed for duration;
   (b) Upon written agreement of all members;
   (c) Upon the death or bankruptcy of any member, unless some percentage of the remaining members agree to continue doing business; or
   (d) Upon determination by a court that it is not reasonably practicable to continue the business.

   Generally, upon the dissolution of an LLC, the LLC must file articles of termination or dissolution with the state in which it was formed and wind up its business activities.

13. **Miscellaneous Provisions.** Similar to a partnership agreement, the LLC operating agreement may include numerous other provisions. For example, it may provide that members may not transfer their interest in the LLC to others without first offering it to existing LLC members. Provisions should be included for dispute resolution, amendments to the operating agreement, location of books and records, reimbursement for expenses, and any other matters pertinent to the operation of the business.

PRACTICE TIP

If you work closely with several LLC clients, keep their operating agreements handy. Consider drafting a one-page index or table of contents as the first page of the agreement so that you can readily find critical operating agreement provisions relating to distributions, duties, withdrawal, and transfers of LLC interests. Highlight provisions that you find you refer to over and over again, or place notes in the margins next to key provisions. Remember that if the operating agreement does not address a certain issue, your state LLC statute will control.

E. Transferability of Interest

Most states and the ULLCA provide that a member's financial interest in an LLC, namely, the right to profits or distributions, is personal property, and as such may be freely assigned to another. The assignment, however, carries with it only the assignor's right to profits. It does not entitle the new owner to be a member of the LLC with rights of participation unless the operating agreement so provides or *all* of the other members consent (although some states require only a majority vote).

F.   Dissociation and Dissolution of LLCs

Under the ULLCA, although many events (such as an individual LLC member's death or bankruptcy) cause a dissociation, fewer events require dissolution and winding up. Naturally, a well-written operating agreement should discuss such issues. The following rules apply under ULLCA §§ 601, 602, 603, and 701 (although they may be modified by the LLC operating agreement).

Events Causing Dissociation.   A member is dissociated from an LLC if any of the following events occur:

- The member provides notice of his or her express will to withdraw;
- An event agreed to in the operating agreement;
- A transfer of all of a member's interest in the LLC;
- A member's expulsion;
- A member's bankruptcy; or
- A member's death.

Remember that unless provided otherwise in the operating agreement, a member has the right to dissociate from an LLC at any time, by express will. The dissociation may be wrongful (because it is in breach of a term of the operating agreement, which may give rise to damages), but the member will be able to dissociate nonetheless. The usual effect of a dissociation is that the member no longer has the right to participate in the management of the LLC.

Events Causing Dissolution and Winding Up.   Under ULLCA § 701, an LLC will dissolve and its business must be wound up if any of the following events occur:

- An event specified in the operating agreement;
- All members consent to dissolve (note that some states, including California and New York, provide for dissolution on majority vote and do not require unanimity);
- The passage of 90 days without any LLC members; or
- Upon entry of a judicial decree that it is not reasonably practicable to carry on the LLC business or that the managers are acting fraudulently, illegally, or are oppressing the rights of LLC members.

In the event of a dissolution, the LLC's business must be wound up. Assets will first be applied to repay creditors. Any surplus remaining will be paid to the LLC members in accordance with their rights to distributions. The LLC then terminates its existence by filing articles of termination or dissolution with the secretary of state (and withdrawing its qualification from any states in which it conducts business as an LLC).

Under the ULLCA and most state statutes, failure to file an annual report or pay any fees when due will result in an **administrative dissolution** of the LLC. An LLC may be reinstated by the secretary of state within two years upon compliance with the annual report or fee requirements.

Administrative dissolution
Dissolution of a business entity for some technical reason, such as failure to file annual reports

G.　Conversions, Mergers, and Domestications

Under Article 10 of the 2006 ULLCA, an entity such as a partnership may convert to the LLC form (and vice versa), it may merge with and into an LLC (and vice versa), or a foreign LLC may become a domestic LLC, upon filing the appropriate forms and filing fees with the state agency. As an example of a conversion, in 2006, the corporation America Online Inc. converted to AOL LLC, a limited liability company. Conversions, mergers, and domestications do not affect property owned by the converting, merging, or domesticating entity or its debts or obligations. These transactions cannot be used to evade liability.

H.　Taxation of LLCs

An LLC offers the advantage of the pass-through tax status of a partnership. All income, whether distributed or not, flows through to the individual members, who declare and pay their share of the LLC income on their individual federal tax returns. Similarly, losses sustained by the LLC may be used to offset members' other income and thereby decrease tax liability. Although the LLC does not pay taxes, it will file the same informational tax return used by general partnerships, limited partnerships, and limited liability partnerships (see Chapter Three). Like other entities, the LLC may elect to be taxed as a corporation at corporate tax rates by "checking the box" on tax Form 8832.

I.　LLPs Versus LLCs

There has been a staggering explosion in the number of LLCs since they were first recognized in 1977. For example, by 1996, nearly one in every six new business registrations nationwide was for an LLC. The universally accepted reason for the popularity of the LLC is its unique combination of flexible management, full protection from liability afforded to its members, and favorable pass-through tax status. As a measure of the popularity of LLCs, the number of LLC organizational filings grew from approximately 119,000 in 1995 to approximately 697,000 in 2002. In fact, in 2002, 40 percent of all new businesses in the United States formed as LLCs.

With the number of organizational structures to choose from (including sole proprietorships, general partnerships, limited partnerships, LLPs, LLCs, and corporations), one might ask why some businesses select one structure over another. The choice between an LLP and an LLC may seem particularly confusing when one considers that both the LLP and the LLC offer protection from personal liability for negligence (and in LLCs and in the 48 full shield jurisdictions, LLPs afford protection against liability arising from both tort and contract). Both LLPs and LLCs offer pass-through partnership tax status.

According to some experts, the traditional professions, such as law, accounting, and medicine make up the majority of LLPs, and businesses in the "emerging" professions, such as marketing, computer consulting, and management services, tend to select the LLC form. The rationale for the selection of the LLP form by professionals is that these professions have traditionally operated as partnerships, and, thus, because the LLP is simply a variety of partnership (although one offering protection from personal liability), the LLP form is comfortable and familiar to most professionals. By contrast, the LLC, with its full protection from personal liability whether arising in tort or contract, may be attractive to emerging professions, where the liability landscape is largely unsettled.

In the broadest sense, there are few significant differences between LLPs and LLCs in terms of liability (at least in LLP full shield states), management, flexibility, and taxation. There are, however, some significant economic variations from state to state that may help to explain why some forms are dominant in some states. For example, although Texas was the first state to recognize LLPs and its laws were specifically designed to protect lawyers from liability, law firms in Texas tend to operate as LLCs rather than LLPs, probably because the state imposes an application fee and annual fees of $200 on each LLP partner. Thus, a law firm with 200 partners would pay $40,000 annually to be recognized as an LLP in Texas. In sum, the selection of one entity over another is often based on a complex interplay of considerations of liability, taxation, organizational custom, and fees and taxes.

J. Role of Paralegal

Paralegals are commonly engaged in the following tasks in connection with LLCs:

- Conducting research regarding formation of the LLC, including any requirements as to signals for its name;
- Checking name availability and reserving a name (if state permits);
- Drafting the articles of organization (see Figure 6-1);
- Drafting the operating agreement (partnership agreements and corporate bylaws provide a good starting place; see Appendices B and C) and amending the same, if necessary; and
- Maintaining the LLC's documents and filing annual reporting forms, if required by the state.

Case Illustration
Non-Liability of LLC Members

Case: *Curole v. Ochsner Clinic, LLC*, 811 So. 2d 92 (La. Ct. App. 2002)

Facts: The plaintiff physician sued his former employer, a clinic operating as an LLC, and several of its other member physicians, alleging defamation and other torts. The civil district court granted the defendants' motion to change venue on the ground that venue was not proper in the county in which an individual LLC member resided. The plaintiff appealed, alleging that venue was appropriate because one of the individual physicians employed by the LLC, Dr. Quinlan, resided in the county.

Holding: The court of appeal affirmed, holding that the plaintiff did not plead sufficient allegations to show that Dr. Quinlan acted outside the scope of his authority as chief executive officer of the entity or contrary to the interests of the LLC. A member of an LLC is not personally liable in his capacity solely as a member for any debts or obligations of the LLC. Thus, venue did not lie where the individual LLC member resided.

Key Features
of LLCs

◆ LLCs offer their members full protection from personal liability whether it arises in tort or contract. Only the LLC has liability for its debts and obligations.
◆ LLCs may be managed by their members (member-managed) or by appointed managers (manager-managed). A manager need not be an LLC member.
◆ LLCs are formed by the filing of articles of organization with the secretary of state.
◆ LLCs are governed by their operating agreements.
◆ In many instances, a member's dissociation does not cause a dissolution of the LLC.
◆ The LLC provides the pass-through taxation of a general partnership.

Internet Resources

State LLC statutes: www.law.cornell.edu
                       www.findlaw.com

Text of ULLCA: www.nccusl.org

State forms: www.nass.org (this site provides links to each state's secretary of state for access to LLC organization forms)

Tax forms: www.irs.gov

General information: www.findlaw.com
www.llc-usa.com
www.megalaw.com

Business forms: www.allaboutforms.com (forms for operating agreements and other LLC forms)

Key Terms

Limited liability company
Members
ULLCA
Articles of organization

Operating agreement
Member-managed LLC
Manager-managed LLC
Administrative dissolution

Discussion Questions

Fact Scenario. Cook & Cole, LLC, is a limited liability company engaged in providing restaurant services in several states. The entity has an operating agreement, but it is silent on several issues. The firm is managed by all if its 10 members. Use the ULLCA to answer the following questions (and identify the controlling ULLCA provision).

1. Doug, one of the LLC members, agreed to personally guarantee a loan for money borrowed from Bank of America. If the LLC fails to pay this loan, who will be liable for it?

2. Pete is a prospective new LLC member. Can Pete contribute a promise to provide accounting services for the LLC next year rather than contributing cash to the LLC?

3. The LLC's operating agreement is silent about distributions of profit. The LLC would like to distribute $200,000 profit to its members. How will this be divided?

4. Mike, an LLC member, owes money on his Visa credit card. The credit card issuer has obtained a judgment against Mike for the $5,000 Mike owes. What rights does the credit card issuer have? Discuss.

5. The LLC would like to ensure that third parties only deal with members Diana and Theresa in any transactions relating to real estate. How might the LLC go about ensuring that third parties understand that other LLC members have no authority to purchase real estate for the LLC?

6. The LLC failed to file its annual report in two states this year and was dissolved. May the LLC be reinstated? How long does the LLC have to apply for reinstatement?

Net Worth

1. Access the Web site for the Georgia Secretary of State. In 2007, how many domestic limited liability companies were formed? How many domestic for-profit corporations were formed that year?
2. What is the fee to reserve a name for an LLC in California? For how long may it be reserved?
3. What is the fee in Texas to file a certificate of conversion of a Texas corporation to a Texas LLC?
4. Access the Web site for the restaurant Five Guys Burgers and Fries (Five Guys Enterprises). What business structure has this company adopted?

7

◆ ◆ ◆

Introduction to Corporations

◆ ◆ ◆

A. Introduction

Corporations are the first form of business enterprise examined thus far that exist separately from their members, so that the death, withdrawal, or bankruptcy of the owners of the corporation, the shareholders, never affects the legal existence of the corporate entity.

Like limited partnerships, limited liability partnerships, and limited liability companies, **corporations** are creatures of statute and can only be created by compliance with various statutory formalities. In contrast to partnerships, which derive their existence from the agreement of their members, corporations derive their existence from the state. A corporation may be composed of one shareholder or of hundreds of thousands of shareholders.

According to legal theory, the corporation is a *person*. In fact, the root word for "incorporate" is *corpus*, the Latin word for "body." Thus, incorporation results in the existence of a new body or person that exists independently from its owners. This new person is liable for the contracts it signs, the money it borrows, and the obligations it incurs. Because a corporation is an artificial person (rather than a natural person) it can act only through its duly appointed agents, namely, its directors and officers. Nevertheless, none of the people involved in a corporation will have personal liability for its losses or obligations.

A corporation is governed by the laws of the state in which it is incorporated. Moreover, a corporation that is formed in one state and that does business in another is subject to the laws of both jurisdictions. Corporations that operate in every state are thus subject to a patchwork quilt of laws.

Although each state has its own statutes governing corporations formed within its borders (and those authorized to conduct business in the state), nearly all state statutes are based on the 1984 revised **Model Business Corporation Act (MBCA)** drafted by the American Bar Association. The various state statutes relating to corporations are thus somewhat similar, but there are still variations

Corporation
A legal entity created by a state to carry out business

MBCA
Model Business Corporation Act; act on which individual statutes governing corporations are based

from state to state. See Appendix A for a citation to each state's corporation statutes. The text of the MBCA is available at the Web site of the American Bar Association (see Internet Resources at the end of this chapter). Publicly traded corporations are also subject to various federal laws relating to the trading of securities.

In addition to the statutes governing corporations, some states have a rich and complex body of case law interpreting those statutes. Thus, to understand fully the requirements of any one state, both its corporation statutes and the cases interpreting those statutes must be reviewed.

In addition to being governed by various statutes and cases, corporations are also governed by two basic documents: the *articles of incorporation,* which provides basic information about and is needed to create the corporation, and the *bylaws* of the corporation, its own internal rules for operation.

B. Corporate Powers and Purposes

Each state's statutes grant certain powers to the corporation to enable it to conduct its business. MBCA § 3.02 provides a fairly typical listing of **corporate powers** granted by statutes. Among the powers are the following:

Corporate powers
List of activities enumerated by a state in which a corporation can engage

1. To sue and be sued and to defend in the corporation's own name (rather than in the names of the shareholders, directors, or officers);
2. To make and amend bylaws for regulating the corporation's business;
3. To purchase, acquire, own, hold, improve, sell, lease, or mortgage real or personal property;
4. To enter into contracts, incur liabilities, borrow money, issue bonds, and lend money;
5. To elect directors and appoint officers, employees, and agents;
6. To establish benefit plans for directors, officers, agents, and employees;
7. To make donations (both for the public welfare and those that further the corporation's business, such as political donations);
8. To be a member or manager of a partnership or other entity and to purchase and hold shares or other interests in other entities;
9. To transact any lawful business; and
10. To exist perpetually.

A state's statutes provide the maximum authority for a corporation, and a corporation may not engage in any activity inconsistent with state statutes. In the event the articles or bylaws conflict with the state statutes, the statutes will govern.

A corporation's purposes are different from its powers. Its purposes are the goals and objectives it intends to achieve, such as developing real estate or operating a chain of restaurants. State statutes usually provide that a corporation may be organized for any lawful purpose. Corporations use their powers to achieve their purposes.

C. Types of Corporations

There are several types of corporations. Most of these will be discussed further in the following chapters, but a brief introduction to the various types of corporations will be helpful to understand the modern business corporation, the primary focus of discussion in this text.

1. Domestic Corporations

A corporation is a **domestic corporation** in the state in which it is organized. If ABC, Inc. is incorporated in Utah, in Utah it is regarded as a domestic corporation.

Domestic corporation
A corporation operating in the state of its incorporation

2. Foreign Corporations

A corporation formed in one state and doing business in another state is referred to in the second state as a **foreign corporation**. Thus, using our example, if ABC Inc. conducts business in several states, it is a domestic corporation in Utah and a foreign corporation in the other states in which it does business. Corporations organized in other countries are sometimes referred to as foreign corporations, but the correct term for such entities is **alien corporations**.

Foreign corporation
A corporation operating in a state other than its state of incorporation

Alien corporation
A corporation formed in another country

3. Federal or State Corporations

Entities formed under the authority of a federal or state law may also be corporations. For example, the Tennessee Valley Authority is a federal corporation formed to develop the resources of the Tennessee Valley. Similarly, many towns and cities are incorporated.

Federal or state corporation
An entity formed under the authority of a federal or state statute for some public good

4. Public Corporations

Public corporations (or *publicly held* or *publicly traded* corporations) are corporations whose shares are sold to the public at large, such as Microsoft Corporation and General Mills, Inc.

Public corporation
A corporation whose shares are sold to the public at large

5. Privately Held Corporations

A privately held corporation is often formed by a small group of family members or friends and its share ownership is limited to these individuals. These **privately held corporations** do not offer their shares to the public and are generally smaller enterprises.

Privately held corporation
A corporation whose shares are usually owned by a small group, often family or friends

6. Nonprofit Corporations

A **nonprofit** (or "not-for-profit") **corporation** is one that is formed not for the purpose of making a profit but for scientific, educational, or religious purposes

Nonprofit corporation
A corporation formed not to make a profit but for a public benefit, religious purposes, or the mutual benefit of its members

or for the mutual benefit of its members. For example, the American Cancer Society is a nonprofit corporation, as is the National Capital Area Paralegal Association.

7. Close Corporations

Close corporation
A corporation whose shares are held by a small group of shareholders that is allowed to act informally

A **close corporation** is one whose shares are held by a few people, usually friends or family. A corporation elects to be a close corporation under state law. This status allows it certain flexibility with regard to corporate formalities. For example, shareholders in a close corporation are allowed to participate in management of the corporation and yet retain their limited liability status. Shareholders in a close corporation usually agree not to sell their shares to any third party without first offering them to the corporation or to each other.

8. Professional Corporations

Professional corporation
A corporation organized by professionals, such as doctors

A **professional corporation** is one formed for the purpose of practicing a profession, such as law, medicine, or accounting.

9. S Corporations

S corporation
A corporation that avoids double taxation by passing through all of its income to its fewer than 100 shareholders

S corporations (called such after the Internal Revenue Act subchapter that allowed for their creation) are not truly different types of corporations but are smaller corporations that are formed to minimize the drastic effect that double taxation has on small business corporations. Corporations that meet certain criteria (those with no more than 100 individual shareholders, who may not be nonresident aliens, among other criteria) may elect S status. In this event, the corporation does not pay federal tax on income it earns; all of the income is passed through to the shareholders, who then pay tax at their appropriate rates. Corporations that are not S corporations are called **C corporations**.

C corporation
A corporation that is not an S corporation and that is subject to double taxation

10. Parent and Subsidiary Corporations

Parent corporation
A corporation that creates another corporation (the subsidiary)

A corporation that creates another corporation is called a **parent corporation**. Typically, the parent holds all or a vast majority of the stock of the corporation it has formed, called the **subsidiary corporation**.

Subsidiary corporation
A corporation created by another (the parent)

D. Advantages and Disadvantages of Incorporation

1. Advantages

Limited Liability. Probably the greatest advantage of selecting the corporate form for doing business is the limited liability protection the corporation offers its shareholders, directors, and officers. Only the corporation itself is responsible for its obligations and debts. Shareholders in a corporation may see their stock fall in value, and, in a worst-case scenario, become worthless. Nevertheless, they have no personal liability for corporate obligations. Similarly, directors and officers are not liable for corporate obligations unless they act with gross negligence or breach their duties of due care.

Corporate Deductions.   Although corporations are taxpaying entities, they are entitled to a wide range of deductions that can be used to offset corporate income. Items such as rent, insurance, and salaries may be deducted from the corporation's income before determining the amount on which the corporation will pay tax. Other typical deductions include interest expenses, costs for legal and accounting services, and the costs of benefit and retirement plans.

Continuity of Existence.   A corporation may endure perpetually. Whereas sole proprietorships terminate on the death of the sole proprietor and general partnerships may dissolve upon the death of a partner, a corporation may survive the death of its shareholders and the transfer of their stock to other parties.

Transferability of Share Ownership.   A person's ownership interest in a corporation is shown by a document called a **stock certificate**. The stock certificate is not what is owned; it merely represents ownership in a corporation. Shares (or stock) in a corporation are freely transferable. A simple phone call to a broker will initiate the purchase or sale of stock. Alternatively, a stockholder may transfer the stock to another merely by endorsing the reverse side of the stock certificate, much like one endorses a check over to another person. The easy transferability of share ownership contrasts with other forms of business, which may dissolve upon a full transfer of the owner's interest.

> **Stock certificate**
> The document that represents ownership in a corporation

2.   Disadvantages

Double Taxation.   The biggest disadvantage of corporate existence is **double taxation**. As a separate person or entity, the corporation's income is subject to taxation at specific rates applicable to corporations. This is in stark contrast to sole proprietorships, general partnerships, limited partnerships, limited liability partnerships, and limited liability companies, all of which pass through all the income earned by the business to the owners, who then pay tax at whatever rate is applicable to them. After paying taxes on its income, the corporation may then distribute some of its profits to its shareholders in the form of cash dividends. These distributions received by the shareholders must be declared as income and are thus subject to taxation. Thus, the same money is taxed twice: once when the corporation receives it and then again when the shareholders receive it, although in 2003, Congress reduced the taxation rates on dividends.

> **Double taxation**
> Concept in corporate law in which money earned by a corporation is taxed

Avoiding Double Taxation.   Various measures may be taken to avoid double taxation. They include the following.

S Corporations.   Some corporations may avoid the burden of taxation by electing to be S corporations, in which case all income earned by the corporation is passed through to the shareholders, who pay tax at their appropriate rates. There are several restrictions as to the election of S status, and it is not an option for any corporation having more than 100 shareholders. S corporations are discussed in Chapter Fifteen.

Small Corporations Whose Shareholders Are Employees. Small corporations whose stock is held by a few family members or friends all actively employed by the corporation can reduce the burden of double taxation. Although these corporations will pay tax on the income they receive, rather than distributing profits in the form of dividends to their shareholders, they will distribute profits in the form of salary increases or bonuses to their employee-shareholders. Although the recipient of the salary or bonus must still pay tax on that money received, the payment of such salaries or bonuses is a deduction for the corporation that can then be used to offset other corporate income. Such an approach cannot be taken by large corporations such as Nike Inc., which would have no justifiable reason to pay salaries or merit bonuses to its hundreds of thousands of shareholders.

Section 1244 stock
Stock upon the sale of which (at a loss) receives favorable tax treatment and is taxed as an ordinary loss

Section 1244 Stock. "Small business corporations" may automatically qualify under § 1244 of the Internal Revenue Code (26 U.S.C. § 1244) for the shareholders to receive certain favorable tax treatment on the sale of their stock at a loss. For § 1244 purposes, a "small" business relates not to how many people will be in the corporation, but to the amount of money the corporation plans to raise by selling stock, which may not exceed $1 million. If the requirements of § 1244 are met, any stock sold at a loss will automatically receive favorable tax treatment.

Qualified small business stock
Stock issued by a qualified corporation that provides certain tax benefits on the gain realized on the sale of the stock

Qualified Small Business Stock. Another way corporations can avoid or minimize the effect of double taxation is through the provisions of § 1202 of the Internal Revenue Code (26 U.S.C. § 1202), enacted to allow individuals who hold **qualified small business stock** for more than five years to exclude one-half of any gain they realize on the sale of such stock. The remaining one-half of the gain is taxed as a capital gain. A qualified small business must have total gross assets of less than $50 million at the time the stock is issued, and at least 80 percent of its assets must be used in certain trades and businesses.

PRACTICE TIP

Corporations must be accurately named and described in all documents relating to the entity. Thus, note the correct name of the corporation, the state of its incorporation, and whether it has elected S status or is a C corporation on the inside of the client's file or on a master list you keep near your desk. Having this critical information handy will save you from having to flip through reams of paper.

Formalities of Organization and Operation. Forming a corporation requires strict compliance with the laws of the state of incorporation. Incorporation fees are charged, and preparing the documents will likely require the assistance of an attorney. Moreover, each state imposes annual filing and reporting requirements

FIGURE 7-1
Advantages and Disadvantages of Corporations

Advantages	*Disadvantages*
Limited liability for directors, officers, shareholders	Double taxation
Wide range of business deductions	Formalities of organization, expense of organization and maintenance
Easy transferability of shares	Centralized management (rather than management by owner-shareholders)
Continuity of existence	

on corporations either incorporated in or doing business in that state. After a corporation is formed, it must continue to comply with various statutory formalities, such as requirements for annual shareholders' meetings and annual reports filed with the states in which it conducts business. The corporation must also file a tax return each year with the Internal Revenue Service, and various state taxes may also be imposed. These reporting and filing requirements make the corporation the most difficult business enterprise to form and maintain.

Centralized Management. Although shareholders own the corporation, they do not manage it. Shareholders vote for directors, who then govern the corporation as a board and appoint officers to manage the daily business affairs of the corporation. Thus, individuals who wish to manage and operate a business personally may prefer to operate as sole proprietors, general partners, partners in limited liability partnerships, or members of limited liability companies. Of course, for those individuals who prefer to invest their capital in an entity and not manage it, centralized management conducted by an experienced board of directors of a corporation provides certain advantages. In a small corporation, management is not centralized because the few shareholders elect themselves as directors and appoint themselves as officers and thus manage the enterprise themselves. See Figure 7-1 for a chart summarizing the advantages and disadvantages of corporations.

E. Role of Paralegal

More paralegals are employed in corporate law than in any other field except litigation. Paralegals in the corporate practice field engage in a variety of activities, including the following:

- Preparing to form the corporation by gathering forms and obtaining information about filing fees and annual reporting requirements;

- Forming the corporation by preparing its articles of incorporation;
- Preparing corporate bylaws;
- Maintaining corporations by preparing various resolutions, notices of meetings, and minutes of meetings;
- Engaging in corporate transaction work, such as mergers and acquisitions, the sale of stock, or corporate employment issues; and
- Engaging in fact-gathering and legal research so that determinations can be made as to whether S status should be elected, whether the corporation should be organized as a for-profit corporation or as a nonprofit corporation, whether the corporation should elect to be organized as a close corporation, or whether the corporation should be organized as a professional corporation.

Case Illustration
Protection of Shareholders from Liability for Corporate Obligations

Case: *First Realvest Inc. v. Avery Builders Inc.*, 600 A.2d 601 (Pa. Super. 1991)

Facts: The plaintiff sued the defendant corporation and its two shareholders for breach of contract. The trial court held that the individual defendants had no personal liability for the contract.

Holding: The court affirmed. When a party enters into a contract with a corporation, no action will lie against the shareholders of that corporation for breach of the contract. Although the plaintiff had alleged that the individual shareholders should be liable because they drew out profits from the corporation, the court noted that shareholders routinely draw out corporate profits. To impose liability on shareholders for corporate promises merely because the corporation is formed for their benefit and they draw out profits would render the corporate form useless.

Key Features
of Corporations

◆ Corporations are persons and exist separately from their owner-shareholders.
◆ Corporations offer limited liability for their shareholders, officers, and directors, because the corporation itself is liable for its own debts and obligations.

- ◆ Corporations may exist perpetually.
- ◆ Ownership of stock in corporations is easily transferred.
- ◆ Corporations are subject to double taxation: The income of the corporation is taxed, and when profits are distributed to shareholders, the shareholders also pay tax on money received.
- ◆ Corporations are usually expensive to form and maintain.
- ◆ Management of corporations is centralized in a board of directors; the owner-shareholders do not manage the typical large business corporation.

Internet Resources

State statutes:	www.law.cornell.edu www.findlaw.com
Text of MBCA:	www.abanet.org/buslaw/ committees/CL270000pub/ nosearch/mbca/home.shtml
Tax forms and information:	www.irs.gov
General information:	www.nass.org (for links to each state's secretary of state and general information and forms) www.ilrg.com (for links to each state's statutes, forms, and corporate filing information) www.lectlaw.com (for information on businesses in general and corporations in particular) www.findlaw.com www.tannedfeet.com www.megalaw.com

Key Terms

Corporation	Domestic corporation
MBCA	Foreign corporation
Corporate powers	Alien corporation

Federal or state corporation	C corporation
Public corporation	Parent corporation
Privately held corporation	Subsidiary corporation
Nonprofit corporation	Stock certificate
Close corporation	Double taxation
Professional corporation	Section 1244 stock
S corporation	Qualified small business stock

Discussion Questions

Fact Scenario. ABC Inc. is a small corporation, incorporated in Oregon, with four shareholders, who are all also employees. The corporation operates a restaurant. Use the MBCA to determine your answers.

1. The corporation would like to reduce its tax liability. What might the corporation do?

2. The corporation owes $12,000 to Bank of America. Who is liable to pay this debt? Why?

3. The corporation is owed $30,000 arising out of a breach of contract signed for ABC Inc. by Ray, the president of the corporation. Who will be the plaintiff in an action arising out of this breach of contract? Why?

4. The corporation would like to expand and do business in the State of Washington. What should it do? What is the corporation called in Oregon? What is it called in Washington?

5. The corporation would like to contribute money to a political action committee that advocates for restaurateurs. May it do so?

6. The corporation would like to sponsor a 5K race to raise money for the local library. May it do so?

Net Worth

1. Access www.investordictionary.com. What is the definition of "shareholder"?

2. Access www.corporateinformation.com. Locate information about Starbucks Corporation. What is its ticker symbol? When does its fiscal year end? What type of shares does it offer?

3. Locate the MBCA through the American Bar Association Web site. What is the definition of "shares" provided in § 1.40?

8

◆ ◆ ◆

Formation of Corporations

◆ ◆ ◆

A. Introduction

Forming a corporation involves a certain amount of preparation and planning. Careful thought must be given to choosing a jurisdiction in which to incorporate, choosing a corporate name, engaging in any preincorporation activities necessary to ensure the corporation will be ready to engage in business upon formation, actually creating the corporation, and then completing certain activities so the corporation can begin to function.

B. Preincorporation Activities

1. Activities by Promoters

The people involved in planning and organizing a corporation are usually referred to as **promoters.** During the process of planning the corporation, the promoters are joint venturers, who thus have fiduciary duties to each other and to the proposed corporation. They also have the usual joint and several personal liability of joint venturers. Upon creation of the corporation, these joint venture relationships terminate and are replaced by various corporate relationships.

Promoters often enter into agreements with third parties prior to actual creation of the corporation. For example, a promoter may make arrangements to lease office space for the proposed corporation. Problems may arise if for some reason, such as a falling-out among the promoters, the corporation is never formed. The landlord is left with an empty office that he may have remodeled to suit the specific needs of the proposed corporation. Courts have used a variety of theories to hold the promoters personally liable for their **preincorporation contracts** and thereby protect innocent third parties with whom the promoters have dealt. Generally,

Promoter
One involved in organizing a corporation

Preincorporation contracts
Agreements entered into by promoters on behalf of a yet-to-be-formed corporation

93

only when there is an express intention to release the promoter from liability will the promoter be able to avoid liability for agreements entered into before the corporation is formed. This is the approach of MBCA § 2.04, which provides that persons purporting to act on behalf of a corporation, knowing there was no incorporation, are jointly and severally liable for liabilities created while so acting.

Ratification
Approval of a transaction

Relation back
Doctrine that certain actions are viewed as having occurred on an earlier date

If the corporation is formed, it will usually ratify the preincorporation agreements, either by express **ratification** at a meeting of the new corporation's board of directors or by implied action, for example, by moving into the new office spaces. Ratification **"relates back"** to the date the preincorporation contract was entered into, so it is as if the promoter never entered into the agreement, and the corporation is a party from the date of that agreement. Unless the promoter is expressly released from these contractual obligations, he may remain liable under the terms of any agreement he has entered into. Generally, only larger businesses that require a great deal of preincorporation planning require promoters. Most smaller businesses will complete their incorporation process, which is typically easily accomplished, before engaging in any contractual activities.

2. *Preincorporation Share Subscriptions*

Preincorporation share subscription
Offer to purchase shares in a corporation before its formation

Promoters may also undertake activities to raise capital for the proposed corporation. Historically, some states required that the corporation have a certain amount of capital before it could begin operating. From a practical standpoint, some corporations merely desire to be assured they will have a certain amount of capital upon their formation. **Preincorporation share subscriptions,** or offers to purchase stock when the corporation is later formed, are often used to accomplish this goal. The subscription, which is irrevocable for a certain period of time (usually three to six months), is a simple written agreement by which one person offers to purchase a certain number of shares at an agreed-upon price when the corporation is later formed. If the corporation is formed and accepts the offer, the subscriber or offeror must pay for the stock as agreed or face liability for breach of contract.

C. Selection of Jurisdiction in Which to Incorporate

A business may incorporate in any United States jurisdiction. Some states have more flexible corporate laws than others, and thus some consideration should be given as to which state will be selected for the state of incorporation. Generally, however, if the corporation intends to conduct its business solely in one state, for example, Ohio, that should be the first choice for incorporation unless there is something particularly unfavorable about Ohio corporation laws. For larger corporations that will operate nationwide, perhaps other jurisdictions should be considered. Because the corporation will be subject to regulation and, in most cases, taxation in all of the states in which it conducts business, it might as well select the jurisdiction for incorporation with the most permissive and favorable corporation statutes.

1. *Delaware Incorporation*

Delaware is well known for having pro-business and flexible statutes. For example, Delaware provides significant protection to corporations against hostile takeovers. Delaware designed its statutes to be attractive to corporations and takes pride in referring to itself as the "Incorporating Capital of the World." Approximately 60 percent of Fortune 500 companies are incorporated in Delaware. Delaware also offers low filing fees and a customer-oriented service staff. The state accepts documents by facsimile transmission and operates until midnight to afford quick incorporation if needed. Most other states have also modernized their corporation statutes, but Delaware continues to be the gold standard.

2. *Factors in Selecting a Jurisdiction*

There are several factors to consider in determining where to incorporate:

- Incorporating in one state and doing business in another will subject the corporation to filing and reporting requirements and fees in both states.
- Some states favor their own domestic corporations by awarding public contracts to their own domestic corporations rather than corporations formed outside the state.
- States that are attractive to corporations often have substantial case law to serve as a guideline in the event of later problems or disputes. Such a well-developed body of law lends predictability to businesses.
- The costs of incorporation should be considered as well as annual reporting requirements and taxes. For example, Delaware has no sales tax and does not impose state income tax on corporations that do not conduct any actual business in Delaware. In California, however, corporations pay a minimum annual tax rate of the greater of 8.84 percent of their net income or $800 just for the privilege of being organized or qualified in the state, even if they do no business there.

D. The Corporate Name

1. *Selection*

The corporation's name is critical to its marketing and business strategy. Thus, careful consideration should be given to its selection. The name must comply with all statutory requirements. For example, most states require that the name include a corporate signal, such as "corporation," "company," or "incorporated," or an abbreviation thereof. Most states preclude the use of "bank," "trust," or "insurance" in the name (unless the corporation provides such services) and the use of any words, such as "United States," that would imply an association with a federal or state agency.

As is always the rule, the corporation may not select a name that is the same as or confusingly similar to that used by another domestic corporation or that used by a foreign corporation doing business in the state. Thus, a corporation that will operate nationwide must ensure that its name is available in all jurisdictions and does not infringe that of another entity. Corporations that intend to operate throughout the United States should conduct nationwide name availability searches by consulting experts, such as Thomson CompuMark, at (800) 692-8833, or CT Corsearch, at (800) 732-7241. It is much more cost-effective to determine name availability early in the incorporation process rather than to devote significant sums to developing consumer recognition of a name only to be precluded from using the name in all states.

2.　Name Availability, Reservation, and Registration

Incorporation matters are handled in almost all states by the secretary of state, although some states use other departments or agencies (such as Maryland, in which incorporations are handled by the Department of Assessments and Taxation). For ease and simplicity, this text refers to "secretary of state" when discussing the public agency responsible for corporate activity.

The secretary of state has the responsibility for determining if a corporate name is available for use. In most states, availability can be determined by a single telephone call to the office of the secretary of state. Most states now allow online searching of corporate names through their Web sites. Phone numbers, addresses, and Web sites for the secretaries of state are given in Appendix A. Alternatively, many of the attorney's services identified in Figure 8-1 will check name availability. When considering a corporate name, those selecting the name should have a few alternatives available so that if one name is refused, an alternative can be checked. Even if a secretary of state refuses a corporate name on the basis that it is too similar to another corporation's name, nearly 40 states allow use of the name if the other party consents to such in writing.

Name reservation
Process of reserving a name for a corporation while its incorporation papers are being prepared

If the name is available, it should be reserved for the proposed corporation during the period of time the articles of incorporation are being prepared. Some states allow a **name reservation** by telephone; most states require a written reservation request. Most states provide downloadable forms on their Web sites for name reservations. Many states, including Delaware, allow name reservations to be made through the Internet. A minimal fee is charged, and the reservation is usually good for 30 to 120 days. During the time the reservation is in existence, the name may not be used or taken by any other corporation. (See Figure 8-2 for a sample name reservation form.)

Name registration
Process of reserving a name in a foreign jurisdiction

A process somewhat similar to name reservation is **name registration.** A name registration is used by a foreign corporation to preserve its corporate name in a state in which the corporation eventually intends to do business. For example, assume a corporation formed in Iowa achieves great success and decides to expand to neighboring states. During the period in which the corporation is planning this expansion, it should register its name in other states. A name registration keeps a corporate name available for a substantial length of time, often one year. Not all states permit name registration. If a state does not permit registration, a corporation can form a subsidiary corporation in other states to act as a **name-saver** to ensure the corporate name is available when the corporation eventually enters the state.

Name-saver
Corporation formed by another for purpose of reserving a corporate name in a foreign jurisdiction

---

FIGURE 8-1
Corporate Service Companies

Attorneys Corporation Service, Inc.
3021 W. Magnolia Blvd.
Burbank, CA 91505
(800) 462-5487
www.attorneyscorpservice.com

Corporation Service Company
2711 Centerville Road
Wilmington, DE 19808
(800) 927-9800
www.incspot.com

CT Corporation
111 8th Avenue
New York, NY 10011
(800) 624-0909
www.ctadvantage.com

The Company Corporation
(a wholly owned subsidiary of
    Corporation Service Company)
2711 Centerville Road, Suite 400
Wilmington, DE 19808
(800) 818-0204
www.incorporate.com

Additionally, the following Web sites of the states of California and Delaware, respectively, list numerous companies and individuals that will serve as registered agents for service of process:

www.ss.ca.gov/business/bpd_service_companies.htm (California)
http://corp.delaware.gov/agents/agts.shtml (Delaware)

Like sole proprietors and partnerships, corporations may operate under a fictitious or **assumed name.** A corporation may wish each of its divisions to have a distinctive name. In some states, such as California and Florida, the same forms used by sole proprietors are used by corporations to operate under a fictitious name (see Figure 2-2).

Assumed name
A name under which a business operates that is not the name under which it was formed

E. Articles of Incorporation

The document prepared and filed with the secretary of state that creates a corporation is generally called the **articles of incorporation** (although some states, including Delaware, use the term *certificate of incorporation* or may use the term *charter*). The articles of incorporation serve as the corporation's constitution.

All states provide forms for the articles of incorporation. Nearly all states post downloadable forms on their Web sites. Use of the forms is not mandatory. Generally, the articles are easily prepared. The articles, of course, must comply with state statutory requirements. Including additional or optional provisions in the articles is permissible; however, once filed, articles of incorporation are somewhat difficult and costly to amend because amendment typically requires shareholder

Articles of incorporation
The document that creates a corporation; also called the *certificate of incorporation or charter*

FIGURE 8-2

New York Application for Reservation of Name

Application for Reservation of Name
Under §303 of the Business Corporation Law

NYS Department of State
Division of Corporations, State Records and Uniform Commercial Code
One Commerce Plaza, 99 Washington Avenue
Albany, NY 12231-0001
http://www.dos.state.ny.us

PLEASE TYPE OR PRINT

APPLICANT'S NAME AND ADDRESS

NAME TO BE RESERVED

RESERVATION IS INTENDED FOR (CHECK ONE)

New domestic corporation (The name must contain "Incorporated" or "Inc." or one of the other words or abbreviations in §301 of the Business Corporation Law.)

New domestic professional service corporation (The name must end with "Professional Corporation" or "P.C.")

Foreign corporation intending to apply for authority to do business in New York State*

Proposed foreign corporation, not yet incorporated, intending to apply for authority to conduct business in New York State

Change of name of an existing domestic or an authorized foreign corporation*

Foreign corporation intending to apply for authority to do business in New York State whose corporate name is not available for use in New York State*

Authorized foreign corporation intending to change its fictitious name under which it does business in this state*

Authorized foreign corporation which has changed its corporate name in its jurisdiction, such new corporate name not being available for use in New York State*

X_____   _____
Signature of applicant, applicant's attorney or agent   *Typed/printed name of signer*
(If attorney or agent, so specify)

INSTRUCTIONS:

1. Upon filing this application, the name will be reserved for 60 days and a certificate of reservation will be issued.
2. The certificate of reservation must be returned with and attached to the certificate of incorporation or application for authority, amendment or with a cancellation of the reservation.
3. The name used must be the same as appears in the reservation.
4. A $20 fee payable to the Department of State must accompany this application.
5. Only names for business, transportation, cooperative and railroad corporations may be reserved under §303 of the Business Corporation Law.

*If the reservation is for an existing corporation, domestic or foreign, the corporation must be the applicant.

DOS-234 (Rev. 5/08)

approval and filing with the secretary of state. Thus, many experts recommend that the articles comply strictly with what the state requires and that optional provisions be included in the corporation's bylaws, because bylaws are comparatively easy to amend and are not a public document open for public review.

1. *Elements of Articles of Incorporation*

Although there is some variation from state to state, the provisions generally required to be included in the articles of incorporation are as follows:

Name. The corporation's name must be set forth in the articles and must comply with any state requirements as to required signals, such as "Inc.," and so forth. The name should have been previously reserved and the articles timely filed during the reservation period so that the name has been "locked up" for the corporation.

Registered Address. The articles must set forth the street address (a post office address is seldom acceptable) of the corporation's initial registered office in the state to facilitate communications with the corporation. If the corporation does not intend to do business in the state and has incorporated there only to take advantage of liberal corporate statutes, it can make arrangements with a corporate service company to serve as its registered office in the state. Service companies provide numerous other services as well, such as assistance in reserving the corporate name and filing the articles with the secretary of state. (See Figure 8-1 for identification of some service companies.)

Agent for Service of Process. In nearly all states, the corporation must designate an individual or a corporation in the state to receive service of legal process (the summons and complaint that initiate legal action). Once again, if the corporation does not intend to do business in the state, it can engage a service company to act as its agent. In most states, the secretary of state is also authorized to accept service of process on behalf of the corporation. Generally, changing the registered address or registered agent for a corporation is fairly easy; it does not require the complex procedures required for amending the articles. Under most state laws (and MBCA § 14.20), failure to have a registered office or registered agent for 60 days is grounds for administrative dissolution of a corporation. Many state Web sites identify the agents for service of process for corporations doing business in the state. Enter a company's name and you will be given the date of incorporation, status (active or dissolved), and the identity of its agent who will accept service of process.

Purposes. Many states require the corporation to set forth its purposes in the articles. Most, however, also allow the corporation to use a *full purpose* or **broad purpose clause** rather than specifying its actual purposes. A broad purpose clause typically provides that "the purpose of the corporation is to engage in any lawful act or activity for which a corporation may be organized under the laws of this state." The advantage of using such a clause is that it allows the corporation to grow and expand into other activities without necessitating an amendment to its articles. The MBCA and many states do not require a purpose clause.

Broad purpose clause
Clause in corporate articles that states the corporation may engage in any legal activity; also called *full purpose clause*

Ultra vires **doctrine**
Seldom-used legal theory that certain acts are invalid as being beyond a corporation's powers

Years ago, when corporations were universally required to state their specific purposes, corporations would occasionally exceed their stated purposes. Such acts were said to be ***ultra vires***, literally acts "beyond the powers" of a corporation. The early view was that any act beyond a corporation's powers or purposes was null and void, and either party to a contract could disaffirm the act or contract. This approach led disappointed parties to a contract to assert the doctrine in order to escape their obligations. Later, as broad purpose clauses became common, the *ultra vires* doctrine eroded: If the corporation can engage in any lawful act, then few acts can be challenged on the basis that they are beyond the power or purposes of the corporation. Thus, the *ultra vires* doctrine is primarily of historical interest today.

MBCA § 3.04 reflects the modern approach: Neither the corporation nor any third party doing business with the corporation may escape its respective duties on the theory that the corporation lacks authority to act. Nevertheless, shareholders may seek to enjoin the transaction, the directors and officers can be sued for engaging in *ultra vires* acts, and the state attorney general may seek dissolution of the corporation for *ultra vires* acts.

Description of Stock. The corporation's shares must be described in the articles. There are three general rules:

1. If the corporation will issue more than one type or class of shares (for example, common and preferred stock), all of the provisions, privileges, and restrictions relating to each class must be set forth.
2. The corporation must identify the number of shares it has the authority to issue. This number, called the **authorized shares,** forms an upper limit on the shares the corporation may issue. If the corporation wishes to issue stock in an amount greater than the number identified in the articles, it will need to amend its articles. In some states, filing fees are based on the authorized number of shares identified in the articles. Thus, the number selected should be sufficient to accommodate anticipated growth but not so high as to result in excessive filing fees.
3. Many states require that the corporation state the par value of its stock. **Par value** is the nominal or face value of a share of stock. It is the minimum amount for which a share of stock may be issued. If par value is $1, stock may be sold for more than $1 but not less. Under the MBCA, there is no requirement of identifying par value. The MBCA has eliminated the concept of par value.

Authorized shares
The number of shares set forth in a corporation's articles that the corporation has authority to issue

Par value
The minimum amount for which a corporation's stock can be sold

Although these rules may seem complex, the statement in the articles can be quite simple: "The corporation has the authority to issue 20,000 shares of common stock with a par value of $1 per share." In states that follow the MBCA, if only one class of stock is to be issued, such as common stock, the articles need only state the number of shares that the corporation is authorized to issue and the statement, "The corporation is authorized to issue 25,000 shares of stock" will suffice.

Incorporators. The names (and usually the addresses) of the incorporators (those preparing the articles) must be provided. The incorporators must also sign the articles. In many cases, attorneys and paralegals act as incorporators. (See Figure 8-3 for sample articles of incorporation.)

2. Optional Provisions in Articles of Incorporation

After the required elements are included, most states and the MBCA allow the inclusion of optional provisions in the articles. It must be remembered, however, that any additional provisions may necessitate going through the somewhat complex and expensive process of amending the articles later.

Among the more common optional provisions found in articles of incorporation are the following:

- Number, names, and addresses of the initial board of directors;
- Period of duration of the corporation;
- Provisions requiring a greater than majority vote for certain corporate actions, such as requiring two-thirds shareholder approval for a merger; or
- Provisions eliminating or restricting the personal liability of directors and officers (other than for some intentional, willful, or criminal act) and provisions permitting the corporation to indemnify directors or officers if they incur liability while acting in good faith.

3. Preemptive Rights

The articles of incorporation may provide for shareholders' preemptive rights. A **preemptive right** is the right of a shareholder, when new shares are being issued, to purchase as much of the newly issued stock as is needed to maintain her then-current ownership interest in the corporation. In essence, a preemptive right is a type of right of first refusal. Before the corporation may sell stock to any outsiders, the current shareholders must be given the opportunity to purchase stock in an amount equal to their present ownership interest in the corporation. For example, assume that when a corporation is formed, Tess and Bill own 58 percent and 42 percent, respectively, of the corporation's stock. If the corporation wishes to issue 1,000 shares and the shareholders have preemptive rights, Tess would have the right to purchase 580 shares and Bill would have the right to purchase 420 shares. If they elect not to exercise their preemptive rights, the corporation may then offer the stock to third parties.

Preemptive rights allow shareholders to maintain their proportionate interest and control in a corporation; the corporation will not be able to flood the market with shares and thereby reduce the current shareholders' power and control.

Preemptive rights are somewhat disfavored because they impose burdensome requirements on corporations to provide notice to existing shareholders rather than simply issuing stock quickly to raise needed capital. Thus, in most states (and under MBCA § 6.30), if preemptive rights are to exist, they must be included in the articles of incorporation. Failure to specify that preemptive rights are given typically means they do not exist.

Preemptive rights
Right of shareholder to buy pro rata share of newly issued stock before it is offered to nonshareholders

FIGURE 8-3
Nevada Articles of Incorporation

ROSS MILLER
Secretary of State
206 North Carson Street
Carson City, Nevada 89701-4299
(775) 684 5708
Website: www.nvsos.gov

Articles of Incorporation
(PURSUANT TO NRS CHAPTER 78)

USE BLACK INK ONLY - DO NOT HIGHLIGHT   ABOVE SPACE IS FOR OFFICE USE ONLY

1. Name of Corporation:

2. Registered Agent for Service of Process: (check only one box)
☐ Commercial Registered Agent: _____ Name
☐ Noncommercial Registered Agent (name and address below) **OR** ☐ Office or Position with Entity (name and address below)

Name of Noncommercial Registered Agent OR Name of Title of Office or Other Position with Entity

Street Address   City   Nevada   Zip Code

Mailing Address (if different from street address)   City   Nevada   Zip Code

3. Authorized Stock: (number of shares corporation is authorized to issue)
Number of shares *with par value:*   Par value per share: $ Number of shares *without par value:*

4. Names and Addresses of the Board of Directors/Trustees: (each Director/Trustee must be a natural person at least 18 years of age; attach additional page if more than two directors/trustees)
1) Name
Street Address   City   State   Zip Code
2) Name
Street Address   City   State   Zip Code

5. Purpose: (optional; see instructions)
The purpose of the corporation shall be:

6. Name, Address and Signature of Incorporator: (attach additional page if more than one incorporator)
Name   X _____ Incorporator Signature
Address   City   State   Zip Code

7. Certificate of Acceptance of Appointment of Registered Agent:
I hereby accept appointment as Registered Agent for the above named Entity.
X _____
Authorized Signature of Registered Agent or On Behalf of Registered Agent Entity   Date

This form must be accompanied by appropriate fees.   Nevada Secretary of State NRS 78 Articles
Revised on 7-1-08

4. Filing of Articles of Incorporation

Once the articles are prepared, they must be filed with the appropriate state agency, usually the secretary of state. Each state's requirements vary slightly. Failure to comply with the state's requirements will result in the state's refusal of the articles of incorporation.

In most states, the incorporator simply mails the articles to the office of the secretary of state with an appropriate cover letter and the required filing fee. The secretary of state reviews the articles and may return a copy stamped "Approved" or "Filed" or may return a formal certificate of incorporation. Many states now permit online filing of the articles of incorporation with payment of fees by credit card.

Other states impose additional requirements. For example, in Illinois, a copy of the articles of incorporation must be recorded in the county in which the corporation's registered office is located. Other states require that the corporation publish notices in newspapers. Thus, a careful reading of the state statutes is required to ensure that all statutory requirements are followed.

In most states, and under MBCA § 2.03, corporate existence begins upon the filing of the articles of incorporation (unless the articles specify a delayed effective date).

PRACTICE TIP

If you work in an active corporate practice, you need to create a working corporate binder with all forms and filing fee schedules. Download extra copies of the forms and fee schedules from the secretary of state's Web site. When projects arise and you are asked to check name availability, reserve or register a corporate name, draft articles of incorporation, or prepare a client's annual corporate report, you will have everything you need at your fingertips. Make notes as to Web site addresses, which forms may be submitted online, telephone numbers of helpful people at the secretary of state's office, whether duplicate copies are required, and so forth. Aim for efficiency so that every project is more streamlined and efficient than the one before.

F. Post-Incorporation Activities

1. Bylaws

Bylaws are rules that govern the operation and management of a corporation. The bylaws are prepared by the attorney or paralegal and presented for adoption at the first organizational meeting of the corporation. Bylaws are easily amended. Thus, any provision that might change, for example, an annual meeting date, should be included in the bylaws rather than in the articles of incorporation. The bylaws are not filed with any public agency; they are simply maintained by the corporation in a looseleaf binder along with minutes of meetings and other corporate records. Most law firms have standard sets of bylaws. These can then be readily adapted to meet the needs of various corporate clients. Additionally, form books and service companies routinely offer sets of prepared bylaws.

Bylaws
Internal rules governing corporate procedures and operation

Following are the typical items usually provided in corporate bylaws:

Introductory Information.   The first few sections of the bylaws will set forth the name of the corporation, its principal office address, and any other office locations.

Information About Directors.   The bylaws should contain various provisions relating to the managers of the corporation, that is, the board of directors, including the following:

- **Requirements for Position.** If the directors must be shareholders in the corporation or residents of the state of incorporation, this should be specified.
- **Number, Tenure, and Compensation.** The number of directors the corporation will have (or a specified range, such as "not less than three nor more than nine") as well as when and how they will be elected or removed from office should be set forth. Compensation of directors and reimbursement of their expenses should be addressed.
- **Authority to Manage.** The directors should be given express authority to manage the business and affairs of the corporation. Any limitations on their authority should be set forth with particularity. If the board will have any committees, such as a compensation committee, its membership and duties should also be described. Authority to declare and pay dividends to the shareholders should be granted to the directors.
- **Meetings.** The bylaws should indicate when and where regular meetings of the directors will be held (weekly, monthly, and so forth); when and how **special meetings** (any meetings between regularly scheduled meetings) will be held; how many directors constitute a **quorum** (the minimum number of directors required to transact business); how meetings will be conducted and adjourned; and whether directors may take action telephonically or without a formal meeting (that is, by unanimous written consent).
- **Liability.** If the corporation plans to indemnify directors for acts taken in good faith, this should be stated in the bylaws. Few people would agree to act as directors if they believed they could be held liable for some mere error in business judgment. Thus, unless directors act in bad faith or with reckless disregard of the corporation's interests, they are generally reimbursed or indemnified for costs and expenses incurred in defending themselves.

Information About Officers.   The bylaws should identify the corporate officers. The most typical officers are president, vice president, secretary, and treasurer. The bylaws should specify each officer's duties and discuss removal of officers, filling their vacancies, and their compensation.

Information About Shareholders.   Just as the bylaws should contain all information relating to directors and officers of the corporation, so should they also include information relating to the owners of the corporation, the shareholders. The following provisions are usually included: information about shareholders' annual and special meetings, including notices of meetings; quorum requirements for

---

Special meeting
A meeting held between regularly scheduled meetings

Quorum
Minimum number of persons required to transact business

shareholders' meetings; method of voting, including voting by proxy; any restrictions or limitations on voting; and authority of shareholders to inspect the shareholders' list and other corporate records.

Miscellaneous Information.　　The bylaws typically include the following:

- The form of stock certificate and any information relating to issuance of shares;
- Information about location and inspection of corporate records;
- Identification of the **tax year** of the corporation, which may be a calendar year (January 1 through December 31) or some other 12-consecutive-month period; and
- Information relating to banking.

(A form of bylaws for a corporation is provided in Appendix C.)

Tax year
An annual accounting period for keeping records and reporting income and expenses

2. Corporate Supplies

As soon as the corporation is formed, its supplies should be ordered by the law firm. The supplies are usually ordered from one of the various companies the law firm generally does business with, and consist of three items:

- The corporate **seal**, used to authenticate documents (and seldom used in modern times);
- The **minute book**, which is a binder used to contain minutes of meetings of directors and shareholders; and
- The **stock certificate book**, which resembles a large checkbook and contains stock certificates that can be issued to purchasers of the corporation's stock. (See Figure 8-4 for a sample stock certificate.)

Seal
Instrument used to emboss documents to verify authenticity

Minute book
Binder or book used to maintain minutes of corporate meetings and other records

Stock certificate book
Book containing stock certificates to be issued to shareholders

3. Organizational Meeting

Although a corporation is formed upon the filing of its articles of incorporation, it needs a first or **organizational meeting** to complete its incorporation activities and commence business. Almost all states and the MBCA require either an organizational meeting or the preparation of a written document in lieu of holding an organizational meeting. The organizational meeting is usually held at the law firm and is attended by the incorporators, the initial directors and officers of the corporation, and any anticipated shareholders.

The law firm usually prepares an agenda for the meeting, and the following matters are usually acted upon:

- If directors were not named in the articles of incorporation, they are elected by the incorporators or shareholders at the organizational meeting. These initial directors serve until the first shareholders' meeting, at which time their successors will be elected.

Organizational meeting
First corporate meeting held to launch corporation

FIGURE 8-4

Sample Stock Certificate

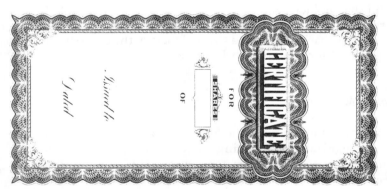

- Officers are appointed by the directors.
- The corporation's bylaws are adopted.
- Preincorporation contracts are ratified.
- Preincorporation share subscriptions are accepted.
- The form of corporate seal and stock certificate are presented for approval.
- Banking, tax, and accounting information are discussed, and the directors usually discuss whether it is desirable, when feasible, for the corporation to elect S corporation status to avoid double taxation (as discussed in Chapters Nine and Fifteen).
- The directors authorize the officers to begin issuing stock and fix the consideration for each share.
- The directors discuss miscellaneous matters, such as whether the corporation should qualify to do business in other jurisdictions and whether the corporation should adopt any employee benefit plans.

In small corporations, electing directors and appointing officers is a formality because the people involved in the corporation are family members or friends and the parties have agreed long before the meeting on how the corporation will be managed.

After the meeting, the law firm prepares minutes of the meeting, which are signed by the secretary and placed in the minute book. These minutes serve as a guide to the corporation for preparing minutes of subsequent meetings. (A form for minutes of an annual shareholders' meeting is provided as Figure 10-2.)

Most states and the MBCA do not require a formal in-person organizational meeting. Instead, they allow the incorporators to agree unanimously in writing to all of the matters that would ordinarily be discussed at the organizational meeting. However, many law firms prefer that an in-person meeting be held as an opportunity to emphasize corporate responsibilities (such as requirements for annual shareholders' meetings) and to respond to questions. Such in-person organizational meetings often are not necessary for experienced and sophisticated clients.

See Figure 8-5 for an incorporation checklist, which can be used as a step-by-step approach for organizing corporations.

4. Annual Report

Although it is not due immediately after incorporation, most state statutes and MBCA § 16.22 require the corporation to submit an **annual report** to the secretary of state providing basic information about the corporation, such as the number of authorized shares, the number of shares that have been issued, and identifications of directors, principal officers, and the agent for service of process. Most states automatically mail the report form to the corporation for completion. The annual report is often prepared by the paralegal and will be accompanied by filing fees and required tax payments. Most states now allow electronic filing of annual reports.

Annual report
Form required to be filed annually in most states providing information about the corporation

FIGURE 8-5

Incorporation Checklist

1. Select jurisdiction in which to incorporate. Consider whether business will be local in nature or whether extraterritorial expansion is planned.
2. Identify corporate name (and possible alternatives). Research required "signals" in state of incorporation.
3. Determine name availability by checking with secretary of state.
4. If business will be conducted nationally or expansion is planned, consider a full-scope nationwide name search.
5. If name is available, reserve name, and docket period of name reservation.
6. Gather the following information so articles of incorporation can be prepared:
   - Determine identity of incorporators
   - Determine principal address of corporation within the state of incorporation
   - Identify registered agent (or make arrangement with attorneys' service company to serve as registered agent)
   - Identify initial directors
   - Identify stock of company
     ◆ Common or preferred stock (if preferred, identify preferences and special rights)
     ◆ Number of authorized shares
     ◆ Par value or no par value
7. Gather incorporation forms and schedule of filing fees from secretary of state.
8. Prepare articles of incorporation, have them signed and filed.
9. Order corporate kit/supplies.
10. Prepare bylaws and provide them to proposed directors for review and comment.
11. Confirm incorporation to client, and schedule first organizational meeting. Prepare notice of meeting or waivers of notice.
12. Prepare agenda for first organizational meeting. Items should include:
    - Election of directors
    - Appointment of officers
    - Approval of bylaws
    - Ratification or adoption of preincorporation contracts or actions, including legal and incorporation fees
    - Acceptance of preincorporation stock subscriptions
    - Discussion of applying for status as S corporation
    - Confirmation of § 1244 stock
    - Review of articles, seal, form of stock certificate
    - Authorization of issuance of shares
    - Authorization of application for Employer Identification Number (Form SS-4)
    - Review of miscellaneous matters, if not in bylaws (selection of fiscal year, selection of bankers and accountants, and discussion of qualifying in foreign jurisdictions)
13. Prepare minutes of first organizational meeting and send to client for signature by secretary of corporation and placement in minute book.
14. Docket date for next meeting.
15. Docket date for submission of annual report to secretary of state.

G. Defects in Incorporation Process

On occasion, a defect in the incorporation process becomes important. For example, assume that Lee Hunter is owed $50,000 by ABC Inc. and the corporation has only $30,000. Lee, as a creditor, may begin investigating various corporate documents to find out if there is some error in the incorporation process that would allow him to hold the shareholders personally liable for the remaining $20,000 owed to him.

Historically, courts reviewed the nature of the defect and classified the corporation as either a **de jure corporation** (literally, one "of right"), which had complied strictly or substantially with state law and could not be attacked by anyone, or a **de facto corporation** (literally, "in fact"), a corporation that failed to comply substantially with state law and could be attacked by its creator, the state, but not by third parties. If the corporation were neither de jure nor de facto, it could be attacked by a third party such as Lee.

Modern statutes and the MBCA have eroded the use of the de jure and de facto doctrines. For example, MBCA § 2.03(b) provides that the secretary of state's filing of the articles is "conclusive proof" that the corporation is validly formed and is thus invulnerable to attack by third parties (although it can be challenged by the state of incorporation). Thus, there are far fewer cases today alleging that shareholders should be liable for corporate debts due to defects in incorporation than there were years ago. In sum, the secretary of state's filing of the articles is the demarcation point. Before this, the promoters have personal liability; after this, the corporation is viewed as validly formed (and may only be attacked by the state).

De jure corporation
A corporation that has substantially or strictly complied with statutory requirements and is unassailable

De facto corporation
A corporation that did not substantially comply with statutory requirements and can only be challenged by the state

H. Role of Paralegal

Paralegals play an extremely active role in forming a corporation. They generally engage in the following activities:

- Drafting agreements to be entered into by promoters, defining their rights and obligations to each other and to the proposed corporation;
- Drafting preincorporation share subscriptions and, if necessary, assignments of those subscriptions;
- Conducting legal research to ensure the corporation is incorporated in a jurisdiction beneficial to it;
- Assisting in selection of corporate name, conducting research as to required corporate "signals" in name, and checking name availability;
- Reserving the name so it is available for the corporation (see Figure 8-1) and docketing the date the reservation expires to ensure that the incorporation process is completed before the reservation expires;
- Preparing and filing articles of incorporation (see Figure 8-3);
- Registering the name in foreign jurisdictions if the corporation intends to operate in other states;
- Drafting bylaws for the corporation (see Appendix C);
- Ordering the corporate supplies (see Figure 8-4 for sample stock certificate);

- Preparing the agenda for the organizational meeting and taking minutes of the meeting or preparing a written consent document in lieu of organizational meeting; and
- Docketing the dates for required corporate meetings and annual reports.

Case Illustration
Corporate Ratification Eliminates Liability of Promoters

Case: *Tin Cup Pass Ltd. Partnership v. Daniels*, 553 N.E.2d 82 (Ill. App. Ct. 1990)

Facts: Promoters signed a lease for the benefit of a proposed corporation that was named on the lease. Due to a problem with the initially planned corporate name, the corporation was ultimately formed under a different name. When the corporation failed to pay rent for the premises, the plaintiff lessor sued the promoters. The trial court held that the promoters were not individually liable for the lease obligations.

Holding: The appellate court affirmed. The court determined that the parties' intent should control. In this case, the parties intended that the ultimate lessee would be a corporation. The fact that the corporation was created under a different name is not significant, particularly where, as here, the corporation ratified the lease by recognizing it and treating it as valid. In such a case, the promoters will not be personally liable.

Key Features
in Forming Corporations

- ◆ Corporations are planned and organized by promoters. Agreements made by promoters bind the promoters personally until they are released from liability thereon.
- ◆ Interested investors often offer or subscribe to purchase stock when the corporation is later formed. The offer is irrevocable for some period of time.
- ◆ Consideration should be given as to the jurisdiction in which to incorporate. Some states have laws that are more flexible and permissive than others.
- ◆ The corporate name must usually include a signal showing the entity is a corporation. The name should be reserved prior to incorporation.

- ◆ The document that creates a corporation is called the articles of incorporation. It must comply with state statutes.
- ◆ Bylaws must be prepared for the corporation. Bylaws provide internal rules for the operation of a corporation.
- ◆ Corporations must hold a first or organizational meeting to commence the corporation's business.

Internet Resources

State corporation statutes:	www.law.cornell.edu www.findlaw.com
Text of MBCA:	www.abanet.org/buslaw/committees/ CL270000pub/nosearch/mbca/home. shtml
Secretaries of state:	www.nass.org (this site provides links to each state's secretary of state for access to forms for name reservations and articles of incorporation and basic information about the incorporation process)
S election forms:	www.irs.gov
Forms for articles of incorporation and other formation documents, including bylaws:	www.siccode.com/forms.php www.allaboutforms.com www.lectlaw.com

---

Key Terms

Promoter	Preemptive rights
Preincorporation contracts	Bylaws
Ratification	Special meeting
Relation back	Quorum
Preincorporation share subscription	Tax year
Name reservation	Seal
Name registration	Minute book
Name-saver	Stock certificate book
Assumed name	Organizational meeting
Articles of incorporation	Written consent
Broad purpose clause	Annual report
Ultra vires doctrine	De jure corporation
Authorized shares	De facto corporation
Par value	

Discussion Questions

Fact Scenario. Peter and Rachel, promoters for a corporation to be formed, have entered into agreements to purchase various textbooks for the corporation. The corporation will engage in tutoring and educational services in Indiana.

1. The corporation is never formed. Who is liable to pay for the textbooks?
2. Assume that the corporation is formed. How can Peter and Rachel ensure that they have no further liability for any contracts made prior to incorporation?
3. In which state should the business be incorporated? Why?
4. Discuss whether the following names would be acceptable for the corporation:
   - Exclusive Tutoring
   - Teach Your Tots, Inc.
   - U.S. Tutoring
   - Teach & Tutor Co.
5. Discuss the advisability of placing the following items in the articles of incorporation or in the bylaws:
   - Identification of the corporation's stock as common or preferred
   - Information about the location of the regular meetings of the board of directors
   - Information about where the corporation intends to maintain its bank accounts
   - Information about the duties of the corporation's secretary
   - A provision allowing the shareholders to exercise preemptive rights
6. Assume that one of the corporation's clients has not paid a bill and recently discovered that when the articles of incorporation were filed, the corporation's street address was identified as "Ellwood" rather than "Elmwood." Under the MBCA, will the client be able to avoid paying the bill on the basis of this error? Discuss.
7. The corporation wishes to expand into Michigan and Ohio. What steps should the corporation take?
8. Prior to incorporation, and on February 1, Rachel's sister Hope agreed to purchase 50 shares of stock in the corporation when it was later formed. May Hope revoke this subscription? Under the MBCA, by what date should the corporation be formed so that it can accept this subscription?

Net Worth

---

1. In Delaware, are the following corporate names acceptable?
   - Rebecca's Design & Décor Syndicate
   - Rebecca's Design & Décor Club
2. Access the Web site for the California Secretary of State and determine whether the following names are available.
   - Ralph's Electric Inc.
   - Daisy's Florist Inc.
   - Mountain Scribe, Inc.

[Handwritten notes in margin: Delaw Code / Title 8 / Corporations / Chapter 1 / Section 102]

[Handwritten notes at bottom: Donut Delight, Inc / Joe's Red Hots, Inc. Fish Holding, Inc.]

3. Access the Web site for the Florida Secretary of State. Who is the agent for service of process for Burger King Corporation?

4. Access the Web site for the Indiana Secretary of State. What is the fee to reserve a corporate name in Indiana? How long will the reservation last?

5. Access the Web site for the Wisconsin Secretary of State. What is the fee to file articles of incorporation for a for-profit corporation? What is the fee for expedited service?

9

◆ ◆ ◆

Corporate Financial Structure

◆ ◆ ◆

A. Introduction

All corporations need capital or money to operate and expand their business activities. Generally, to raise money, corporations either sell stock to investors or borrow money from various lenders. The stock sold to investor-shareholders and the evidence of the corporation's obligation to repay borrowed money are referred to as *securities*. There are two types of securities: **Equity securities** are shares of a corporation sold to investors called *shareholders* or *stockholders* (the terms are synonymous) and **debt securities**, which are often in the form of bonds, are evidenced by documents that show the corporation's obligation to repay money it has borrowed. Corporations may also simply borrow money from banks and other lenders, in which case a loan agreement or a promissory note will be executed by the corporation to evidence its obligation to repay the loan (see Figure 9-2 for form of simple promissory note). Bonds are often used by corporations in connection with long-term loans that are secured by corporate property; in the event of a default by the corporation in repaying the bond, the bondholder will seize the property pledged to satisfy the debt. Bonds are thus debt instruments used by corporations to raise money. According to dicta in one case, the terms *bonds, debentures*, and *notes* are generally used interchangeably. *Metro. Life Ins. Co. v. RJR Nabisco*, 716 F. Supp. 1504 (S.D.N.Y. 1989). The federal government and cities also issue bonds to raise money.

Although the terms *stocks* and *bonds* are often referred to in the same breath, these two types of securities are vastly different from each other. A shareholder who owns equity securities (or shares) in a corporation is an insider, an owner of the corporation, who is entitled to vote on various corporate issues, may receive distributions of profits (called dividends), and receives assets of the corporation if it liquidates. A creditor or **bondholder**, on the other hand, is an outsider, not a corporate owner, and is entitled merely to be repaid the amount loaned to the corporation under agreed-upon terms.

Equity security
A security representing ownership interest in an enterprise (often called a *share*)

Debt security
A security representing an obligation of the corporate issuer (which may be a *bond*)

Bondholder
One to whom a debt is owed by a corporation

Many experts believe that stocks have a greater potential for return than bonds; however, stocks carry a greater risk of loss and can fluctuate wildly in value. Bonds are more stable because the investor can predict in advance the expected return. Moreover, in the event the corporation liquidates, bondholders, as creditors of the corporation, will receive assets before shareholders. Investors are thus usually advised to diversify their portfolios with a combination of stocks and bonds.

Issuance of each type of security offers certain advantages and disadvantages to a corporation. When a corporation issues stock, it receives capital that need not be repaid because shareholders expect to make money either by receiving dividends or upon the eventual sale of the stock. Each new share of stock issued, however, dilutes the control of the existing shareholders. The issuance of bonds offers the advantage to the corporation of receiving capital without causing a loss of power to current shareholders. Moreover, the corporation may deduct any interest it pays to its creditors and bondholders. Nevertheless, the debt or bond must be repaid by the corporation at some time, usually with interest. Thus, most corporations issue a mix of securities, depending on their needs and market conditions. The directors will decide whether to raise money by issuing stock (equity financing) or by borrowing money (debt financing).

Approximately 50 percent of American families now own stock. However, the majority of stock sold on the national exchanges is not held by individual investors but by institutional investors, such as mutual funds, TIAA-CREF, and Barclays.

The public sale of corporate securities, whether stock or bonds, is subject to regulation by applicable state laws and by the federal Securities Act of 1933 and the Securities Exchange Act of 1934 (see Chapter Fifteen). All of these laws are designed to protect the public from fraud. Many small issuances of stock are exempt from such regulation.

B. Equity Securities

1. Introduction

The corporation's equity securities are identified in the articles of incorporation, which set forth the number of shares the corporation is authorized to issue. Such shares are thus referred to as **authorized shares**. When the corporation issues shares to third parties, the shares are referred to as **outstanding shares**. Owners of outstanding shares are entitled to vote and participate in corporate distributions. Large publicly traded corporations have significant numbers of outstanding shares. For example, as of 2008, General Mills had 336 million shares of common stock issued and outstanding. The difference between authorized shares and outstanding shares is important because only issued and outstanding shares are entitled to vote at corporate meetings and to receive dividends.

The decision to issue shares, and the price thereof, is made by the board of directors acting in the best interest of the corporation. The number of shares authorized by the articles act as a ceiling or limitation on the number of shares that can be issued, and the directors must honor any preemptive rights granted to shareholders by the articles. The articles may authorize more than one type or class of shares. For example, a class of shares may be issued that has certain rights or

Authorized shares
The number of shares the corporation has the authority to issue according to its articles

Outstanding shares
Shares issued by a corporation and held by investors

preferences over other types of shares. This stock is usually referred to as **preferred stock**.

A shareholder has three ownership interests in a corporation: the right to vote (usually one vote per share), the right to participate in distribution of dividends (if declared by the board and if the corporation is solvent), and the right to receive net assets upon the corporation's liquidation (after creditors, including bondholders, have been paid).

Preferred stock
Stock in a corporation that carries certain rights and privileges

2. Par Value Stock

In addition to the directors' duty to establish the value of the stock while acting in the corporation's best interests, there is another limitation relating to the amount for which stock can be issued. The **par value** of the stock as set forth in the articles of incorporation is the nominal or face value set for each share. It is the minimum amount for which stock may be issued. Thus, if the par value is $10, a share of stock can be issued for $10 or any amount in excess of this but cannot be issued for an amount less than $10. This explains why par value is usually set at such a low amount (often $1 or even 10 cents). The par value of General Mills's common stock is 10 cents. Par value is not equivalent to market value. In fact, because par value is usually so low, corporations hope that market value is far in excess of par value.

Par value
The lowest price for which stock may be sold

Some states allow the directors to issue stock for less than par value if the directors determine this is in the best interests of the corporation. In general, shares issued for less than the par value are referred to as **watered stock**.

In most states, corporations now have the option either of stating a par value for the stock in the articles of incorporation or of stating that there will be no par value. The MBCA typifies the modern trend in not requiring any par value to be stated. If no par value is stated in the articles, the directors can sell the stock for whatever price the directors determine, so long as this price is reasonable. Shares issued at approximately the same time, however, must be issued for approximately the same consideration, unless there is a valid business reason for the price differential.

Watered stock
Stock issued for less than its par value

3. Consideration for Shares

According to the MBCA and most modern statutes, shares may be issued for consideration consisting of any tangible or intangible property or benefit to the corporation, including cash, promissory notes, services performed, contracts for services to be performed, or other securities of the corporation. This flexible approach allows the corporation to issue its shares for almost anything, so long as there is some benefit to the corporation. Once the board of directors determines what consideration should be paid for the stock, that determination is deemed conclusive as far as adequacy is concerned.

4. Stock Certificates

Corporations may issue stock without physically delivering a certificate to the shareholder. Shares issued without the formality of stock certificates are

Uncertificated shares
Stock issued without actual stock certificates

called **uncertificated shares**. The ownership of such shares is recorded in the corporate books, and the holders of uncertificated stock have the same rights as owners of stock evidenced by paper certificates. The issuance of uncertificated stock simply reduces the paperwork burden on a corporation engaged in volume trading of its stock. For today's modern corporations, with their rapid trading of stock, use of actual paper certificates is uncommon.

When paper certificates are used, their content and form are controlled by state statute. MBCA § 6.25 provides that share certificates must provide the following information: the name of the issuing organization and the state law under which it is organized; the name of the person to whom the share is issued; and the number and class of shares. The share certificate must be signed on behalf of the corporation (either manually or by facsimile signature) by two officers of the corporation, usually the president and secretary. For large corporations, manual issuance of certificates would be a daunting task, and corporations often thus engage the services of a **transfer agent**, often a bank or trust company, which maintains a supply of blank certificates with facsimile signatures of the officers. The transfer agent also records transfers of shares and may act as the corporate **registrar** and maintain the list of shareholders.

Transfer agent
An individual or entity that processes and issues a corporation's stock certificates

Registrar
An individual or entity that maintains a corporation's list of shareholders

On occasion, shareholders own fractions of shares. This generally occurs when the corporation declares a share dividend. For example, if a corporation declares a dividend of 1 share for every 100 shares owned, the owner of 150 shares would be entitled to receive $1\frac{1}{2}$ shares. The owner of a fractional share is entitled to fractional voting rights, dividends, and other shareholder rights. Alternatively, the corporation may issue scrip rather than a stock certificate for the fractional share. **Scrip** is a document evidencing ownership of a partial share. When the shareholder has accumulated sufficient scrip to total one share, the scrip may be surrendered to the corporation for a certificate evidencing one full share. The holder of scrip is not entitled to exercise any shareholder rights, including voting rights for these partial shares.

Scrip
A document showing ownership of a partial share

5. Classes of Stock

Most corporations issue only one type of stock, generally referred to as common stock. A corporation may, however, if its articles so provide, authorize the issuance of more than one class of stock. These additional classes may have some benefit or preference over the common stock and are therefore called preferred stock. Thus, corporations have great flexibility in their financial structuring. Generally, the holders of preferred stock have elected a more conservative approach to investing than owners of common stock because dividends are almost always paid on preferred stock in a predetermined amount, thus providing a reasonably certain cash return.

Common stock
Ordinary stock of a corporation having no special privileges

Common Stock. If a corporation does not specify in its articles of incorporation the type of stock to be issued and only one class of stock is authorized, it will be **common stock**. Common stockholders have no obligation to the corporation or to its creditors except to pay the consideration required for issuance of the shares. The holders of common stock usually enjoy the following rights:

- **Voting Rights.** Each outstanding share of common stock is typically entitled to one vote on each matter voted on, and fractional shares are entitled to corresponding fractional votes. It is possible to have different classes of common stock, each having different voting rights. For example, Common A shareholders may be entitled to two votes per share and Common B shareholders may be entitled to one vote per share. Every shareholder within a class, however, must be treated uniformly.

- **Distribution Rights.** There is no requirement that a corporation ever pay distributions or dividends to its shareholders. Dividends, whether in the form of cash, property, or other shares of the corporation, are paid within the discretion of the board, assuming profits permit. If an individual owns 10 percent of the Common A stock, she will be entitled to 10 percent of whatever distribution is declared by the board of directors for Common A shareholders.

- **Liquidation Rights.** Upon **liquidation** of the corporation (the winding up of its business affairs), the corporation must satisfy its creditors, including bondholders. The shareholders are then entitled to their proportionate share of the corporation's net assets.

- **Other Rights.** In addition to the typical rights of common shareholders described above, common shareholders may also have preemptive rights (usually only when provided by the articles of incorporation) or cumulative voting rights (see Chapter Ten), which allow them, in an election for directors, to multiply the number of shares owned by the number of directors being elected and cast these as they like.

Liquidation
The winding up of a business and its affairs

Preferred Stock. A class of stock that has some sort of right or preference over another class is preferred stock. The creation of preferred stock must be authorized by the articles of incorporation; the articles must describe the preferences, limitations, and rights of these shares. Preferred stock may be used by a corporation to attract investors with a more conservative approach who desire steady and predictable returns on investments. Preferred stock generally has the following features:

- **Voting Rights.** Preferred stock may or may not have voting rights. So long as one class of stock has unlimited voting rights, other classes may have limited or no voting rights. One reason that preferred shareholders often have no voting rights is that they can rely on their contractual rights guaranteed by the articles of incorporation. Therefore, they do not need to participate in corporate management through voting.

- **Distribution Rights.** A typical feature of preferred stock designed to attract investors is a preference in distributions. In many cases, these are **cumulative distributions**, meaning that if the distribution is not paid during any given year, it simply adds up, and the corporation is required to pay these cumulative distributions to the preferred shareholders before distributions are paid to common stockholders. This cumulative dividend

Cumulative distribution
Distributions that add up and must be paid once a corporation has funds to do so

Noncumulative distribution
A distribution that does not accumulate and is lost if it cannot be paid

is generally built into the stock itself. For example, the articles of incorporation may state that each share of preferred stock is entitled to a $5 annual cumulative dividend or to receive annually 4 percent of the preferred stock's stated value. A **noncumulative distribution** means that the distribution does not accumulate. Thus, if the corporation has insufficient profits to pay a distribution to a shareholder for two years, the shareholder simply loses the right to the distribution. These distribution rights allow preferred shareholders to predict their income from their stock holdings with some degree of certainty.

- **Liquidation Rights.** The holders of preferred stock may be entitled to a stated distribution (for example, $3 per share of preferred stock) upon liquidation. These distributions are paid only after creditors are paid but before common shareholders receive any assets in liquidation.
- **Conversion Rights.** Preferred shareholders may be given the right to convert their preferred shares into cash or some other security, usually common stock (either at an agreed-upon price or an agreed-upon ratio). **Conversion rights** allow preferred shareholders to convert their preferred shares to common shares if the common shares are doing extraordinarily well or are providing better returns than the preferred shareholders are receiving.
- **Redemption Rights.** Preferred stock may be issued with **redemption rights** by which the corporation has the power to reacquire the shares from the shareholders or to **call** the shares back, or, alternatively, the shareholder has the right to compel the corporation to redeem or buy back the shares. This latter right, called a **put**, offers preferred shareholders the advantage of having a ready buyer for their shares. Usually, shares so reacquired by the corporation are retired and restored to the status of authorized but unissued shares.

Conversion right
Right to convert preferred stock into some other form of equity security, usually common stock

Redemption right
Right to compel a stockholder or a corporation to sell or buy stock back

Call
Right of corporation to require shareholder to sell stock back to corporation

Put
Right of shareholder to require corporation to buy stock from shareholder

See Figure 9-1 for a chart comparing common and preferred stock.

PRACTICE TIP

For each active corporate file on which you work, create a Client Data Sheet. The sheet may be maintained in paper form and attached to the inside of the client's general file or may be maintained electronically in your computer files. The Client Data Sheet should provide all of the critical information relating to the client, including accurate corporate name, date and state of incorporation, and a full description of its stock. The number of authorized shares should be noted as well as identification of the classes of stock. If preferred stock has been issued, list its rights (for example, whether dividends are cumulative, whether the stock carries conversion rights, and so forth). The Client Data Sheet will be an invaluable resource. Nearly all contracts and transactions to which the corporate client is a party must give this information. Thus, maintaining it in one specific file will allow you to retrieve these critical data efficiently.

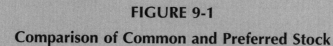

FIGURE 9-1
Comparison of Common and Preferred Stock

	Common Stock	*Preferred Stock*
Voting Rights	Usually one vote per share	Voting rights may or may not exist; articles will specify.
Distribution Rights	No right to distributions; distributions declared in discretion of board and corporation must be solvent.	Distributions are usually "guaranteed" and may be cumulative (meaning that if profits do not permit a distribution, right to distribution carries over until corporation can pay it).
Liquidation Rights	Shareholders receive assets after distribution to creditors and then to preferred shareholders.	Shareholders receive assets after creditors and before common shareholders; distribution may be guaranteed.
Conversion Rights	No conversion rights	Shareholders may have right to convert their preferred shares into some other type of shares (usually common).
Redemption Rights	No redemption rights	Shareholders may be able to compel corporation to purchase their stock at agreed-upon price.

C. Debt Securities

1. Introduction

In addition to issuing stock to raise money, corporations may also borrow money from banks, financial institutions, or individuals. A *debt security* is the instrument that evidences the corporation's debt to another, called a **debt security holder**. The debt security holder is not an owner of the corporation, as is a shareholder, and thus does not have any voting rights or rights to distributions. The debt security holder is simply a creditor who is entitled to be repaid the principal amount of the debt at the appropriate time with the stated interest.

Debt security holder
One to whom a corporate obligation or debt is owed

2. Unsecured Debt

Corporations may borrow money without pledging any property as collateral or security for the debt. In such a case, the creditor has no right to any corporate asset upon default by the corporation and will simply have to sue the corporation to receive repayment of the debt. Such a debt security is referred to as being **unsecured**. Often, the corporation's obligation will be set forth in a loan agreement or in a simple document called a **promissory note**, by which the corporation merely promises to repay money borrowed at a specified time and with specified interest. Promissory notes are often used for short-term financing needs of the corporation. Figure 9-2 shows a form of simple promissory note.

Unsecured debt
Debt for which no collateral is pledged

Promissory note
A written agreement by which one party promises to repay money borrowed from another party

FIGURE 9-2
Unsecured Promissory Note

$50,000   January 1, 2009

For value received, the undersigned, Bailey & Bailey, Inc., a corporation organized and existing under the laws of the State of California, promises to pay to William McMullen, at 2450 Beacon Hill Drive, Los Angeles, California, the sum of Fifty Thousand Dollars ($50,000) with interest from January 1, 2009, until paid, at the rate of five percent (5%) per annum, all due and payable on December 31, 2012. This note may be paid in full at any time without any penalty charges. The undersigned waives demand, presentment, and protest, and all notices thereof and agrees to remain bound hereunder notwithstanding any extension, modification, or waiver by the holder of this note. Should suit be commenced or an attorney employed to enforce the terms of this note, Bailey & Bailey, Inc., agrees to pay such additional sum as a court might order reasonable as attorneys' fees. Principal and interest payable in lawful money of the United States.

Bailey & Bailey, Inc.

By: _____
Title: _____

3.   Secured Debt

Secured debt
Money borrowed by a corporation backed by collateral that can be seized in the event of nonpayment

Bond
Instrument issued with intent of raising money for an entity

Mortgage bond
Document by which real estate is pledged as collateral to secure payment of a debt (also called a *mortgage note*)

Security agreement
Document by which personal property is pledged as collateral to secure payment of a debt

Financing statement
Document filed with secretary of state to provide notice of a security interest

When the corporation's obligation to repay money is **secured**, upon corporate default in repayment, the creditor may seize some specific corporate asset that has been pledged as collateral to ensure the corporation will repay its loan. The document evidencing the corporation's obligation to repay (often a **bond**) will specify the principal amount due, the interest required, the date of repayment, the property pledged to secure repayment of the loan, and perhaps provide other rights to the bondholder or lender.

If the property pledged by the corporation is real estate, the document used by the parties is usually called a **mortgage bond** (or *mortgage note*), and the corporation should be required to insure the real estate, keep it in good condition, pay the taxes due on it, and keep it free and clear of other encumbrances. The mortgage will be recorded with the county recorder where the land is located. If the property pledged by the corporation is personal property (for example, cars, computers, or equipment), the parties will prepare a **security agreement** and then file with the secretary of state a **financing statement** describing the property to provide notice that the lender has a security interest in the stated property. Recording the creditors' interests in corporate real estate or personal property allows other potential lenders to determine the level of the corporation's debt. Many states allow online searching of financing statements filed with the state, and paralegals routinely assist clients who will be loaning money to others in conducting searches (called *UCC searches*, after the Uniform Commercial Code governing the granting of security interests) of these records to ensure that the borrowers have not already pledged security interests in personal property.

4. Common Features of Debt Securities

Because investors can always place their money in banks and receive interest thereon, the corporation may introduce various features or provisions in its debt securities to induce investors to loan money to the corporation. Following are some common features introduced into debt securities to make them attractive to lenders:

- **Higher Interest.** If the corporation pays a lender interest that is higher than that commonly paid by banks, lenders will find it attractive to loan money to the corporation.
- **Redemption Terms.** The corporation may agree not to pay off or "redeem" the debt prior to the date the parties agreed upon for repayment. An early payoff by the corporation would deprive the lender of the interest it expected to receive over the life of the loan. Thus, the corporation may introduce favorable **redemption terms** to assure the lender that it will receive the bargained-for interest. The corporation may agree not to redeem the debt before its stated maturity date or to pay a penalty or premium to the lender if the debt is redeemed or paid off early.
- **Conversion Terms.** Debt securities may be convertible into equity securities, or shares of the corporation. Such **conversion terms** would allow the creditor to trade in debt for shares and become a shareholder in the corporation without using actual cash to buy the shares.
- **Priority and Subordination Rights.** A corporation may agree with a lender that it will never give another debt **priority** over the lender's debt and will always keep later borrowings junior or **subordinate** to the lender. Such terms assure the lender that it will be paid first.
- **Voting Rights.** A few states, including Delaware and New York, authorize the articles of incorporation to allow debt security holders to vote on certain issues, including election of directors. This is not a common approach.

Redemption terms
Terms relating to a borrower's right to pay off or redeem a debt prior to its maturity date

Conversion terms
Right of a lender to convert a debt security to an equity security

Priority
Process of making one obligation senior to others

Subordination
Process of making one obligation junior to others

See Figure 9-3 for a comparison of equity and debt securities.

D. Taxation of Corporations

1. Introduction

Because a corporation is viewed as a separate entity or person created under the authority of the state, it must pay taxes just as other persons do. Corporations are subject to federal taxation and may be subject to state and local taxation as well. The taxation of a corporation is accomplished by corporate tax rates different from those for natural persons. The taxation of a corporation is a significant feature of corporate existence and distinguishes the corporation from other forms of business (sole proprietorships, general partnerships, limited partnerships, limited liability partnerships, and limited liability companies), in which the money earned is simply passed through to the individuals involved, who pay tax at the rate established by the Internal Revenue Code for individuals.

FIGURE 9-3
Comparison of Equity and Debt Securities

Equity Securities ("Stock")	*Debt Securities (often in the form of "Bonds")*
Shareholder is an owner of the corporation and is entitled to vote and receive distributions, if earnings permit.	Creditor or bondholder is an outside creditor of the corporation and is entitled to timely repayment of the debt.
Issuance of shares produces cash for the corporation.	Borrowing money produces cash for the corporation.
Issuance of shares dilutes power of existing shareholders but costs the corporation nothing.	Borrowing money does not dilute the power of existing shareholders but money borrowed must be repaid.
If corporation is insolvent, no distributions will be paid to any shareholder.	Creditor or bondholder will be entitled to periodic payments of interest and principal or repayment of the debt.
Corporation may not deduct distributions to shareholders (and distributions are taxed to the shareholder recipients).	Corporation may deduct interest paid to creditors and bondholders and thereby reduce its taxable income.
In event of liquidation, shareholders receive assets after outside creditors and bondholders.	In event of liquidation, creditors and bondholders receive assets before shareholders.

---

2. Double Taxation

Double taxation
Taxation of corporate income at two levels, once when received by corporation and then again when distributed to shareholders

Corporations are subject to **double taxation**. Corporations pay tax at specified corporate rates on income; then when net profits are distributed to shareholders, the shareholders pay income tax on distributions received at the applicable tax rates. Figure 9-4 shows the current tax rates for individuals and corporations. Corporations are, however, entitled to deductions for various expenses, such as rent, salaries, interest paid to lenders, and contributions to employee benefit plans. Corporations report their taxable income on IRS Form 1120.

In mid-2003, Congress reduced individual taxes on dividends to 15 percent (5 percent for the lowest two brackets) and agreed to eliminate taxes entirely in 2008 for the lowest two brackets. These dividend reductions are scheduled to expire in 2010.

Large publicly held corporations simply accept double taxation as a cost of doing business. Smaller corporations, however, may minimize double taxation through the use of various means, including electing S corporation status (in which all income earned by the corporation is passed through to the shareholders, who must number fewer than 100, who pay at their individual rates). S corporations are discussed in Chapter Fifteen. In small corporations in which shareholders are actively employed, these employee-shareholders do not receive dividends; rather, they may receive salary increases or bonuses, which, although they may be taxable to the employee-shareholders, are deductible by the corporation as expenses. Corporations that are not S corporations are called C corporations.

FIGURE 9-4
Federal Taxation (2008)

Taxable Income
(Taxpayer Filing Singly)

Taxable Income Over	But not over	Tax	Tax +%	On amount over
$0	$8,025	$0.00	10	$0
8,025	32,550	802.50	15	8,025
32,550	78,850	4,481.25	25	32,550
78,850	164,550	16,056.25	28	78,850
164,550	357,700	40,052.25	33	164,550
357,700		103,791.75	35	357,700

Taxable Income
(Married Taxpayers Filing Jointly)

Taxable Income Over	But not over	Tax	Tax +%	On amount over
$0	$16,050	$0.00	10	$0
16,050	65,100	1,605.00	15	16,050
65,100	131,450	8,962.50	25	65,100
131,450	200,300	25,550.00	28	131,450
200,300	357,700	44,828.00	33	200,300
357,700		96,770.00	35	357,700

Taxable Income for Corporations

If taxable income is Over	But not over	Tax is	Of the amount over
$0	$50,000	15%	$0
$50,000	$75,000	$7,500 + 25%	$50,000
$75,000	$100,000	$13,750 + 34%	$75,000
$100,000	$335,000	$22,250 + 39%	$100,000
$335,000	$10,000,000	$113,900 + 34%	$335,000
$10,000,000	$15,000,000	$3,400,000 + 35%	$10,000,000
$15,000,000	$18,333,333	$5,150,000 + 38%	$15,000,000
$18,333,333		35%	$0

Similarly, a corporation may elect to obtain funds through debt financing (by borrowing money) rather than through equity financing (by issuing shares) because interest paid to creditors is a deductible corporate expense, whereas

Thin incorporation
A corporation whose debts are disproportionately high to its equity

dividends paid to shareholders are not deductible. To ensure the corporation does not encumber itself by issuing only debt securities, the Internal Revenue Service has devised the theory of **thin incorporation**, which discourages corporations from issuing too many debt securities. If the IRS deems the debt to be excessive, the IRS may then characterize interest payments on debt as dividends, which are then nondeductible to the corporation and subject to taxation by the recipient.

Accumulated earnings tax
Tax penalty imposed on corporations that retain earnings beyond reasonable business needs

To discourage corporations from simply holding on to profits rather than distributing them (thereby reducing the impact of double taxation), the IRS has devised certain penalties that give corporations strong incentive to distribute profits to shareholders rather than hoarding them. Thus, if a C corporation accumulates earnings beyond the reasonable needs of its business to avoid having shareholders pay income taxes on earnings that should have been distributed to them, the corporation will be subject to an **accumulated earnings tax** in the current amount of 15 percent of the accumulated taxable amount retained in excess of $250,000. Imposing this penalty encourages corporations to distribute income to shareholders, who then pay tax on the money they have received.

3. State and Other Taxes

Franchise fee
Fee imposed on business for privilege of doing business in a state

Corporations that transact business in a state are usually subject to that state's income tax, if any. Some states assess tax based on the revenue generated in the state; other states impose a flat tax rate on corporate income. Additionally, most states impose a special tax on corporations merely for the privilege of being incorporated or authorized to do business in the state. Usually called a **franchise fee**, the tax may be the same flat fee assessed to all corporations or the tax may be based on annual income. Corporations may also be subject to property and sales tax. Thus, corporations are subject to a dizzying array of taxes.

E. Role of Paralegal

Although advice given to corporations regarding the relative advantages and disadvantages of issuing equity and debt securities (and the tax consequences thereof) is the purview of the attorneys and accountants advising the client, there are a number of activities in which the paralegal will be involved:

- Monitoring the issuance of stock to ensure that a sufficient number of shares are authorized by the articles of incorporation to accommodate any such issuance;
- Preparing minutes of directors' meetings approving the issuance of equity and debt securities;
- Amending the corporation's articles of incorporation to increase the number of authorized shares, if necessary (including preparing notices and minutes of directors' and shareholders' meetings authorizing such an amendment);
- Assisting the corporation in its bookkeeping activities to ensure interest payments are timely made to lenders; and

- Conducting searches of county and state records (UCC searches) to determine existence of mortgage bonds/notes and security agreements that pledge corporate property as collateral.

Case Illustration
Rights of Preferred Shareholders Are Subordinate to Creditors

---

Case: *Warren v. King*, 108 U.S. 389 (1883)

Facts: Preferred shareholders claimed that they were entitled to have their shares of stock declared to be a lien on the property of the company.

Holding: Holders of preferred stock occupy a position inferior to all creditors. They have no claim on the property of the company superior to that of creditors who became creditors subsequent to issuance of the preferred stock. They are not preferred as to any but the holders of common stock, and their rights must be determined by the language of the stock certificate.

Key Features
of Corporate Financial Structure

- To raise money, corporations will issue stock (equity securities), which show ownership interest in the corporation, or bonds (debt securities), which are loans to the corporation. Corporations may also borrow money by executing loan agreements or promissory notes.
- Shares issued by a corporation must be authorized by the articles of incorporation.
- The par value of a share is the nominal face value of the share and is the lowest price for which it can be sold.
- If stock has no par value, it may be sold for whatever amount the directors determine is in the best interests of the corporation.
- Corporations may have more than one class of stock.
- Common stock is ordinary stock of the corporation and usually has voting rights, distribution rights, and liquidation rights (distribution and liquidation rights are exercised after preferred stockholders exercise their rights).
- Preferred stock has some sort of right or preference other classes do not have, often as to cumulating dividends, conversion (changing preferred stock to common stock), or redemption (a buyback of the stock by the corporation).

◆ Debt securities may be unsecured, in which case, in the event of a default, the creditor simply sues to recover the money owed by the corporation.

◆ Debt securities may be secured by corporate real estate or personal property; in the event of a default the creditor may recover the property pledged as security or collateral.

◆ Debt securities may have favorable redemption terms (so the corporation does not pay off the debt early) or conversion terms (so the securities can be converted into equity securities or shares).

◆ Corporations are said to be subject to "double taxation": The corporation pays tax on the money it receives, and shareholders then pay tax on distributions made to them. Interest paid on bonds is a deductible expense for the corporation.

Internet Resources

State corporation statutes:	www.law.cornell.edu www.findlaw.com
Text of MBCA:	www.abanet.org/buslaw/committees/ CL270000pub/nosearch/mbca/home. shtml
Secretaries of state:	www.nass.org (this site provides links to each state's secretary of state for access to forms and online UCC searching in many states)
Internal Revenue Service:	www.irs.gov (site provides tax information and forms)
Company information:	www.hoovers.com (site provides addresses and basic information about many U.S. companies)
Forms for promissory notes and security agreements:	www.ilrg.com www.siccode.com/forms.php

Key Terms

Equity security	Outstanding shares
Debt security	Par value
Bondholder	Watered stock
Common stock	Promissory note
Preferred stock	Uncertificated shares
Authorized shares	Transfer agent

Registrar
Scrip
Liquidation
Cumulative distribution
Noncumulative distribution
Conversion right
Redemption right
Put
Call
Debt security holder
Bond
Unsecured debt

Secured debt
Mortgage bond
Security agreement
Financing statement
Redemption terms
Conversion terms
Priority
Subordination
Double taxation
Thin incorporation
Accumulated earnings tax
Franchise fee

Discussion Questions

Fact Scenario. H & A Inc. is a California corporation authorized to issue 500,000 shares of common stock and 20,000 shares of preferred stock, which preferred shares have the right to cumulative dividends.

1. The corporation has not issued any dividends for three years. This year the corporation will issue a dividend. Describe the rights of Peter, a preferred shareholder, and the rights of Carrie, a common shareholder.

2. Identify one advantage and one disadvantage to corporations of issuing stock and of issuing bonds.

3. Discuss three features that the corporation could introduce into its bonds to induce investors to purchase the bonds.

4. The corporation is holding its annual meeting to elect its directors. What are the rights of Peter, Carrie, and Bill (a bondholder)?

5. Peter has conversion rights. What advantage does this afford him?

6. Why would Bill prefer that the corporation not redeem his bond prior to its maturity date?

7. The corporation has not distributed any dividends in three years because it has been setting aside $400,000 that it plans to use to expand its business operations in the western states. Is there any risk to the corporation in adopting this strategy?

Net Worth

1. Access the Web site for the SEC and review the Form 10-K for the Washington Post filed on ~~February 28, 2008~~. Review the cover sheet. April 3, 2011
   a. How many shares of Class A common stock were outstanding?
   b. How many shares of Class B common stock were outstanding?

2. Access the Web site for Berkshire Hathaway, Inc. and locate the proxy statement for the 2008 annual shareholders' meeting.
   a. Where was the meeting held?
   b. How many votes do shares of Class A stock carry?
   c. How may votes do shares of Class B stock carry?
3. Access the Web site for Investorwords. What is the definition of a debenture?
4. Access the UCC search database for New York. Conduct a UCC search on Orville Blythe. When was the UCC statement filed? When will it expire or lapse? Who is the secured party?

10

♦ ♦ ♦

Corporate Management

♦ ♦ ♦

A. Shareholders' Rights and Responsibilities

1. Introduction

Shareholders (or *stockholders*, a synonymous term) are the owners of a corporation. Yet these owners do not manage the corporation (although shareholders in smaller corporations are more actively involved than shareholders in large, publicly traded companies). Shareholder participation in corporate management is indirect and is generally limited to voting. Shareholders do not vote on day-to-day management matters but rather are restricted to voting on the election (and removal) of directors and fundamental changes to the corporation, such as amending the articles of incorporation and mergers. Shareholder voting rights take place at two types of meetings: annual meetings and special meetings. Alternatively, most states allow shareholders to take action without a meeting if they unanimously agree to some action in writing.

As to shareholder responsibilities, generally, shareholders have only one responsibility: to pay for the stock issued to them. Once the stock is paid for, shareholders are not liable to the corporation or to its creditors for the corporation's debts and obligations. Although the shareholder's stock may plummet in value to zero, a shareholder generally has no liability for corporate obligations. Shareholders' rights, responsibilities, liabilities, and duties are governed by state statutes, the articles of incorporation, and the corporate bylaws.

Shareholder
An owner of a corporation; also called *stockholder*

2. Inspection Rights

Shareholders have the right to be informed of the affairs of the corporation. Most state statutes provide an absolute right to shareholders to inspect most records, such as articles, bylaws, and minutes of shareholders' meetings. Other states, such as

Delaware, provide that the inspection must be for a proper purpose. This is also the approach of MBCA § 16.02. Additionally, in most states, shareholders have a right to review the list of shareholders at any time so long as the review is for a proper purpose. Some states, however, require that the shareholder own a certain minimum amount of stock before being allowed to inspect corporate records.

3. Voting Rights

Shareholders exercise their limited role in the operation of the corporation primarily through voting. The articles of incorporation may grant, deny, or limit voting rights. For example, one class of shares might have nonvoting stock. Other types of voting include the following:

Straight voting
Voting in which each share of record has one vote

Cumulative voting
Method of voting in election for directors in which each share carries as many votes as there are directors being elected

- **Straight Voting.** Generally, each share of record is entitled to one vote for each director's position to be filled or for each issue being considered. Thus, if Eve has 100 shares, she may cast 100 votes for or against a merger. This is called **straight voting** and is the most common form of voting.
- **Cumulative Voting. Cumulative voting** may be provided for in the articles of incorporation or mandated by state statute. Cumulative voting applies only to the election of directors, not to other corporate issues, such as voting on mergers or dissolution. If cumulative voting rights exist, each share is multiplied by the number of vacancies to be filled on the board of directors. The votes may then be cast in any manner desired by the shareholder. Thus, if Eve has 100 shares and five directors are being elected, Eve will have 500 votes to cast however she likes. To maximize the advantage of cumulative voting, which is intended to allow some representation of minority shareholders on the board of directors, minority shareholders tend to "dump" all their votes on one candidate rather than dilute the impact of cumulative voting by spreading their votes among the nominees. In most states (and under MBCA § 7.28(b)), cumulative voting is permissive, meaning that the articles may provide for cumulative voting; if the articles do not so provide, no cumulative voting exists. In a few states, including Arizona, cumulative voting is mandated by statute (for corporations that are not traded publicly).

4. Shareholders' Meetings

Shareholder voting occurs at two types of meetings: annual meetings and special meetings. The bylaws or the notice of the meeting will specify the place of the meeting. The meeting may be at the corporation's principal office or it may be rotated around the country to allow shareholders living in various locations to attend an occasional meeting.

Annual meeting
Yearly meeting of shareholders

- **Annual Meetings.** Most state statutes require that corporations hold annual meetings of shareholders. The primary business conducted at the **annual meeting** is the election of directors, although other business may take place. The time and date of annual meetings is usually set forth in the corporation's bylaws, which might provide, for example, that the annual meeting will be held the first Monday in May of each year.

- **Special Meetings. Special meetings** are shareholder meetings held between annual meetings. Shareholders need some mechanism to call meetings between annual meetings to investigate mismanagement or to vote on removal of directors. Similarly, corporate management needs a mechanism to call a meeting to consider an unexpected event, such as a merger proposal. Most states provide that the board of directors of a corporation may call a special meeting or that shareholders owning 10 percent or more of the outstanding stock may demand that the corporation call a special meeting.

Special meeting
A meeting held between regular or annual meetings

Notice of Meetings. All jurisdictions require that shareholders receive notice of all meetings. Notice requirements may be very detailed; therefore, state statutes must be carefully reviewed to ensure that notice is properly given. See Figure 10-1 for a sample notice of an annual shareholders' meeting.

Shareholders Entitled to Notice. To determine the shareholders who will receive notice, the corporate bylaws will usually provide a **record date**, or a date selected in advance of the meeting. Any shareholder who owns shares on the record date will receive the notice. Many bylaws provide that the record date will be 30 days before the meeting. Thus, if the meeting date is May 1 and the record date is April 1, a shareholder who owns shares on April 1 will receive the

Record date
A date selected in advance of a meeting or event

FIGURE 10-1
Notice of Annual Meeting of Shareholders

Notice is hereby given that the Annual Meeting of Shareholders of V-Tech, Inc., will be held in the Mayflower Suite of the Sheraton Manhattan Hotel, located at 790 Seventh Avenue, New York, New York 10019, on June 1, 2009, at 10:00 a.m. Eastern Standard Time, for the following purposes:

1. To elect five directors to serve until the next annual meeting or until their successors have been elected and qualified.
2. To ratify the appointment of PricewaterhouseCoopers as the Company's independent registered public accountants for the next fiscal year; and
3. To transact such other business as may properly come before the meeting or any adjournment thereof.

Only shareholders of record at the close of business on May 2, 2009, are entitled to notice of and to vote at the meeting or any adjournments thereof.

May 2, 2009   By order of the Board of Directors
New York, New York   Ellen N. Franklin, Secretary

notice and be entitled to vote even if the shareholder sells his shares between the record date (April 1) and the meeting date (May 1). Similarly, an individual who buys shares after the record date is set is simply out of luck: He will not be entitled to vote at the upcoming meeting.

Contents and Timing of Notice. The notice must specify the date, time, and place of the meeting. Under MBCA § 7.05(a), the notice must be given no fewer than 10 and no more than 60 days before the meeting. Notice of a special meeting must describe its purpose. Erring on the side of caution, most corporations specify the purposes for all meetings, whether annual or special. Notice is generally effective when it is mailed. Most corporations include an annual report with the notice of an annual shareholders' meeting. The annual report explains the company's performance, includes financial information, and provides other information of interest to shareholders. Paralegals are routinely involved in preparing and reviewing annual reports.

Defective Notice. If the corporation fails to meet its obligations with regard to its notice requirements, the meeting is invalid and may be attacked by any shareholder who did not receive proper notice. There are, however, two alternatives a corporation may use to try to save an otherwise invalid meeting. First, a shareholder may sign a written waiver of notice, expressly waiving his right to receive notice. Second, a shareholder may consent in writing to action taken at the meeting.

Shareholder Lists. After the record date is determined, the corporation prepares an alphabetical list of shareholders, which must be made available to shareholders for inspection through the meeting date. Making the shareholder list available for inspection promotes shareholder discussion and perhaps banding together by shareholders to vote as a group to achieve certain goals.

Quorum
The minimum number of shareholders or directors required to be present before action can be taken

Quorum. No action may be taken at any shareholder meeting unless a certain minimum number of shares, called a **quorum**, is present. Generally, a quorum is a majority of shares entitled to be cast on a given matter. Thus, if 1,000 shares are entitled to vote on the election of directors, 501 shares must be present for the meeting to be held. If no quorum is present, the meeting must be adjourned. Although the articles may modify the quorum, in most states (including California and New York) they may not reduce the quorum to less than one-third of the shares entitled to vote at the meeting.

Proxy
Written authorization from one directing another to vote his shares

Proxies. Most states and the MBCA allow shareholders to vote by proxy if they are unable or do not wish to attend a meeting. A **proxy** is a written authorization instructing another person to vote one's shares on one's behalf. The closest analogy to a proxy form is an absentee ballot. The proxy may be specific and may direct the proxy holder (who is an agent of the shareholder) to vote a certain way, or the proxy may be general and authorize the proxy holder to cast the shareholder's votes in the proxy holder's discretion. Proxies may generally be revoked at any time before they are exercised by communicating the revocation to the corporation's secretary or attending the meeting and voting in person. Proxies are used to ensure that a quorum is present. For example, General Electric Company had more than 600,000 shareholder accounts of record as of early 2008. No facility can accommodate that number of shareholders. Thus, most shareholders vote by proxy rather than voting in person at a meeting.

Conducting the Meeting. At the meeting, items on the agenda are presented in the form of resolutions, which the shareholders then vote on. Some states require that approval by a majority is required to take action. However, MBCA § 7.25(c) and many states provide that a measure (other than election of directors) passes when the votes for that measure exceed the votes cast against it. This allows a measure to pass without receiving a majority vote. For example, if 100 voting shares are outstanding, a quorum would be 51. If 51 shares are present (either in person or by proxy) and corporate statutes require a majority vote to take action, at least 26 of those shares must vote affirmatively. Under the MBCA approach, however, the measure could pass with fewer than 26 votes, for example, if 20 shares voted in favor, 18 shares voted against the action, and 13 shares abstained.

As to election of directors, under MBCA § 7.28(a) and most state statutes, directors are elected by a **plurality** of votes, meaning that the candidate who receives the most "for" votes wins, even if the candidate does not receive a majority of the votes. For example, if candidates Amy, Bob, and Cole receive 45, 30, and 25 votes, respectively (and 100 shares are voting), Amy has won by a plurality. She may not win by majority vote unless she receives at least 51 out of the 100 votes.

As discussed below, numerous shareholder proposals have been made recommending that directors be elected by majority rather than plurality vote. In an extreme situation, in a plurality-vote case, a director could be elected with one vote, because the only two options available to shareholders of many publicly traded companies is to either vote "for" or "withhold" for a director. Ninety such proposals were made during the 2005 proxy season. Several companies, including Intel, have voluntarily adopted majority voting in director elections.

Shareholders may enter into **voting agreements** by which they specify in writing in advance how they will vote. Such an agreement allows shareholders to band together to seek control.

Meeting Minutes. There is very little regulation as to the conduct of meetings. Large corporations tend to have more formal meetings, and voting is by written ballot, which lends certainty. Smaller corporations (whose shareholders own equal numbers of shares) tend to use voice voting or a show of hands. Minutes of the meeting are usually prepared by the corporation's secretary. To provide protection against later challenges, the minutes should recite that notice was timely sent, that a quorum was present, that a measure passed by sufficient vote, and so forth. The **minutes** are usually a summary of the meeting rather than a verbatim transcript. MBCA § 7.08 provides only that the rules adopted for and the conduct of any shareholders' meeting must be fair to the shareholders. See Figure 10-2 for sample minutes of a shareholders' meeting.

Plurality
The number of votes received by one in an election when the candidate does not have a majority of votes; counting only votes "for" a nominee and not counting votes "against" or withheld

Voting agreement
An agreement among shareholders specifying how they will vote

Minutes
Written record of events occurring at a meeting

FIGURE 10-2
Minutes of Annual Meeting of Shareholders

An annual meeting of the shareholders of V-Tech, Inc., a New York corporation (the "Corporation"), was held on June 1, 2009, at 10:00 a.m., in the Mayflower Suite of the Sheraton Manhattan Hotel, 790 Seventh Avenue, New York, New York 10019, for the purpose of electing directors of the Corporation, voting on the approval of Pricewaterhouse-Coopers as the Corporation's independent registered public accountants, and transacting such other business properly before the meeting.

Harry S. Hunter, Chief Executive Officer, acted as Chairman, and Ellen N. Franklin acted as Secretary.

At 10:00 a.m. the Chairman called the meeting to order.

The Secretary announced that the meeting was called pursuant to Section 602 of the Business Corporation Law of New York and Article III of the bylaws of the Corporation.

The Secretary announced that the meeting was held pursuant to notice properly given as required under the laws of the State of New York and the bylaws of the Corporation or that notice had been waived by those entitled to receive notice under the bylaws. Copies of any written waivers executed by those persons entitled to receive notice will be attached to the minutes of this meeting by the Secretary. The Secretary read the minutes of the last annual meeting of shareholders. The minutes were approved and placed in the Corporation's minute book.

The Secretary announced that an alphabetical list of the names of shareholders and the number of shares held by each was available for inspection by any person in attendance at the meeting.

The Secretary announced that a quorum was present at the meeting.

All of the directors of the corporation were present at the meeting. The following other person was present: Helen Hays, Chief Financial Officer of the Corporation.

The reports of the President and Chief Financial Officer were presented to the shareholders and were placed in the Corporation's minute book.

The Chairman then called for the election of directors of the Corporation.

Upon motion duly made, seconded, and carried, the following persons were elected to the board of directors of the Corporation, to serve as directors until their successors are elected at the next annual meeting of shareholders of the Corporation and qualify:

> William Mulholland
> Holly McMullen
> Paul X. Ryan
> John Lillard
> Greg Young

The Chairman then called for the approval of PricewaterhouseCoopers as the Corporation's independent registered public accountants.

Upon motion duly made, seconded, and carried, PricewaterhouseCoopers was approved as the Corporation's independent registered public accountants upon the same terms and conditions set forth in the Notice of this Annual Meeting of Shareholders and placed in the minute book.

There being no further business before the meeting, on motion duly made, seconded, and unanimously carried, it was adjourned.

Date:_____   _____
                                                Ellen N. Franklin, Secretary

---

PRACTICE TIPS

- Make sure your Corporate Data Sheet for each corporate client identifies the corporation's annual meeting date, notice requirements, quorum requirements, and the like.
- To calculate the timing of notices and record dates, use the calculator at www.timeanddate.com.

---

5. Shareholder Action Without a Meeting

Under MBCA § 7.04(a) and most state statutes, shareholders may take action without formally meeting, thereby allowing business to be conducted without the expense of holding meetings if all shareholders entitled to vote on an issue consent to the proposed action in writing. The corporate secretary will prepare a written consent action reflecting the action to be taken and will distribute it (or counterpart copies of the document) to all shareholders to sign. Once signed by the last shareholder, the measure is effective. Shareholders may consent to action electronically by e-mail. Action by written consent is primarily designed to simplify corporate formalities for smaller corporations when it may be difficult for shareholders to get together for meetings.

Although the MBCA and most states require that the consent be unanimous, Delaware and some other states require only the same number of votes that would be required to take action at a formal meeting (usually, a majority vote). In fact, a recent amendment to the MBCA allows a corporation to permit shareholder action by written consent by a majority vote (rather than unanimous) if the articles of incorporation so provide. MBCA § 7.04(b). Such a provision allows larger and publicly traded corporations to take actions more expeditiously and without the necessity of a meeting. When action is taken by less than unanimous written consent, the MBCA requires that notice of the action be given to nonconsenting shareholders. If a corporation elects its directors by cumulative voting, however, such directors may not be elected by less than unanimous written consent.

The rationale for the preference in most states for requiring unanimous consent is that in the absence of a meeting, there is no opportunity for debate and discussion.

6. Other Shareholder Rights

Shareholders may have preemptive rights, which give them the right to purchase as many newly issued shares as will maintain the shareholder's proportionate ownership interest in the corporation. Shareholders may have the right to receive dividends if the corporation is solvent and the directors decide to declare dividends.

Buy-sell agreement
Agreement among
shareholders regarding their
rights to purchase and sell
stock in a corporation and
usually imposing some
restriction on those rights

Legend
A notation marked on a
stock certificate indicating
the stock is subject to some
restriction or limitation

Shareholders also have the right to transfer their shares to others, unless they have entered into agreements restricting the transfer of their shares. Such agreements, typically used only in small corporations, usually require that a shareholder who wishes to sell stock must first offer it to the corporation and/or to the other shareholders. If the corporation and the other shareholders decline to purchase the shares, the shares may then be sold to an "outsider." Small corporations use such agreements, often called **buy-sell agreements**, to prevent the intrusion of outsiders. Generally, any restrictions on stock transfers (or voting) must be referred to by a notice or **legend** on the face of the stock certificate, which informs potential purchasers that the stock is subject to some restrictions as to its sale or voting.

7. Modern Trends

Modern technology is having a significant effect on shareholder meetings. Effective January 1, 2009, all publicly traded companies are required to post their proxy materials (namely, the proxy statement and the annual report) on the Internet and then provide their shareholders with notice of the availability of these proxy materials 40 days before the meeting. Companies may also mail their proxy materials and if shareholders request materials by mail, they must be provided at no charge. Shareholders may also now vote by telephone or by accessing a Web site. In fact, the SEC reported that by the 2006 proxy season, nearly 90 percent of shareholders of publicly traded companies voted electronically or telephonically. These advances help the corporation reduce printing and postage costs and also enhance shareholder participation in corporate governance. Some experts predict that companies will eventually hold "cybermeetings," with shareholders all over the world participating via the Internet. At present, the primary barrier to cybermeetings is ensuring the confidentiality and security of voting.

Another new trend, which has been adopted by MBCA § 1.44 and SEC rule, is to allow the delivery of a single annual report and proxy statement to shareholders who share the same last name and address, unless contrary instructions are received from a shareholder. This practice, known as **householding**, is designed to reduce printing and postage costs.

Householding
Practice of sending only one
report and proxy statement
to shareholders with same
surname at same address

8. Shareholder Actions

Disgruntled shareholders may take two types of actions against a corporation: direct actions and derivative actions.

Direct action
Action initiated to address
direct harm done to the
complainant

1. **Direct Action.** A **direct action** (or individual action) is litigation initiated by a shareholder who has been directly injured by some act of the corporation, such as a refusal of voting rights or a denial of a dividend when every other shareholder received a dividend. If numerous shareholders are similarly situated, they may bring a class action so that all their rights are adjudicated at the same time.

Derivative action
Action initiated to enforce a
right owned by another

2. **Derivative Action.** A **derivative action** is brought by a shareholder to enforce a cause of action owned by the corporation but that it will not enforce. In brief, the shareholder sues the corporation to compel it to

enforce corporate rights. The shareholder is the plaintiff and both the corporation and any wrongdoer are the defendants. The shareholder is not suing for direct injury done to herself; the action "derives" from the shareholder's ownership interest in the corporation, which will not sue the wrongdoer (perhaps because the wrongdoer is a director or has a familial or other relationship with the corporation). If the shareholder is successful, any recovery goes to the corporation; the shareholder, however, is usually reimbursed for costs and expenses incurred in the litigation.

To reduce frivolous suits against corporations, Congress enacted the Private Securities Litigation Reform Act (15 U.S.C. §§ 78u-4) in late 1995. The Act requires plaintiffs to state in specific detail any allegations of misrepresentation rather than merely generally alleging misconduct and then using discovery to obtain specificity and perhaps uncover claims. Although the number of lawsuits declined for several years after passage of the Act, the number rose sharply in early 2008, primarily due to a surge in cases related to the collapse of the subprime mortgage market. The median loss alleged in the subprime cases is $4.5 billion. It can be difficult, however, to recover damages from a troubled company, as shown by the fact that the median recovery in settled cases in early 2008 was less than 3 percent of claimed losses. It remains to be seen what the fallout will be from the spectacular financial collapses of 2008 and the government bailout of the banking sector and Wall Street approved in October 2008. The 2008 financial collapse is discussed below.

9. Piercing the Corporate Veil

Although the general rule is that shareholders have no personal liability for a corporation's debts and obligations, there are exceptions to this rule. Shareholders may certainly agree to accept personal responsibility for corporate obligations. For example, a newly formed small corporation may have trouble obtaining a bank loan unless all of the individual shareholders agree to guarantee the loan personally.

Because the corporation shields the shareholders from liability, it is said that there is a "veil" between the corporation and the shareholders such that creditors are not able to **"pierce the veil"** to hold individual shareholders liable for corporate obligations. Nevertheless, courts will pierce the veil whenever it is necessary to prevent fraud or injustice. Although this standard gives courts great flexibility in determining the circumstances under which liability may be imposed on shareholders, in actual practice, piercing-the-veil cases tend to share a common element: The shareholders have not acted as if the corporation is a separate entity; rather, they view the corporation as their mere **alter ego** or business conduit.

The usual piercing-the-veil case involves a creditor who has not been fully paid by a small corporation. For example, assume a creditor is owed $50,000 by ABC Inc. If the corporation has only $10,000 in its bank accounts, the creditor is unlikely to be happy with such a small recovery and will begin examining the corporate books and records to see if he can pierce the veil and hold the shareholders liable for the remainder of the debt.

Piercing the veil
Holding individual shareholders liable for corporate obligations

Alter ego
Doctrine alleging separate corporate existence has been ignored by shareholders

Following are the three most frequent examples of conduct that leads to piercing of the veil:

1. **Commingling of Assets.** The corporation is a separate person. Therefore, it has its own bank accounts and funds. If shareholders "dip into" corporate accounts when they are low on funds or if the corporation borrows money from the shareholders to meet its obligations (without a formal loan agreement), **commingling of assets** has occurred. It does not matter whether the money is repaid. If the shareholders disregard the fact that the corporation is a separate entity, they may be liable in a piercing-the-veil suit.

2. **Lack of Formalities.** If the corporation never issues stock, never appoints officers, and never holds meetings, the veil may be pierced, and liability may be imposed on individual shareholders. When corporate owners do not treat the corporation as a separate entity that must comply with various legal formalities, there is little reason why courts should. Thus, corporate clients must be counseled on the importance of observing corporate formalities.

3. **Inadequate Capitalization.** Shareholders may be liable for corporate obligations when the corporation is so inadequately capitalized that it could not expect to meet its responsibilities. Failure to ensure that the corporation has sufficient funds to meet its needs works an injustice on creditors.

The usual piercing-the-veil case is brought against a small corporation whose shareholders are all active in managing the business (and are usually so busy managing the business that they forget to respect the corporation as a separate entity). Large corporations such as Ford Motor Company do not allow shareholders access to corporate funds, routinely hold their meetings according to law, and are usually adequately capitalized.

Commingling of assets
Combining funds owned by different individuals or entities

B. Directors' Rights and Responsibilities

1. Introduction

Directors
Those who manage a corporation

Corporations are managed or governed by individuals called **directors**, and a corporation must have a board of directors. Directors' duties and powers derive from state statutes, the articles of incorporation, and the corporate bylaws. Directors have full authority for determining corporate policy and exercise this authority in their regular and special meetings. Each director has one vote, and generally a simple majority is required to take action, although all states allow directors to take action without a meeting if they act by unanimous written consent. Directors owe duties of due care and good faith to the corporation. Generally, directors are not liable for a mere error in judgment unless their action (or lack thereof) is clearly and grossly negligent.

2. Functions of Directors

Directors are charged with exercising all corporate powers and managing the entire business affairs of a corporation. Although directors may delegate many duties to officers or committees, certain duties, such as authorizing dividends, filling vacancies on the board, and amending bylaws may not be so delegated. Among other duties, directors are responsible for the following: appointing and supervising officers; determining all financial matters (including issuing stock and bonds and obtaining loans); determining products, services, and employee benefits and compensation; authorizing distributions; amending bylaws; and exercising responsibility for all corporate operations.

3. Election, Term, Vacancies, and Removal of Directors

A few states require at least three directors, but most states and the MBCA permit a corporation to have a single director. Corporations with more than one director typically authorize an odd number of directors to minimize the chance of deadlock. A corporation may also have a range of directors. Although the articles or bylaws may set minimum and maximum age standards and residency requirements, the trend is to avoid such limitations, although older statutes often required that directors be residents of the state of incorporation.

If the initial directors are not named in the articles of incorporation, they will be elected at the corporation's first organizational meeting. These directors serve until the first annual shareholders' meeting. Directors are then elected at the first annual meeting and at every annual meeting thereafter, unless their terms are staggered. In a **staggered system**, the directors do not all face election at the same time; their terms are divided into groupings, much the way the United States Senate is a staggered system. Although all senators have six-year terms, only one-third of the 100 senators stand for election every two years. A staggered or classified system promotes continuity in the board and may make a hostile takeover more difficult because it would take several elections for an aggressor to take control of an entire board.

Staggered system
Method of corporate governance in which not all directors are elected at the same time or election

If a vacancy occurs on the board due to resignation, retirement, or death, the vacancy is filled either by the shareholders or by the remaining directors. Most statutes and bylaws allow the remaining directors to fill the vacancies. The newly appointed director steps into the shoes of his or her predecessor and serves for the remainder of the predecessor's term.

At common law, once directors were elected, they could be removed by shareholders only "for cause," which usually meant fraud, incompetence, or dishonesty. The modern approach is to recognize that because the shareholders are the owners of the corporation, they should be allowed to remove directors with or without cause. Shareholders who are dissatisfied with a director will usually demand that the corporation call a special meeting for the stated purpose of removing that director.

Generally, directors may not remove other directors, although some states allow directors to remove a director who has been convicted of a felony or who has been adjudged to be of unsound mind.

4. Directors' Meetings

Just as there are two types of shareholder meetings (annual and special), there are two types of directors' meetings, regular and special.

1. **Regular Meetings.** Most boards meet at regularly scheduled intervals, such as once per month or once per quarter. The board conducts its business and manages the corporation at these meetings.
2. **Special Meetings.** A special meeting is any meeting held between regular meetings. A special meeting may be called to discuss a merger proposal or some other important matter that cannot wait for the next regular meeting.

5. Meeting Requirements

Location and Notice.   The place of the meeting, whether regular or special, may be specified in the bylaws or may be determined by the directors. Usually, meetings may be held anywhere. Directors are generally not entitled to notice of regular meetings because it is their duty to manage the corporation and they are expected to know when the board regularly meets. As for special meetings, most statutes require only reasonable advance notice. Like shareholders, directors may also give up or waive their right to receive notice of any meeting, either before or after the meeting.

Quorum and Proxies.   Directors may not take action at any meeting unless a quorum is present. Generally, a quorum consists of a majority of the number of directors as fixed in the articles or bylaws. For example, if the corporation has nine authorized directors, at least five must be present at a meeting for business to be conducted. Because directors are charged with the duty of managing the corporation, they may not vote by proxy in most states.

Conduct of Meetings.   Action taken at a directors' meeting is usually by simple majority vote. Because there are seldom more than 15 directors of any corporation, a voice vote or show of hands is usually acceptable. If the vote is not unanimous, each director's respective vote should be recorded in the minutes of the meeting so that if liability arises with regard to action taken at the meeting, it can readily be determined which directors, if any, violated their duties to the corporation. As with shareholder meetings, there are no required procedures, and directors' meetings may be quite informal. There is no mandated format for minutes, but they should reflect the resolution of or action taken on each matter and recite that notice was properly given (if required), that a quorum was present, and any other pertinent matters. A resolution may be phrased as follows: "RESOLVED THAT the proposed lease between the corporation and Smith Wakefield Co. is commercially reasonable and in the best interests of the corporation and the lease is hereby approved."

6.   Directors' Action Without a Meeting

Because it can be difficult for directors to get together for a meeting, all states (and MBCA § 8.21) permit directors to take action without a meeting if they unanimously consent in writing. **Written consents** are now very common methods for accomplishing board action. A document expressing the action to be taken is circulated to all directors for signature (or the directors sign separate documents), and the document is then placed in the corporate minute book. As is the case for shareholders' action by written consent, action by written consent of the directors must usually be unanimous because without a meeting, there is no opportunity for discussion and debate. See Figure 10-3 for form of written consent action by directors.

Written consent
Document reflecting action taken by agreement in writing rather than action taken in person at a meeting; generally, must be unanimous

7.   Compensation and Inspection Rights

In most states and under the MBCA, directors may fix their own compensation. In theory, the safeguard against directors establishing inappropriately high compensation for themselves is the fact that the shareholders have the ability to remove directors. Most large corporations pay directors significant salaries as well as stipends for attending meetings.

To fulfill their duties to the corporation, directors have the right to inspect corporate records and books. If a director uses her right of inspection for an improper purpose, such as obtaining the list of corporate clients to sell to a competitor, she may be liable for breach of her fiduciary duties to the corporation.

8.   Directors' Standards of Conduct, Liability, and Indemnification

Introduction.   The general standard of conduct for directors is set forth in MBCA § 8.30, which provides that a director must discharge his or her duties in good faith and in a manner reasonably believed to be in the best interests of the corporation. Directors must exercise the care that a person in similar circumstances would reasonably believe appropriate.

Conflicts of Interest.   If a director has a conflict of interest (for example, a director's spouse will benefit from a transaction the corporation is contemplating), MBCA § 8.62 allows such a transaction so long as the director discloses the potential conflict and a majority of disinterested directors approve the transaction. Some states are even more permissive. For example, Delaware allows the transaction so long as the director discloses the conflict and the transaction would be fair to the corporation in any event.

Business Judgment Rule.   Courts are somewhat reluctant to impose liability too readily on directors for fear that no one would agree to serve as a director if his decisions were constantly second-guessed. Thus, most jurisdictions have adopted the **business judgment rule**, which immunizes directors from liability for decisions made so long as the directors had a reasonable basis for their decision and

Business judgment rule
Rule immunizing directors and officers for action taken so long as they acted in good faith

FIGURE 10-3
Action by Written Consent of Directors

The undersigned, constituting all of the Directors of V-Tech, Inc. (the "Corporation") hereby take the following actions by written consent pursuant to Section 708 of the Business Corporation Law of New York and Article V of the bylaws of the Corporation as if present at a meeting duly called pursuant to notice.

> RESOLVED, the Directors approve the hiring of Kara Powell as Vice President of Human Resources for the Corporation to perform such duties and at a salary and upon terms and conditions as determined by the President of the Corporation.
> RESOLVED, the Articles of Incorporation for the Corporation shall be amended to change the name of the Corporation to Velocity Inc., which action shall be voted on by the shareholders of the Corporation pursuant to a special meeting to be called therefor by the President of the Corporation.
> RESOLVED, that the Corporation shall instruct its counsel to initiate litigation against the Corporation's landlord for defects at the principal office of the Corporation.

The officers of the Corporation are hereby authorized to take appropriate action to effect the purposes of these resolutions.

Date: _____

_____
William Mulholland

Date: _____

_____
Holly McMullen

Date: _____

_____
Paul X. Ryan

Date: _____

_____
John Lillard

Date: _____

_____
Greg Young

acted in good faith. In fact, a presumption exists that the board acted with sound business judgment, and so long as some rational business purpose can be found for board action or inaction, the directors will be protected from liability.

Reliance on Others.　Because directors cannot be expected to know all matters relating to the corporation, they are entitled to rely on information and opinions of others, including employees, officers, experts, attorneys, and accountants. Generally, this reliance must be reasonable, meaning that directors may not bury their heads in the sand when they have actual knowledge or should make inquiries that would make reliance unreasonable. For example, directors could rely on an appraisal of a parcel of real estate performed by a professional appraiser; however, relying on advice from a neighbor's son taking a real estate class would not be "reasonable."

Extent of Liability and Defenses.   Directors who violate their fiduciary duties may be personally liable for the injury caused to the corporation by their breach. For example, directors may be personally liable for the payment of distributions to shareholders in violation of the articles of incorporation or state statutes. Directors may also be liable for the acts of employees or officers who have been improperly supervised.

It is generally not a defense to liability that a director was a "marquee" director, that is, one elected only to lend prestige to the board of directors. Similarly, it is no defense that a director was inexperienced or could not attend board meetings. Once a person accepts the position of director, she is subject to the duty of due care. Board members have a duty to be informed of corporate activities. Once a director realizes he cannot perform his duties because of age, disability, or inexperience, he should act in the best interests of the corporation by resigning.

Modern Practice: Insurance, Statutory Limitations, and Indemnification.   Fearing litigation, many prospective directors and officers refuse to serve unless the corporation procures **director and officer liability insurance (D & O insurance)** to insure against claims of breach of duty made against directors and officers. In most instances, such insurance also provides for attorneys' fees and costs. The cost of D & O insurance can be extremely high, and generally such insurance does not cover acts that are willful, reckless, or illegal.

> **D & O insurance**
> Insurance procured to protect directors and officers from claims and lawsuits

Due to rising insurance costs and increased litigation against directors and officers, many states have enacted statutes allowing corporations to limit the exposure of directors. These statutes usually allow the articles of incorporation to include a provision eliminating or limiting the personal liability of a director (or officer) to the corporation or to its shareholders so long as an act was in good faith.

Corporations may agree to **indemnify** or reimburse directors or officers from liability incurred by them in defending lawsuits brought against them. Generally, corporations will only indemnify corporate management if the managers acted in good faith. Thus, the corporation has no duty to indemnify a director who acted with gross negligence or illegally.

> **Indemnification**
> Reimbursing another for injury sustained by the other; "holding one harmless" from allegations against the person

9. Delegation of Authority

The board of directors has the authority to delegate some of its functions to officers or to various committees. These committees, such as compensation committees or audit committees, assist the board by carrying out ordinary corporate activities. The directors are required, however, to supervise carefully those to whom duties have been delegated.

10. Corporate Scandals, Reform, the Sarbanes-Oxley Act, Governance Guidelines and Trends, and the 2008 Financial Crisis

Recent Corporate Scandals.   The collapse of Enron Corp. and other spectacular corporate crashes in 2001 and 2002 produced increased debate about the conduct and responsibilities of corporations and their boards of directors. Board members of Enron received $70,000 annually merely for serving on the board. Explanations for causes of the scandals included excessive compensation given to corporate managers (causing them to focus on short-term profits rather than long-term corporate stability), lack of accounting oversight, euphoria among analysts (causing them to "hype" questionable stocks), lack of regulatory oversight, and simple greed. The fallout included an estimated $200 billion in lost savings, lost jobs, and retirement losses for employees. Another consequence is a lack of investor confidence in the American financial markets, fostered by the spectacle of a parade of former high-flying CEOs doing the "perp walk" on their way to their indictments.

Proposals for Reform. The most important reform advanced to prevent another series of corporate scandals and recession was the passage of the corporate and accounting law, the Sarbanes-Oxley Act of 2002 (15 U.S.C. §§ 7201 et seq.), the most significant securities legislation since the 1930s. Among its provisions are the creation of a Public Company Accounting Oversight Board to establish accounting standards and conduct investigations; increased penalties for securities fraud; provisions for strong corporate audit committees, all of whose members must be independent from corporate management; requirements that CEOs and CFOs certify that company financial statements fairly present their companies' financial condition; provisions mandating that companies publish information in their annual reports assessing the effectiveness of their internal financial reporting control structure and procedures; requirements that the SEC review public filings of publicly traded companies at least once every three years; provisions allowing the SEC to bar directors and officers from serving in public companies if they are found to be "unfit" for service in a public company; and forbidding investment bankers from supervising the research of their analysts who recommend stocks to investors.

Governance Guidelines and Trends. As a direct result of investor pressure and a strong signal of increasing shareholder power, many corporations have adopted **governance guidelines** to improve corporate operations. Many of the guidelines call for diversity in boards of directors, require more **independent directors** (meaning those who have no business or familial relationship with the corporation or its managers), require periodic audits and reviews of corporate operations, and impose mandatory stock ownership by directors (to ensure their interests are closely aligned with those of shareholders). The governance guidelines for both General Motors and Microsoft are available on their Web sites, at www.gm.com and www.microsoft.com, respectively.

In the past few years, shareholders have become increasingly activist, resulting in a number of additional reforms and trends in corporate governance practice. Among the trends seen in the past few years are the following:

- As discussed above, one of the proposals activist shareholders have made is to replace plurality voting in elections for directors with majority voting. Because many publicly traded corporations afford their shareholders only two voting options (specifically, either to vote "for" a director or to "withhold" a vote), theoretically, a director could be elected with one vote (assuming one shareholder voted "for" the director and all other shareholders "withheld" their votes). Requiring a majority vote would ensure

Governance guidelines Formal written policies relating to management of corporations

Independent director Director with no business or family relationships with corporation or its managers

that directors who are elected enjoy more widespread shareholder support. In fact, nearly 60 percent of Fortune 500 companies implemented some form of majority voting in director elections prior to the 2008 proxy season. PROXY Governance, Inc., a proxy advisory service, has noted that majority voting is thus on its way to becoming an industry standard.

- Closely related to the trend of electing directors in public corporations by majority rather than plurality vote, 2006 amendments to the MBCA provide that public corporations may adopt alternative voting systems for director elections in their articles of incorporation. (If the articles do not so provide, plurality voting remains the standard or "default" rule.) These new amendments also provide that a nominee who receives more votes against election than in favor of election is still elected. The term of that director, however, is shortened to a period of 90 days after the election results. The remaining board members will fill the office, and the director has no right to hold over. MBCA § 10.22.

- A number of shareholder proposals focus on reining in executive pay and more complete disclosures of executive compensation. Called "say on pay" or "pay for performance" proposals, these resolutions reflect growing anger on the part of shareholders about excessive executive compensation (especially for executives whose companies have underperformed) and their desire to link executive compensation directly to company performance. In 1982, the average CEO of a large U.S. company earned 42 times what his or her average employee did; by 2007, the average CEO made 431 times what the average employee did. Generally, say on pay proposals are aimed at giving shareholders only an advisory vote on executive pay. Nevertheless, they provide a way for shareholders to make their views known. Support for such proposals is steadily growing, with 60 proposals filed by shareholders in 2007 and more than 90 in 2008. In early 2009, the new SEC chairman endorsed giving shareholders a nonbinding vote on executive pay. Related to say on pay proposals are "clawbacks," which allow companies to seek recovery of compensation paid to executives when their companies have to restate their financials. New disclosure rules by the SEC require executives to explain their compensation in more detail. Marking the biggest changes in disclosure on executive compensation in 25 years, publicly traded companies must now provide more information in their proxy statements about the value of options and stock granted to their top five executives as well as a total compensation figure that includes all forms of cash and noncash pay (which would allow shareholders to compare pay from one company to another).

- Another clear trend in corporate governance is a move away from using a staggered or classified board of directors toward electing all directors at the same time. Shareholders have successfully argued that electing directors annually rather than every two or three years makes board members more responsive to them and more accountable for financial missteps.

- Many shareholder proposals focus on "social issues." As examples, one shareholder proposal asked Exxon to publish data on climate change, and shareholders proposed 57 resolutions relating to global warming during the 2008 proxy season, nearly half of which were withdrawn after companies made commitments on setting targets for reducing greenhouse gas emissions and reaching other environmentally related goals.

- The SEC continues to consider the means by which shareholders can gain access to the company's proxy statement for the purpose of proposing their own slate of directors. Although SEC Rule 14a-8 allows shareholders to submit proposals (if they own at least 1 percent of the company's voting stock), companies often refuse these proposals because they do not comply with certain technical requirements. This is a decades-long debate, and 22 SEC chairmen have worked on this problem. As of the writing of this text, the SEC has again delayed taking action on this issue.

- Shareholder activism has accelerated with the use of the Internet, which allows shareholders to communicate with each other. Activists have created blogs, used MySpace, and even launched campaigns on YouTube to promote their agendas.

The 2008 Financial Crisis.　Public confidence in the financial markets was further shaken in 2008 with the collapse of well-known American institutions including the Bear Stearns Companies, insurance giant American International Group, Inc. (AIG), Lehman Brothers, and Washington Mutual Bank; the placing of Fannie Mae and Freddie Mac under federal conservatorship; and the resulting government bailout or rescue of these troubled financial institutions in the amount of $700 billion, which was approved in October 2008. Experts have cited numerous causes for these failures, including lack of government oversight, reckless speculation, greed, and the housing and credit crises. In particular, experts have focused on the fact that during the housing boom of the early 2000s, lenders relaxed standards for homebuyers and made subprime loans to these buyers. These risky loans were then packaged into pools and purchased by Wall Street. When the housing market slowed and their interest rates moved upward, homeowners were unable to make their mortgage payments and defaulted on their loans. Lenders and banks then became the "owners" of real estate worth less than what was owed on it. As losses mounted, loans became more difficult to obtain, causing a credit crunch. Without loans, spending slows, causing a further slowdown in the economy.

At the time of the writing of this text, the FBI had begun investigating whether fraud played a role in the problems at Fannie Mae, Freddie Mac, Lehman Brothers, and AIG. The SEC has also opened numerous investigations.

Some of the provisions in the American Recovery and Reinvestment Act of 2009 (the Obama administration's "stimulus bill") include the following measures, aimed at promoting the long-term health of American companies:

- Pay caps on senior officers of companies that receive massive government assistance.
- Compensation provisions that restrict additional compensation to executives to the form of stock that can only be redeemed by the executives after federal bailout money is repaid.
- Provisions allowing shareholders whose companies have received federal bailout funds to provide advisory votes on executive compensation.

- Provisions allowing the government to review bonuses and compensation paid to senior executives at companies who received federal bailout money to determine whether such payments should be recaptured or clawed back.

C. Officers' Rights and Responsibilities

1. Introduction

The traditional **officers** of a corporation are president, vice president, secretary, and treasurer. A corporation may have fewer or more officers, if desired. The officers carry out day-to-day corporate activities and are selected, supervised, and removed by the board of directors. Officers are usually subject to the same standards of care as directors and, like directors, are fiduciaries of the corporation.

Officers
Individuals appointed by directors to carry out various corporate activities

2. Appointment, Tenure, and Functions of Officers

Officers are usually selected or appointed by the board of directors. In fact, it is often said that officers serve "at the pleasure of the board," meaning that the directors have the authority to remove officers at any time, either with or without cause. If an officer serves pursuant to an employment agreement, however, the terms of that agreement must be followed. If the board terminates an officer in breach of the agreement, the corporation may be liable for breach of contract.

Officers perform a broad range of functions, that is, whatever functions are delegated to them by the directors. In large corporations, directors often establish a policy or goal and then charge the officers with achieving that objective.

3. Titles of Officers

The MBCA does not require any specific officers. The corporation's bylaws usually describe the officer positions. A corporation is not limited to the most common officers (president, vice president, secretary, and treasurer); the corporation is free to create other officer positions with other titles. For example, a large corporation may have a treasurer, a chief financial officer, and a comptroller, each of whom has specific duties relating to the financial affairs of the corporation. In most states, one person may simultaneously hold more than one corporation office; however, some states prohibit the same person from acting as both president and secretary, primarily because those are the two officers whose signatures are required on stock certificates and other corporate documents.

- **President.** The president of a corporation usually presides at directors' and shareholders' meetings. Often, the president acts as general manager of the corporation.
- **Vice President.** The vice president acts in the place of the president in his absence and assists the president. Some large corporations will have

numerous vice presidents, such as senior vice president, and executive vice president, vice president of human resources, and so forth.

- **Secretary.** The corporation's secretary has the responsibility for taking minutes of shareholders' and directors' meetings and maintaining the minute book. The secretary also verifies the authenticity of documents and prepares notices of meetings.
- **Treasurer.** The treasurer is the financial officer of the corporation and has the responsibility for receiving, maintaining, and disbursing corporate funds and paying taxes.
- **Other Officers.** Many corporations appoint a **chief executive officer** (the CEO), who will supervise all of the other officers, preside over all meetings, and have primary responsibility for managing the corporation. Some corporations appoint a **chief financial officer** in addition to the corporate treasurer. A **chair** of the board, if appointed, is a board member who presides at directors' meetings and performs such duties as are assigned by the board.

Chief executive officer
Individual who supervises other officers

Chief financial officer
Individual with primary responsibility for all financial matters

Chair
Individual who presides at corporate meetings

4. Authority of Officers

Because the authority given officers comes from the board of directors, officers are agents of the corporation. Thus, the general agency principles discussed in Chapter One apply to them. This authority may be **actual authority** (meaning express authority or direction given to them by the board), **apparent authority** (authority that another believes the officer possesses due to the officer's conduct or position), or **inherent authority** (authority that flows naturally from an officer's position so she can carry out her duties).

Actual authority
Express authority or direction given by one to another

Apparent authority
Authority that one believes another to possess due to the other's conduct or position

Inherent authority
Authority that naturally flows from one's position

5. Officers' Standards of Conduct, Liability, and Indemnification

Officers are subject to the same duties of care and fiduciary duties imposed on directors. Like directors, officers are protected by the business judgment rule and, therefore, liability is usually founded on acts or omissions of clear and gross abuse or negligence. Courts will not second-guess an officer's decision so long as there was some reasonable basis for the decision. Like directors, officers are entitled to rely on advice and reports given by others, so long as that reliance is reasonable.

The various provisions relating to indemnification of directors for liability and litigation costs and expenses apply equally to officers. Similarly, the corporation may purchase and maintain D & O insurance for officers to insure against liability asserted against or incurred by the officer.

D. Role of Paralegal

Paralegals are extensively involved in all phases of maintaining the corporation, especially in maintaining corporate records, which demonstrate that the corporation is in compliance with state statutes and its articles and bylaws and help protect against a piercing-the-veil claim. Paralegals are routinely involved in the following activities:

- Maintaining a tickler system for annual meetings for all corporate clients and sending reminders to clients of annual meeting requirements;
- Preparing and sending out notices (or waivers of notice) for meetings of shareholders and directors (see Figure 10-1);
- Assisting in preparing annual reports;
- Preparing agendas for meetings of shareholders and directors;
- Preparing minutes for meetings of shareholders and directors (see Figure 10-2);
- Preparing written consent actions for shareholders and directors (see Figure 10-3); and
- Maintaining the corporate minute book.

Case Illustration
Extent of Protection of Business Judgment Rule

Case:	*Hall v. Staha*, 800 S.W.2d 396 (Ark. 1990)
Facts:	Shareholders brought a derivative suit alleging, among other things, breaches of fiduciary duty by directors. A third party had offered to purchase the corporation's stock. The directors did not disclose this offer to the shareholders, in part because these directors would not have been employed at their same salaries if the offer were accepted.
Holding:	Although the business judgment rule protects directors from liability for their decisions, it does not protect the actions of directors who have a conflict of interest. In this case, the directors could not claim the protection of the business judgment rule because of their conflicting interest. Moreover, there was little evidence that the directors investigated the effect of the offer on the corporation or the shareholders (who were never informed of the offer). In such a case, the business judgment rule will not protect the directors.

Key Features
of Corporate Management

◆ Corporations involve three groups of people: shareholders (the owners of the corporation), directors (the managers of the corporation), and officers (appointees of the directors).

- ◆ Although shareholders own the corporation, they do not manage it; their participation takes the form primarily of voting to elect and remove directors and for extraordinary corporate action.
- ◆ There are two types of shareholders' meetings: annual meetings (at which directors are elected) and special meetings (those held between annual meetings).
- ◆ Shareholders may vote by proxy (written instructions to another).
- ◆ Shareholders may initiate direct action against the corporation for direct injury to a shareholder or derivative action for injury sustained by the corporation that it refuses to address.
- ◆ Although shareholders ordinarily have no liability for corporate obligations, they may be liable if they disregard the corporate entity by commingling funds, failing to observe corporate formalities, or undercapitalizing the corporation.
- ◆ Directors manage the corporation and are elected by shareholders; they meet in regular and special meetings.
- ◆ Directors and shareholders may act without a meeting if they unanimously consent in writing to take action.
- ◆ Directors and officers have fiduciary duties to the corporation but will usually be protected from liability under the business judgment rule so long as there is some reasonable business purpose for their actions and they did not act illegally or with gross negligence.

Internet Resources

Sarbanes-Oxley Act:	www.sarbanes-oxley.com
State statutes:	www.law.cornell.edu www.findlaw.com
MBCA:	www.abanet.org/buslaw/committees/CL270000pub/nosearch/mbca/home.shtml
General information:	www.megalaw.com www.findlaw.com
Forms:	www.allaboutforms.com www.siccode.com/forms.php (These sites offer forms for notices of meetings, minutes of meetings, corporate resolutions, and other related forms.)
Corporate governance:	www.governanceprofessionals.org (site of Society of Corporate Secretaries & Governance Professionals, offering publications and information on corporate management issues)

www.corpgov.net/links/links.html (site offers
links to numerous resources relating to corporate governance)
www.thecorporatecounsel.net (site offering articles and publications about governance issues)

Key Terms

Shareholder
Straight voting
Cumulative voting
Annual meeting
Special meeting
Record date
Quorum
Proxy
Plurality
Voting agreement
Legend
Minutes
Written consent action
Buy-sell agreement
Householding
Direct action
Derivative action

Piercing the veil
Alter ego
Commingling of assets
Directors
Staggered system
Business judgment rule
D & O insurance
Indemnification
Independent director
Governance guidelines
Officers
Chief executive officer
Chair
Chief financial officer
Actual authority
Apparent authority
Inherent authority

Discussion Questions

Fact Scenario.   Café Coffee, Inc. operates numerous upscale coffee shops in the
Northeast region of the United States. It has 500,000 shares outstanding and
seven directors. Its bylaws state that the annual shareholders' meeting will be
held April 5 and that the record date for the meeting is 30 days before the meeting.
Use the MBCA to answer the following questions.

1. The directors would like to expand into the Southeast region of the United
States. Discuss the quorum and voting requirements for action on this issue by the
directors (both at a meeting and by written consent).

2. The shareholders would like to remove one of the directors although there
is no evidence that the director has been anything other than scrupulously honest.
How would the shareholders go about accomplishing this removal?

3. The corporation is considering purchasing all of its coffee beans from
Beanery Inc. Director Jones owns a significant number of shares in Beanery Inc.
May Jones vote on this transaction? Discuss.

4. After considerable discussion, market surveys, and reports by several corporate committees, the directors decided to expand into the Southeast portion of the United States. Unfortunately, due to a slumping economy, the expansion has been a failure. Are the directors and officers liable for this decision? Discuss.

5. Assume that the articles of incorporation allow for cumulative voting. Susan owns 100 shares of stock.

   a. How many shares constitute a quorum?
   b. What is the record date for the annual shareholders' meeting?
   c. How many votes will Susan have if there is straight voting in an election for directors?
   d. How many votes will Susan have if there is cumulative voting in an election for directors?
   e. How many votes will Susan have if a meeting is held to discuss a merger with another corporation?

6. Assume that Susan did not receive notice of the annual shareholders' meeting. What might Susan do? Is there anything the corporation can do to "save" the meeting?

7. Director Peterson has been ill and has thus resigned from the board. How will this vacancy be filled?

8. If a corporation has only four shareholders, what is the danger to its shareholders if they fail to keep accurate records?

Net Worth

1. Access the Web site of the SEC. Review the Definitive 14A proxy statement for Target Corporation for May 2008. What methods of voting were authorized for shareholders?
2. Access the Web site of the SEC. Review the Definitive 14A proxy statement for Berkshire Hathaway for 2008. What compensation do directors receive for attending each meeting in person or by conference call?
3. Access the Web site of the SEC. Review the first page cover sheet of the annual 10-K report for General Electric Company filed in February 2008 for the fiscal year ended December 31, 2007. How many outstanding shares of voting common stock were there at the time of the filing of the 10-K report?
4. Locate California's Corporations Code. How many shares must a shareholder own to be entitled to inspect corporate records and copy the list of shareholder names?
5. Who is the current chair of the Public Company Accounting Oversight Board?
6. Access the Web site of General Motors. Review its governance guidelines. What level of stock ownership is required for its directors?

11

♦ ♦ ♦

Corporate Dividends

♦ ♦ ♦

A. Introduction

Shareholders not only hope that their shares will increase in value over time, they also hope that the corporation will pay distributions to them during the time they own the stock. Strictly speaking, a **distribution** is a direct or indirect transfer of money or other property (except a corporation's own shares) to shareholders. More modern terminology uses the term **dividend** to refer to a distribution of a corporation's profits to its shareholders and the term *distribution* to refer to some other payment to shareholders, such as a payment when the corporation liquidates. Distributions made at the time of liquidation are often called **liquidation distributions** or *dissolution distributions*. These distributions are discussed in Chapter Fourteen.

There are three types of dividends:

1. **Cash Dividends.** Cash dividends are the most common type of dividend. They are usually sent to shareholders in the form of a check. Some companies allow shareholders to use their cash dividends to immediately purchase additional shares of stock. Under these plans, known as **dividend reinvestment plans** (commonly called DRIPs), these dividends are immediately reinvested at no fee to the shareholder.
2. **Property Dividends.** Property dividends are the least common and may consist of a product the company makes, such as candy or cereal, or discount coupons to be used at the corporation's stores or restaurants. A modern approach is for a corporation to issue shares of its subsidiary as a property dividend.

Distribution
Used strictly to refer to payments to shareholders that are not a sharing of profits; used loosely to refer to any type of payment to shareholders

Dividend
Used strictly to refer to a distribution of a corporation's profits to its shareholders; used loosely to refer to any type of payment made to shareholders

Liquidation distribution
Distribution made to shareholders when a corporation liquidates (also called *dissolution distribution*)

Cash dividend
Cash distribution made by a corporation

Dividend reinvestment plan
Plan allowing shareholders to immediately use their cash dividends to purchase more shares

Property dividend
Distribution of some form of property by a corporation

3. **Share Dividends.** Share dividends are distributions of the corporation's own shares to its shareholders. After a share dividend, although the actual number of shares owned by a shareholder will increase, the shareholder's proportionate ownership is not affected because all other shareholders in the class will be treated similarly.

There are two basic principles that are applicable to dividends:

1. Dividends are allocated to shareholders in direct proportion to their respective ownership interest in the corporation. Thus, if Jan owns 8 percent of the common stock of a corporation, she will receive 8 percent of the dividends paid to common stockholders. Similarly, if the corporation declares a share dividend in the amount of 1 share for every 10 shares outstanding (assume there are 200 shares outstanding) and Tim owns 20 shares, he will receive 2 shares. You can readily see that although the raw number of shares owned by Tim has increased, his proportionate power and control have not changed. Before the share dividend, Tim owned 10 percent of the ownership of the corporation (because he owned 20 out of 200 shares outstanding) and after the dividend he still owned 10 percent of the corporation (because he owned 22 out of 220 shares).
2. Shareholders within a class must be treated uniformly. Thus, all Common A shareholders must be treated the same. A corporation cannot distribute cash dividends to some Common A shareholders and property dividends to the remainder; however, different classes may be treated differently so that Common A shareholders may receive a cash dividend of $1.00 for each share owned and Common B shareholders receive a cash dividend of $2.50 for each share owned. The articles of incorporation must describe the preferences, limitations, and relative rights of classes of stock if more than one class of shares is authorized (MBCA § 6.01).

B. Restrictions Relating to Dividends

Most state statutes specify the manner by which a corporation may distribute dividends as well as the sources from which they may be paid. Because the result of a cash or property dividend is that assets of the corporation are transferred to the shareholders, certain restrictions exist to protect creditors of the corporation and to ensure that a financially unhealthy corporation will not take its few profits and distribute them to its owners.

1. MBCA Approach

MBCA § 6.40 provides two alternative tests to determine whether a corporation can legally pay a dividend:

1. The **equity insolvency test** states that a corporation may pay a dividend only if the corporation is **solvent**, meaning that it must be able to pay its debts as they come due in the ordinary course of business; or

2. The **excess assets test** (sometimes called the *balance sheet test*) provides that a dividend may be paid if after giving it effect, the corporation's assets will exceed its liabilities and any amount that would be required to be paid to satisfy the rights of preferred shareholders in the event the corporation were to liquidate.

Excess assets test
Test to determine if dividends can be paid in which equity or assets exceed liabilities (also called *balance sheet test*)

If the corporation is able to satisfy either of these tests, it may pay the dividend. The primary purpose of these restrictions is to protect the rights of third-party creditors, although the excess assets test also provides some protection to preferred shareholders because it forbids the corporation from paying a dividend if it would not have enough money to satisfy the rights of preferred shareholders in the event of a liquidation.

2. *Legally Available Funds*

A number of state statutes mandate that dividends may be paid only from certain corporate accounts. Generally, these statutes provide that dividends may be paid only from the **retained earnings** account (the net profits accumulated by the corporation) or its **surplus account** (the value of the corporation's net assets that is greater than its stated capital).

Retained earnings
Net profits accumulated by a corporation

Surplus account
Value of corporation's net assets that is greater than its stated capital

3. *Miscellaneous Restrictions*

It is possible that the corporation has agreed with its lenders or bondholders that it will not pay certain dividends. This promise may have been made so that the corporation could borrow needed funds. If such a contractual restriction exists, it must be honored. Additionally, as discussed in Chapter Nine, some classes of stock might have certain preferences over others with regard to dividends. Nevertheless, even preferred stockholders may not receive a dividend if the corporation is insolvent and, in addition, all dividends must be paid out of legally available funds. If the corporation decides to distribute $500,000 in dividends, the preferred shareholders are entitled to receive their dividends first (and these preferred shares are often entitled to some minimum or fixed dividend amount). If the dividends are cumulative, the corporation must pay the current dividends as well as any arrearages owed for previous years before any distributions may be made to other shareholders. To ensure one class of stock does not subsume another, shares of one class may not be used as dividends for another class (unless the articles of incorporation permit or the shareholders of the class from which the distribution is to be made approve the transaction).

C. Procedure for Declaring and Paying Dividends

Procedure. The decision to declare a dividend is made by the board of directors, either by majority vote at a meeting or by unanimous written consent action taken without a meeting. The document reflecting the decision is placed in the corporate minute book. In making their decision, the directors are entitled to rely on the corporation's books of accounts and financial statements, reports of officers, accountants, counsel, or other experts, so long as reliance is reasonable.

The directors will usually establish a record date for determining the shareholders who are eligible to receive dividends. Generally, the rules relating to record dates for a dividend distribution are the same as those for establishing a record date for meetings. Those shareholders who own stock on the record date fixed by the directors receive the dividends. If no record date is established, those individuals who were shareholders on the date the directors declared the dividend are entitled to receive the dividend. Thus, for all dividends, the dividend is paid to the individual who was the shareholder of record on the record date, even if the shareholder sells her stock before the time the actual payment or distribution is made. A shareholder or share without the right to receive a declared dividend is called **ex-dividend**. The ex-dividend date is two business days before the record date. Once the dividend is declared, newspaper financial sections will note the stock is ex-dividend, which often causes the stock price to drop a bit.

Amending the Articles. To distribute share dividends, the corporation must have sufficient authorized but unissued shares to distribute. For example, assume the articles of incorporation for ABC Inc. authorize 300,000 shares to be issued and there are 260,000 shares outstanding. If the corporation desires to distribute one share for every five shares outstanding, it will need 52,000 shares available to it (260,000 divided by five). In this case, the articles of incorporation must be amended to increase the number of shares the corporation is authorized to issue to accommodate this dividend. The MBCA allows directors to adopt this amendment without shareholder approval if the corporation has only one class of shares outstanding. Alternatively, the corporation could use its treasury stock (see Section F) as the source for share dividends.

Right to Dividends. Generally, shareholders receive dividends when and if declared by the board of directors acting in its discretion. Thus, the determination to distribute dividends is a discretionary decision subject to the business judgment of the directors. The corporation may have sufficient profits to permit a distribution but may be saving its money to expand operations or to acquire another corporation. Generally, courts are reluctant to interfere with the management of corporations, and thus, unless the shareholders can clearly prove bad faith or an abuse of discretion by the directors, the directors cannot be compelled to pay dividends.

Although directors are under no obligation to declare dividends, once they have legally declared a cash or property dividend, the decision is irrevocable, and the dividend becomes a debt owing from the corporation to the shareholder. The declaration of a stock dividend is revocable until the stock is actually issued.

After an upswing in dividend payments in the early 2000s, the financial and housing crisis of 2008 caused dividends to be eliminated or suspended. For example, Citigroup (which recorded billions in dollars of losses on mortgage securities) reduced its dividend in 2008 by 41 percent. Other institutions either likewise reduced their dividends or cut them entirely. Similarly, Dana Holding Corporation, which had paid more than 250 consecutive cash dividends since 1936 has not paid a dividend since 2006. In 2009, Standard & Poor's projected that dividends for the S & P 500 companies would fall nearly 14 percent in 2009, the worst decline since 1942. More than half of the companies making dividend cuts in early 2009 were in the financial sector. These decreases engender much public comment in that experts believe that dividends are usually the last thing corporations want to cut because reductions are tantamount to announcing that the company has a cash flow problem.

Effect of Illegal Dividends. If directors pay dividends from unauthorized accounts or while the corporation is insolvent, the distribution is referred to as an unlawful or **illegal dividend**. Shareholders who receive dividends while the corporation is insolvent must usually return them. Shareholders who receive dividends from unauthorized accounts generally must return them only if they knew the dividends were illegal when they received them. Directors who vote for a dividend contrary to any restrictions are personally liable, jointly and severally, for the amount of the illegal dividend that exceeded the amount that could have been lawfully distributed.

Illegal dividends
Distributions paid when corporation is insolvent or from unauthorized accounts

PRACTICE TIP

It is always important that the minutes you take or review be accurate; however, accuracy is even more critical when meetings discuss and authorize dividends because directors who vote for or assent to unlawful dividends are personally liable for such acts. Thus, it is critical that any votes at any directors' meetings that are not unanimous be accurately reflected in the minutes. For example, if director Ruiz votes against a dividend, the minutes should reflect that fact and identify her by name. The written minutes (and any financial reports or expert opinions she reasonably relied on) will then provide a defense for her if it is later alleged she assented to an illegal dividend.

D. Tax Considerations

Because a corporation is a person, it pays taxes on its net profits at the applicable corporate rates. The tax disadvantage referred to as double taxation means that when corporate profits are distributed to shareholders as cash or property dividends, the shareholders receiving those dividends pay taxes on the same money or property for which taxes have already been paid by the corporation. Payments made by a corporation as dividends are not deductible by the corporation.

- **Cash Dividends.** Shareholders must declare and pay taxes on cash dividends received for any dividend in excess of 50 cents. Corporations that distribute more than $10 to any shareholder in any year must report the dividend to the Internal Revenue Service so that the IRS can verify the shareholder declared and paid the appropriate taxes. In mid-2003, Congress reduced individual taxes on cash dividends to 15 percent (5 percent for the lowest two brackets) and agreed to eliminate taxes entirely in 2008 for the lowest two brackets. These dividend reductions are scheduled to expire in 2010. In fact, these favorable tax rates are likely the reason that dividend payments became fashionable in the early 2000s after a period in the 1990s when they were viewed as stodgy and dull. In mid-2004, Microsoft distributed about $32 billion to its shareholders (about $3 per share), the largest one-time dividend payout in Wall Street history. Cash dividends that are immediately reinvested into more shares through DRIPs are also taxable when received.

- **Property Dividends.** Corporate products, such as cosmetics or discount coupons, can be distributed and are called property dividends. Shareholders receiving such property must declare and pay taxes on the fair market value of the property received. This is another disadvantage of property dividends: A shareholder may receive property she has no use for and yet be required to pay taxes on the unwelcome dividend.
- **Share Dividends.** The tax ramifications of share dividends are quite different from those of cash or property dividends. Tax is paid not when the stock dividend is received but when it is later sold. Taxes are not paid when a share dividend is issued because such a dividend is not viewed as a true distribution of value because the shareholder has the same proportion of ownership after the distribution as before, and the corporation has the same assets after the distribution as before.

To encourage the payment of dividends, and as discussed in Chapter Nine, a federal accumulated earnings tax of 15 percent is imposed on a C corporation's accumulated taxable income in excess of that reasonably needed for its business (which is currently presumed to be no more than $250,000, per 26 U.S.C. §§ 531-535). Thus, although a corporation is not required to declare dividends, if the corporation accumulates earnings in excess of that reasonably needed for business purposes, it may be penalized for such accumulated earnings.

A small corporation whose shareholders are actively involved in the business can reduce the burden of double taxation by distributing corporate profits to the shareholder-employees as bonuses or salaries rather than as dividends. In such cases, the bonus or salary is still taxable to the recipient but the corporation's payment of such is a deductible business expense, thus reducing taxation of the money at the corporate level. This strategy is appropriate only for small corporations; a large corporation with thousands of shareholders cannot justify a "salary" for these individuals and the payment of dividends with its attendant double taxation is simply a feature of the corporate landscape.

E. Stock Splits

Stock split
Division of outstanding shares

A **stock split** occurs when an outstanding share is divided into a larger number of shares. The result is to decrease the price per share. The most common stock split is a two-for-one split, in which case a shareholder owning 100 shares would own 200 shares after declaration of the split. Three-for-one, four-for-one, and other splits are also possible.

A corporation often splits its stock to increase the attractiveness of its shares. For example, if ABC Inc.'s stock traditionally trades at $50 per share but suddenly reaches $80 per share, some investors may be reluctant to buy stock at this price, fearing that it will later level off to its traditional price of $50 per share. Thus, to stimulate trading, a corporation may declare a two-for-one stock split (by a directors' resolution at a meeting or unanimous written consent) whereby the stock is now $40 per share. Assuming the corporation is stable, investors may now view the stock as a bargain and may invest heavily. In many cases, after active trading, the stock may achieve its presplit price of $80 and shareholders will have doubled their money. For example, if James owned 20 shares worth $80 each (for a total of $1,600) before the split, a two-for-one split would result in James owning 40 shares worth $40 each (for a total of $1,600) after the split. If the shares return to their presplit price of $80 per share, James will now own 40 shares worth $80 each (for a total of $3,200) and will have doubled his money.

Walmart's stock splits reveal the potential value in stock splits. Walmart has split its stock on a two-for-one basis 11 times since 1970. If you purchased 100 shares of Walmart stock when it went public in 1970 at a total price of $1,650, on October 1, 2008, you would have owned 204,800 shares for a total value of $12,288,000.

The opposite of a stock split is a **reverse stock split**, in which the corporation reduces rather than increases the number of outstanding shares. For example, a ten-for-one reverse split has the effect of requiring that each group of ten shares be exchanged or surrendered to the corporation for the issuance of one new share. Reverse stock splits are often used by a corporation to eliminate smaller shareholders. Many corporations do this to avoid paperwork, time, and effort to communicate with shareholders who hold only a few shares of stock. Additionally, smaller corporations with fewer shareholders may be exempt from various SEC filing requirements.

Reverse stock split
Reduction of outstanding shares

F. Purchase by a Corporation of Its Own Shares

A corporation may acquire outstanding shares from its own shareholders if the corporation has sufficient funds to do so. The corporation may wish to reacquire its shares for a variety of reasons, including a desire to decrease the supply of stock and thereby increase its price, or to prevent shareholders from selling the stock to others, or to increase earnings per share by reducing the total number of outstanding shares.

A repurchase of stock is sometimes referred to as an **exchange** (or *share exchange*) because the corporation is exchanging its cash for shares. A repurchase or buyback is generally treated as a distribution to shareholders. For example, assume there are ten shareholders of the corporation, each owning 100 shares of stock. If the corporation redeems 10 shares from each of them and pays $20 per share, when the buyback is complete, the shareholders will each own 90 shares of stock and the corporation will have transferred or distributed the sum of $200 to each shareholder. Thus, it can readily be seen that a distribution has occurred. Because a repurchase of stock by the corporation is a distribution, the same restrictions that apply to the distribution of dividends apply equally to the repurchase by a corporation of its own shares, namely, limitations as to solvency or requiring assets to exceed liabilities after the purchase.

Exchange
Exchange of cash for shares (also called *share exchange*)

When the corporation reacquires the previously outstanding shares, it may cancel them and thereby return them to the status of authorized but unissued shares or it may hold them as **treasury stock**, namely, shares reacquired by the corporation considered issued but not outstanding.

Treasury stock
Stock reacquired by a corporation that is considered issued but not outstanding

G.   Role of Paralegal

The decision to distribute dividends originates with the board of directors, usually after consultation with financial advisors. Thus, the attorney and paralegal do not generally play a role until after the decision has been made. There are, however, several activities the paralegal will be involved in, including the following:

- Assisting in preparing minutes of the meeting authorizing the distribution or preparing a unanimous written consent agreement reflecting the decision;
- Amending the articles to authorize a sufficient number of shares to accommodate a share distribution or stock split (and preparing notices and minutes of meetings related thereto);
- Reviewing articles of incorporation and state statutes to ensure any preferences are honored; and
- Preparing and filing a statement of cancellation if the corporation repurchases its own shares and then cancels them.

Case Illustration
Directors' Discretion in Declaring Dividends and Authorizing Stock Repurchase

Case: *Kohn v. Birmingham Realty Co.*, 352 So. 2d 834 (Ala. 1977)

Facts: Plaintiff, a minority shareholder, brought an action to compel a corporation to declare a dividend and to enjoin the corporation from buying back some of its common shares. The trial court dismissed the action. The plaintiff appealed.

Holding: The Alabama Supreme Court affirmed. An Alabama corporation can purchase its own shares if the purchase is made from earned surplus and such a transaction will not render the corporation insolvent. These conditions were satisfied here. Moreover, directors have the authority to declare dividends out of earnings, and courts will not interfere with this management function unless there is fraud, abuse of discretion, or misappropriation of corporate funds. In this case, most of the earned income from which a dividend could have been paid was used to repurchase stock. Because there was no fraud or illegality in the stock repurchase, there was no duty to declare a dividend.

Key Features
of Corporate Dividends

- A dividend is a distribution of a corporation's profits to its shareholders.
- Dividends may be in the form of cash, property, or other shares of the corporation.
- Generally, a corporation must be solvent to distribute a dividend, meaning it is able to pay its debts as they come due.
- Most state statutes regulate the funds from which dividends may be paid.
- Dividends must be uniform within a class but may vary from class to class.
- The decision to declare a dividend is made by the board of directors, who will set a record date for determining shareholders entitled to receive the dividend.
- Shareholders who receive cash must pay taxes on the amount received, shareholders who receive property dividends must pay taxes on the fair market value of the property received, and shareholders who receive share dividends pay taxes at the time the share is eventually sold.

Internet Resources

State statutes:	www.law.cornell.edu www.findlaw.com
Text of MBCA:	www.abanet.org/buslaw/committees/ CL270000pub/nosearch/mbca/home.shtml
General information:	www.megalaw.com www.findlaw.com
Forms:	www.allaboutforms.com www.lectlaw.com (for forms for directors' resolutions and minutes of meetings of directors)

Key Terms

Distribution
Dividend
Cash dividend
Dividend reinvestment plan
Property dividend
Share dividend
Liquidation distribution
Solvency
Equity insolvency test

Excess assets test
Retained earnings
Surplus account
Ex-dividend
Illegal dividends
Stock split
Reverse stock split
Exchange
Treasury stock

Discussion Questions

Fact Scenario.   Kitchen & Bath Renovations Inc. has seven members on its board of directors and 200,000 outstanding shares, 150,000 of which are held by Common A shareholders, and 50,000 of which are held by Common B shareholders. The articles of incorporation authorize 250,000 shares of Common A stock and 80,000 shares of Common B stock. Use the MBCA to answer these questions.

1. The corporation would like to issue a stock dividend to its Common B shareholders. May it use Common A stock to do this?

2. The corporation has decided to issue cash dividends to half of its Common A shareholders and stock dividends to the other half of its Common A shareholders. May it do this?

3. At a board of directors' meeting, the directors authorized a cash dividend of $1 per share for every share of Common A stock outstanding and set the record date as May 1 and the payment date as June 1. Jacob sold all of his 500 shares of Common A stock to Ed on May 15. Who will receive the dividend? Discuss. What is the amount of the dividend?

4. Assume the corporation is having difficulty paying its bills and making payroll. Assume that at a directors' meeting voting on this issue, the directors authorized the cash dividend. Director Blair vigorously opposed this dividend. Describe any liability the directors may have for declaring the cash dividend.

5. Assume that the corporation has declared a stock dividend for its Common B shareholders, declaring that for every 100 shares of Common B stock outstanding, the holder will receive an additional share of Common B stock. Ava owns 100 shares of Common B stock. Bob owns 150 shares of Common B stock. Caroline owns 1,000 shares of Common B stock. What dividend will each of these shareholders receive?

6. Assume that the corporation has a significant amount of cash on hand and has not paid a dividend for five years. Is there anything that a shareholder can do to remedy this situation? What danger does the corporation run in not paying a dividend?

7. The corporation would like to declare a two-for-one stock split for both the Common A stock and for the Common B stock. Describe any procedures the corporation should follow to accomplish this goal.

Net Worth

1. Access the SEC's Web site. Locate the section for investors called "Fast Answers" and review the information about stock splits. According to the SEC, when do companies often do a stock split?

2. Access the SEC's Web site and locate the 10K form filed by Dana Holding Corporation for the fiscal year ended December 31, 2007. Review page 4. What dividends are payable on the company's preferred stock? What will happen if the company fails to pay the equivalent of six quarterly dividends on the preferred stock?

3. Access the SEC's Web site and locate Middleton Doll Company's definitive proxy statement DEF 14A filed on September 29, 2008, or its form 8K filed on September 29, 2008. Review Section 8.01. What was the purpose of the company's reverse stock split?

4. Access the SEC's Web site and locate McDonald's form 8K (use the McDonald's ticker symbol of MCD) filed on September 25, 2008, and its accompanying press release. What quarterly dividend was announced? How many times has McDonald's raised its dividends?

5. Access the Web site of Hormel Foods. Access its Newsroom and review its press release dated September 23, 2008. What dividend was announced? How many quarterly dividends had Hormel Foods paid as of that date?

6. Access the Web site for Standard & Poor's.
   a. Review the information factsheet relating to its index called "S & P Dividend Aristocrats." What is the eligibility requirement for a company to be labeled as a Dividend Aristocrat?
   b. Review the "Constituent List" of the Dividend Aristocrats. What is the first company identified?

12

◆ ◆ ◆

Changes in the Corporate Structure and Corporate Combinations

◆ ◆ ◆

A. Introduction

Shareholder participation in corporate life primarily takes the form of voting on election and removal of directors, but there are some matters that result in such significant changes to the corporation that shareholder approval is required. These matters are often referred to as extraordinary matters and consist of amending the articles of incorporation, mergers, consolidations, share exchanges, sales of corporate assets, corporate domestications and entity conversions, and dissolution of the corporation.

B. Amending the Articles of Incorporation

1. Reasons for Amending Articles

According to most state statutes and MBCA § 10.01, a corporation may amend its articles at any time to add or change a provision that was required or permitted in the original articles (or to delete any provision not required). Thus, amendments may be made to add preemptive rights for shareholders, to create new classes of stock, to change par value, and so forth. The most common reasons for amending the articles are to change the corporation's name and to increase the number of shares the corporation is authorized to issue. In sum, if a provision could have been stated in the original articles, it can be included in the amended articles.

2. Procedure for Amending Articles

The most common procedure for amending the articles is discussion of the proposed amendment by the board of directors and then adoption by the board of a resolution setting forth the text of the proposed amendment and directing that it be submitted for shareholder approval. The board must also make a recommendation that the amendment be approved. The board may act at a meeting by majority vote, or the board may act by written consent, which must be unanimous.

Some states and the MBCA allow the directors to make certain amendments to the articles without shareholder approval. Generally, these amendments pertain to routine matters that do not affect the basic rights of shareholders, such as deleting the names and addresses of the initial directors or registered agent, or making a minor change to the corporate name by substituting "Corporation" or "Inc." for a similar word or abbreviation. Additionally, MBCA § 10.05 permits the directors alone to amend the articles of incorporation to increase the number of shares to the extent necessary to permit the issuance of shares as a dividend (if the corporation has only one class of shares). An amendment merely changing the corporation's agent for service of process can usually be effected by the directors without shareholder approval by filing a simple form with the secretary of state.

The amendment may be voted on by the shareholders at their annual meeting or at a special meeting called for the purpose of amending the articles and the notice of which must state the purpose of the meeting.

Most states require only a simple shareholder majority (50 percent plus one) to approve the amendment, but a few states require two-thirds approval. Under the MBCA, the amendment will be approved if more votes are cast in favor of it than against it. If shareholders may act by written consent, this procedure may be used to amend the articles of incorporation.

3. Articles of Amendment

Articles of amendment
Document filed with state that amends articles of incorporation

After the amendment has been approved by the shareholders, the corporation must prepare and file **articles of amendment** with the secretary of state, together with a filing fee. Nearly all states provide sample forms for articles of amendment. Some states also require that the amendment recite that the original articles were amended pursuant to state statute and that the requisite shareholder approval was received (or that shareholder approval was not needed). (See Figure 12-1 for sample articles of amendment.)

Any requirements relating to the original articles must also be followed when amending articles. For example, if the original articles were required to be published, then the amended articles must also be published. If the amendment changes the corporation's name or authorized number of shares, new stock certificates and a new corporate seal should be obtained.

An amendment to a corporation's articles does not affect the rights of third parties. Thus, the fact that a corporation changes its name does not affect litigation filed against the company or its debts or liabilities.

Finally, if the corporation is doing business in other jurisdictions, their state statutes must be reviewed to determine whether an amendment to the articles triggers any filing requirements in those states.

FIGURE 12-1

Articles of Amendment

Page 1 of 1

STATE OF WASHINGTON
SECRETARY OF STATE

Washington Profit Corporation
See attached detailed instructions

☐ **Filing Fee $30.00**

☐ **Filing Fee with Expedited Service $50.00**

This Box For Office Use Only

UBI Number:

ARTICLES OF AMENDMENT
Chapter 23B.10 RCW

SECTION 1
Name of Corporation: *(as currently recorded with the Office of the Secretary of State)*

SECTION 2
Amendments were adopted on this **DATE:**

SECTION 3
Articles of Amendment were adopted by: *(please check one of the following)*

☐   Board of Directors (shareholder action was not required)

☐   Duly approved by shareholders in accordance with Chapter 23B.10.030 and 23B.10.040 RCW

☐   Incorporators (shareholder action was not required)

SECTION 4
Amendments to Articles on File: *(if necessary, attach additional information)*
_____
_____

SECTION 5
Effective Date of Articles of Amendment: *(please check one of the following)*
☐   Upon filing by the Secretary of State
☐   Specific Date: _____ *(Specified effective date must be within 90 days AFTER the Articles of Amendment have been filed by the Office of the Secretary of State)*

SECTION 6
SIGNATURE *(see instructions page)*

This document is hereby executed under penalties of perjury, and is, to the best of my knowledge, true and correct.

X _____
Signature   **Printed Name & Title**   **Date**

Washington Profit Corporation - Amendment   Washington Secretary of State   Revised 09/08

C. Restating the Articles of Incorporation

Over a period of time, a corporation may amend its articles several times. If each document filed with the secretary of state contains only the amending language rather than setting forth the entire content of the articles, the various versions of the articles will be confusing to readers. Thus, almost all states allow a corporation to restate its articles by combining the original articles with any later amendments into one clean document that supersedes all previous documents.

Restated articles
Articles compiled into one readable form with no changes made

Because the **restated articles** do not include any changes, but rather are a composite of previously approved amendments, shareholder approval is not necessary to restate the articles. The directors will approve a restatement either by majority vote at a meeting or by unanimous written consent. The restated articles will be filed with the secretary of state, together with a filing fee.

D. Amending the Bylaws of the Corporation

Changes in the corporation's bylaws are easily accomplished. Generally, unless state statute, the articles, or the bylaws themselves require shareholder participation, the bylaws may be amended solely by the directors. The directors will approve the amendment to the bylaws either by majority vote at a meeting or by unanimous written consent. The new amendment will be placed in the minute book. Because the original bylaws were not filed with the secretary of state, the amended bylaws need not be either.

E. Corporate Combinations

1. Introduction

A corporation may take control of another corporation or increase its size by a variety of means. One corporation may be merged into another, with all of the merged corporation's assets and property transferred to the survivor corporation. A corporation may purchase the assets of another corporation. One corporation may acquire sufficient stock in another that it is able to assume control. The corporations involved in these transactions are usually called **constituents.** Because all of these combinations affect significant rights of shareholders, all are subject, to varying degrees, to the requirement of shareholder approval.

Constituent
Party involved in a merger or other similar transaction

The reasons for such combinations are varied. A corporation may wish to acquire some special process or technology owned by another, to diversify or expand its operations, or to rid itself of a competitor.

2. Mergers and Consolidations

Merger
Combination of two or more corporations into one corporate entity

Mergers.   State statutes permit the combination of two or more corporations into one corporate entity. This combination is called a **merger.** In the classic merger scenario, Corporation A combines with Corporation B. At the conclusion of the combination, one of the corporations (assume Corporation A) ceases to exist. The survivor, Corporation B, acquires everything previously owned by Corporation A: its assets, its contracts, its rights, its obligations, and usually its shareholders. In the example given, Corporation A is referred to as the *merged corporation* or the **extinguished corporation** and Corporation B is called the **survivor.**

Consolidations. A consolidation is similar to a merger. In this transaction, two or more corporations combine to form an entirely new corporation, a different legal entity from either of the two constituent corporations. At the end of the consolidation, all of the combining corporations cease to exist. The newly formed corporation acquires everything previously owned by the constituents: their assets, contracts, liabilities, and shareholders. In a classic consolidation scenario, Corporation A combines with Corporation B to form Corporation X.

Mergers may take place between two or more domestic corporations or between domestic and foreign corporations. Some states and the MBCA allow mergers between corporations and other business entities, such as partnerships and limited liability companies. Mergers between such different business entities are often called **cross-species mergers.**

Because it is nearly always advantageous in a transaction for one of the constituent corporations to survive, consolidations are fairly uncommon. In fact, the MBCA and some states no longer recognize consolidations.

Extinguished corporation
Corporation that does not survive a merger

Survivor
Corporation that survives a merger

Consolidation
Combination of two or more corporations into one new entity

Cross-species merger
Merger between corporation and some other business entity

PRACTICE TIPS

- When a new corporation is formed to participate in a merger or other transaction, it is often referred to as "NEWCO" or "NEWCORP" in all of the pertinent documents. Watch for this entity name; it is a signal that an entirely new corporation is being created solely for the purpose of the transaction.
- Almost all law firms engaged in mergers and acquisitions (M & A) work use detailed timetables that provide a blueprint as to when and what documents are to be prepared and filed. Maintain all your timetables for use in future transactions along with your list of useful contacts at the SEC, helpful Web sites, and so forth.

Procedures for Effecting Mergers and Consolidations. The procedures for accomplishing mergers and consolidations are the same. Any references in this section to mergers also include consolidations.

Director and Shareholder Approval. The first step in the merger process is negotiation between or among the constituent corporations involved. These preliminary negotiations usually lead to a **letter of intent,** a letter-form document setting forth the basic terms of the transaction. This document is later replaced by a definitive agreement. The constituent corporations must then prepare a **plan of merger,** which will, at a minimum, set forth the following: the names of the constituents and the identity of the survivor; the terms and conditions of the merger; the manner of converting the shares of the extinguished corporation into shares of the survivor (or, if desired, the manner of converting the shares

Letter of intent
Initial document setting forth basic understanding of parties to a transaction

Plan of merger
Document setting forth terms of planned merger

of the extinguished corporation into cash, thereby allowing shareholders to be "cashed out"); and any amendments that will be required to be made to the survivor's articles of incorporation as a result of the transaction.

The plan of merger is then submitted to the boards of directors of each constituent corporation for approval. After adopting the plan of merger, the boards of the constituent corporations must submit the plan for shareholder approval and recommend it for approval. Unless this activity occurs at or near the time of the annual meeting, each corporation will need to call a special meeting, the notice of which must specify that the purpose of the meeting is to consider the plan of merger. The plan of merger must be attached to or summarized in the notice. Most states require a simple majority approval by the shareholders of each constituent corporation. Some states, however, require two-thirds approval. The MBCA approach is similar to its approach on amendments to the articles of incorporation: The merger will be approved if more votes are cast in favor of it than against it.

Approval by shareholders of all constituents is required due to the dramatic impact a merger has on the shareholders. Because one corporation will be extinguished, such an extraordinary matter should be approved by its owners. The corporation owned by the shareholders of the survivor will likely be taking on debt and other obligations of the extinguished corporation. Additionally, share ownership in the survivor will be affected because the survivor will usually absorb shareholders of the extinguished corporation and issue them shares of the survivor. This issuance of shares to the newcomers may cause a shift in power and control among the shareholders of the survivor. If the shareholders of the extinguished corporation receive cash rather than shares in the survivor, the survivor's shareholders are affected by what will likely be a large outlay of cash. In either scenario, their approval is required.

Exceptions to Requirement of Shareholder Approval. There are generally two exceptions to the requirement that shareholders of all constituents must approve a merger:

Subsidiary
Corporation formed by another, called the *parent*

Short-form merger
Merger of a subsidiary into a parent

1. **Short-Form Merger.** A merger between a parent and its **subsidiary** (a corporation created by the parent) need not be approved by the shareholders of *either* corporation (or by the board of the subsidiary) if the parent owns at least 90 percent of the stock of the subsidiary. Shareholder approval is simply not needed in this **short-form merger** because the parent has the necessary votes to extinguish the subsidiary; thus voting by the shareholders of the subsidiary would be a superfluous event. Similarly, voting by the parent's shareholders is not needed because the recapture of the subsidiary by the parent does not materially affect their share ownership.

Small-scale merger
Merger involving little transfer of survivor's stock to incoming shareholders

2. **Small-Scale Merger.** A merger need not be approved by the shareholders of the *survivor* corporation if very little of the survivor's stock (namely, less than 20 percent of its outstanding shares) needs to be transferred to the shareholders of the extinguished corporation. Such a **small-scale merger** simply does not have a great impact on the survivor's shareholders because their power and control will not be significantly diluted. Thus, they need not approve it.

Rights of Dissenting Shareholders. It is possible that some shareholders are adamantly opposed to a merger; they may have philosophical or moral objections about a constituent. Therefore, all states allow these **dissenting shareholders** the right to have their shares appraised and to receive the fair value of their shares in cash as of the date of the merger. This right, called an **appraisal right,** is generally a dissenting shareholder's exclusive remedy if she is opposed to a merger.

A dissenting shareholder must follow a fairly elaborate procedure to be entitled to appraisal rights, including notifying the corporation of her intent to demand payment for her shares, voting against the transaction, and returning various forms to the corporation. Assuming compliance with these complex requirements is met, the corporation will pay each dissenter the fair value of her shares. If they choose, shareholders may withdraw from the appraisal process.

Some states allow partial appraisal rights so that a shareholder may dissent regarding some shares owned and be cashed out with respect to those shares and still remain a shareholder as to the remainder of the shares owned. Appraisal rights are not permitted in small-scale mergers (for the survivor's shareholders) because the affected shareholder had no voting rights. Most states also refuse appraisal rights if the shares are listed on a national exchange or there are at least 2,000 shareholders, because there undoubtedly are ready and available buyers for the dissenter's shares. In a short-form merger in which a parent regains its subsidiary, although the subsidiary's shareholders are not entitled to vote on the transaction, within ten days after the transaction becomes effective, the parent must notify the subsidiary's shareholders that they are entitled to assert appraisal rights. The parent's shareholders are not entitled to appraisal rights.

Articles of Merger. After the merger has been approved by the requisite shareholder vote, **articles of merger** must be prepared and filed with the secretary of state with the appropriate filing fee. Most states provide forms for the articles of merger, which must usually set forth or attach the plan of merger. (See Figure 12-2 for a form for articles of merger.)

Effect of Merger. Upon the effective date of the merger, the merged or extinguished corporation ceases to exist, and the survivor corporation takes over all of the extinguished corporation's assets, properties, shareholders, debts, and liabilities. The shareholders of the extinguished corporation (unless they have dissented and have exercised their appraisal rights) will be issued shares of the survivor in return for their shares in the extinguished corporation according to the plan of merger, or, as discussed earlier, they may be cashed out.

3. Share Exchanges

Another way in which a corporation can gain control of another corporation is a share exchange. In a **share exchange,** one corporation acquires all of the shares of one or more classes of another corporation (the **target**). The acquiring corporation receives all of the target's shares, and the target receives shares of the acquirer (or cash). Both corporations may continue to exist; the target's shareholders exchange their shares for shares in the acquiring corporation or for cash. The acquiring corporation is in an identical position to that of the survivor of a

Dissenting shareholders
Shareholders who vote against merger or some other transaction

Appraisal right
Right of dissenting shareholder to have shares purchased at their fair value

Articles of merger
Document filed with state to effect merger

Share exchange
Exchange of the target's shares for shares in the acquiring corporation

Target
An entity that is the subject of an acquisition or takeover

FIGURE 12-2
California Certificate of Merger

State of California
Secretary of State

OBE MERG

CERTIFICATE OF MERGER
(California Corporations Code sections
1113(g), 6019.1, 8019.1, 9640, 12540.1, 15678.4, 15911.14, 16915(b) and 17552)

IMPORTANT — Read all instructions before completing this form.   This Space For Filing Use Only

1. NAME OF SURVIVING ENTITY   2. TYPE OF ENTITY   3. CA SECRETARY OF STATE FILE NUMBER   4. JURISDICTION

5. NAME OF DISAPPEARING ENTITY   6. TYPE OF ENTITY   7. CA SECRETARY OF STATE FILE NUMBER   8. JURISDICTION

9. THE PRINCIPAL TERMS OF THE AGREEMENT OF MERGER WERE APPROVED BY A VOTE OF THE NUMBER OF INTERESTS OR SHARES OF EACH CLASS THAT EQUALED OR EXCEEDED THE VOTE REQUIRED. IF A VOTE WAS REQUIRED, SPECIFY THE CLASS AND THE NUMBER OF OUTSTANDING INTERESTS OF <u>EACH CLASS</u> ENTITLED TO VOTE ON THE MERGER AND THE PERCENTAGE VOTE REQUIRED OF <u>EACH CLASS</u>. ATTACH ADDITIONAL PAGES, IF NECESSARY.

SURVIVING ENTITY
CLASS AND NUMBER   AND   PERCENTAGE VOTE REQUIRED

DISAPPEARING ENTITY
CLASS AND NUMBER   AND   PERCENTAGE VOTE REQUIRED

10. IF EQUITY SECURITIES OF A PARENT PARTY ARE TO BE ISSUED IN THE MERGER, CHECK THE APPLICABLE STATEMENT.

☐ No vote of the shareholders of the parent party was required.   ☐ The required vote of the shareholders of the parent party was obtained.

11. IF THE SURVIVING ENTITY IS A DOMESTIC LIMITED LIABILITY COMPANY, LIMITED PARTNERSHIP, OR PARTNERSHIP, PROVIDE THE REQUISITE CHANGES (IF ANY) TO THE INFORMATION SET FORTH IN THE SURVIVING ENTITY'S ARTICLES OF ORGANIZATION, CERTIFICATE OF LIMITED PARTNERSHIP OR STATEMENT OF PARTNERSHIP AUTHORITY RESULTING FROM THE MERGER. ATTACH ADDITIONAL PAGES, IF NECESSARY.

12. IF A DISAPPEARING ENTITY IS A DOMESTIC LIMITED LIABILITY COMPANY, LIMITED PARTNERSHIP, OR PARTNERSHIP, AND THE SURVIVING ENTITY IS NOT A DOMESTIC ENTITY OF THE SAME TYPE, ENTER THE PRINCIPAL ADDRESS OF THE SURVIVING ENTITY.

PRINCIPAL ADDRESS OF SURVIVING ENTITY   CITY AND STATE   ZIP CODE

13. OTHER INFORMATION REQUIRED TO BE STATED IN THE CERTIFICATE OF MERGER BY THE LAWS UNDER WHICH EACH CONSTITUENT OTHER BUSINESS ENTITY IS ORGANIZED. ATTACH ADDITIONAL PAGES, IF NECESSARY.

14. STATUTORY OR OTHER BASIS UNDER WHICH A FOREIGN OTHER BUSINESS ENTITY IS AUTHORIZED TO EFFECT THE MERGER.   15. FUTURE EFFECTIVE DATE, IF ANY ____ - ____ - ____ (Month) (Day) (Year)

16. ADDITIONAL INFORMATION SET FORTH ON ATTACHED PAGES, IF ANY, IS INCORPORATED HEREIN BY THIS REFERENCE AND MADE PART OF THIS CERTIFICATE.

17. I CERTIFY UNDER PENALTY OF PERJURY UNDER THE LAWS OF THE STATE OF CALIFORNIA THAT THE FOREGOING IS TRUE AND CORRECT OF MY OWN KNOWLEDGE. I DECLARE I AM THE PERSON WHO EXECUTED THIS INSTRUMENT, WHICH EXECUTION IS MY ACT AND DEED.

SIGNATURE OF AUTHORIZED PERSON FOR THE SURVIVING ENTITY   DATE   TYPE OR PRINT NAME AND TITLE OF AUTHORIZED PERSON

SIGNATURE OF AUTHORIZED PERSON FOR THE SURVIVING ENTITY   DATE   TYPE OR PRINT NAME AND TITLE OF AUTHORIZED PERSON

SIGNATURE OF AUTHORIZED PERSON FOR THE DISAPPEARING ENTITY   DATE   TYPE OR PRINT NAME AND TITLE OF AUTHORIZED PERSON

SIGNATURE OF AUTHORIZED PERSON FOR THE DISAPPEARING ENTITY   DATE   TYPE OR PRINT NAME AND TITLE OF AUTHORIZED PERSON

For an entity that is a business trust, real estate investment trust or an unincorporated association, set forth the provision of law or other basis for the authority of the person signing: _____

OBE MERGER-1 (REV 01/2008)   APPROVED BY SECRETARY OF STATE

merger. Because a share exchange is so similar in its effect to a merger, all of the procedural formalities of a merger must be complied with, including providing appraisal rights to dissenting shareholders.

In 2004, the National Conference of Commissioners on Uniform State Laws together with the American Bar Association promulgated a Model Entity Transactions Act to provide a comprehensive framework for changing entity forms, from mergers to share exchanges to conversions and domestications (discussed in Section F below). At the time of the writing of this text, it has only been adopted in Idaho. The text of the Act is available at www.nccusl.org.

4. Purchase of Assets

A corporation may gain control of another by purchasing all or substantially all of its assets. The selling corporation may be paid for its assets in cash or in stock of the acquiring corporation. At the end of the transaction, the acquiring corporation owns additional assets and the selling corporation is often a mere shell, owning little or nothing more than the cash or shares it has recently received. After it has paid its debts and distributed the proceeds of the sale to its shareholders, the selling corporation often dissolves.

Because there is no change in the status of the legal entity of the acquiring corporation and it is simply buying additional assets, it need not secure the approval of its shareholders; the transaction is viewed as within the purview of the directors, who have the sole authority to manage the corporation's business affairs. The selling corporation, however, is undergoing a significant change by disposing of all or substantially all of its assets, and thus it must have approval of its board of directors and shareholders and, in most states, offer appraisal rights to its dissenting shareholders.

A purchase of assets may be quite advantageous to the acquiring corporation because the transaction does not require shareholder approval and, in most cases, the purchasing corporation buys only assets, not liabilities. In effect, the acquiring corporation "goes shopping" and picks and chooses the assets it desires. It seldom, if ever, agrees to assume any liabilities of the target corporation, which retains responsibility for its own obligations. Moreover, there is no need to issue shares because no newcomers are joining the corporation. The acquirer purchases only the assets it needs. Public filings or amendments to articles are usually not necessitated by the **asset purchase** transaction (with the exception of Hart-Scott-Rodino filings, which are required in large transactions, as discussed below). Under state bulk transfer laws, however, the seller must give notice to creditors of the intended transfer (to ensure a seller does not dispose of all assets without first satisfying creditors).

Asset purchase
Purchase of assets of an entity

The MBCA no longer uses the phrase "all or substantially all of its assets." Rather, the Act requires shareholder approval if a sale would leave the selling corporation without a "significant continuing business activity" (generally, a significant business activity exists if the seller retains 25 percent of its assets). MBCA § 12.02.

For the selling corporation, the procedure for effecting a sale of assets closely parallels the procedure for effecting mergers because the result for the seller is the same: discontinuation of its business operations. Thus, after negotiations, the board of directors of the selling corporation approves the transaction and directs that it be voted on by the shareholders. Most states require a simple majority approval by the shareholders, although some states still require two-thirds approval. Appraisal rights are provided to dissenting shareholders. The MBCA approach is similar to its approach on amendments to the articles of incorporation and mergers: The sale of assets will be approved if more votes are cast in favor of the sale than against it.

5. Purchase of Stock

Stock purchase
Purchase of shares of a corporation

A **stock purchase** is highly similar to an asset purchase; however, in this transaction, the acquiring corporation (or individual) purchases all or substantially all of another corporation's outstanding stock rather than its assets. At the conclusion of the transaction, the acquiring corporation, as owner of all of the target's outstanding shares, now controls the destiny of the target and may decide to dissolve it, allow it to function as a subsidiary, or merge the target into the acquiring corporation, in which case the acquiring corporation is responsible for the obligations of the target.

Many stock acquisitions involve negotiations between the management of the constituent corporations. The board of directors of the acquiring corporation does not need shareholder approval to buy the target's stock because the board is simply making a business decision for the best interest of the acquiring corporation. The board of directors of the target will approve the sale and recommend that its shareholders sell their stock to the acquiror. The shareholders are free to decide whether or not to sell their shares.

Rather than dealing with management of the target, the acquiring corporation may deal directly with the target's shareholders. Once the acquiror has a majority of the stock of the target it has the power to remove the target's existing directors and to elect its own slate of directors, thereby controlling the target.

Tender offer
Public offer made by bidder to acquire shares in a target corporation

A public offer made by the acquiring corporation to the shareholders of the target to purchase a substantial percentage of the company's shares is referred to as a **tender offer,** because the acquiring corporation is asking the shareholders to surrender, or tender, their shares to the corporation. The price the acquiring corporation will pay will be higher than the stock's current market value. This increased price induces the shareholders to sell. Federal securities laws strictly regulate tender offers. The Securities Exchange Act of 1934 provides that any person who acquires stock in a publicly traded company and thereby owns more than 5 percent of a class of stock must file an information statement with the Securities and Exchange Commission (SEC), identifying himself and indicating any plans he has for the target (such as liquidating it or merging it with another corporation). The SEC's tender offer rules generally do not apply to tender offers that, if consummated, will result in ownership of 5 percent or less of the target's outstanding shares, which offers are called "mini-tender offers."

6. Hostile Takeovers

Introduction. Not all combinations of corporations are consensual. Although many transactions involve months of planning and negotiating by the constituents, some combinations occur without the consent of the acquired, or target, corporation. Because these combinations are not consensual, they are usually referred to as **hostile takeovers.**

Although hostile takeovers receive a great deal of media attention, they are the exception, not the rule. In most cases, after a period of negotiations between companies, either the transaction dies a natural death or proceeds upon the parties' mutual agreement. In a hostile takeover, however, the aggressor or bidder goes over the head of the target's management and courts the shareholders directly.

One corporation may wish to acquire another to expand its business operations, to acquire new technology and operations, or even to eliminate competition. In some instances, the aggressor may set its sights on a target that should be operating more profitably, but is not, perhaps due to poor management. The aggressor may believe that a takeover of the company and a replacement of management may result in increased profits. In those instances, management of the target naturally feels threatened and may implement a variety of defenses to ward off the takeover.

The Tender Offer. The aggressor may decide to proceed by surprise. It will usually then begin purchasing the target's stock on the open market. Because a purchase of more than 5 percent of a class of stock requires disclosure and filings with the SEC, the aggressor may purchase up to 4.9 percent of the target's outstanding shares (often called a **foothold** or *toehold* or *creeping tender offer*) before identifying itself to the target. The federal law that regulates tender offers, the **Williams Act,** imposes various requirements on acquirors and potential acquirors, primarily through disclosure requirements.

Alternatively, rather than purchase shares anonymously on the open market, the aggressor may publicly announce a cash offer for as much of the target's stock as the aggressor needs to acquire all or majority control. This is also a tender offer that triggers reporting requirements with the SEC. The tender offer informs shareholders that the aggressor will purchase a certain number of shares at a specified price (typically above the current market price). A tender offer is usually announced by advertisement or press release and tender offer materials are provided to the shareholders and filed with the SEC and any national exchange that lists the target's stock. If insufficient shares are tendered, the aggressor will return the tendered shares and abandon its efforts.

Proxy Contest. As an alternative to a hostile takeover, an aggressor corporation may solicit the target's shareholders with a proposal that they vote for the aggressor's management team, which the aggressor promises will perform more successfully than the current management. This is a **proxy contest** (or *proxy fight*); both management and the aggressor will be attempting to obtain proxies from shareholders for their own slate of directors. If the aggressor is successful, it effectively controls the target through control of a majority of its board of directors.

Defensive Strategies. Corporations adopt a number of strategies to avoid being taken over. These **takeover defenses** may be developed even before a tender offer is made to discourage a takeover bid in the first place. However, actions by the target's directors that are taken only to perpetuate their own status and reward themselves rather than promoting the best interests of the corporation and its shareholders may be breaches of fiduciary duty. Following are some takeover defenses:

Golden parachute
Highly favorable financial packages awarded to senior managers in event of a takeover

Poison pill
An anti-takeover measure triggered by a tender offer at which time the target's shareholders are given additional rights (also called *shareholder rights plan*)

Crown jewel defense
Sale of corporate assets by a target to make itself less attractive to an acquirer

Suicide pact
Agreement by corporate managers to resign en masse after a takeover if any are fired; also called a *people pill*

- **Staggered Boards.** It might take an aggressor several years to obtain control of a board of directors that is staggered (meaning one whose directors stand for election at different times).
- **Golden Parachutes.** The corporation may grant senior managers **golden parachutes** requiring that these individuals, if ousted, be compensated in some extraordinary amount. The golden parachutes may make a takeover prohibitively expensive for an aggressor.
- **Poison Pills.** A **poison pill** (or *shareholder rights plan*) is triggered by a tender offer. Once the tender offer is announced, shareholders are automatically given certain rights, such as increased voting rights or rights to acquire additional shares of the target at bargain prices. These rights make acquisition of control by a bidder far more difficult and may be extremely costly.
- **Crown Jewel Defense.** The target may begin selling off its most valuable assets to make itself less attractive to the bidder. This is the **crown jewel defense**. Of course, the risk is that if the bidder abandons its takeover plan, the target may be left so weakened that it must dissolve.
- **Suicide Pacts.** The managers of the target may enter into a **suicide pact** (sometimes called a "people pill") whereby they agree that if any of them are fired after a takeover, they will all resign. Such an en masse walkout leaves the aggressor without any stability or continuity in management.

7. *Government Regulation*

Hart-Scott-Rodino Act
Federal statute requiring notification to government before mergers involving certain amounts or parties

The federal government has the authority to review mergers and acquisitions under the Clayton Act (15 U.S.C. § 12) to ensure that such transactions do not impair competition and result in monopolies. Specifically, the **Hart-Scott-Rodino Antitrust Improvements Act of 1976** (HSR), 15 U.S.C. § 18a, requires that parties to certain merger transactions file premerger notification with the government (specifically, with the Federal Trade Commission and the Department of Justice) and wait for 30 days before closing their transaction. There are threshold limits for HSR notification; at present, HSR filings are not required if the transaction involves less than $65.2 million. Generally, only companies involved in large transactions must so notify the government so that the government can review the transaction and determine whether it should take action to protect consumers. The government may prohibit transactions or require the parties to divest themselves of certain assets or restructure their transaction.

F. Domestication and Entity Conversion

Chapter 9 of the MBCA provides a series of procedures allowing corporations to change their state of incorporation and also allowing corporations to become different business structures. For example, a corporation may change its structure and become a limited liability company, as AOL did in 2006, changing from America Online Inc. to AOL LLC.

1. *Domestication*

Domestication allows a corporation to change its state of incorporation and be governed by the laws of another state. For example, a corporation formed in Pennsylvania may decide to "go public" and prefer to be a Delaware corporation because of the state's flexible and permissive statutes. Similarly, tax savings may justify a change in the state of incorporation.

The procedures for effecting a domestication are nearly identical to those for mergers. The board of directors will adopt a **plan of domestication** and submit it to the shareholders for approval. The notice of the shareholders' meeting must specify that its purpose is to consider the plan of domestication, and the plan must be included with the notice. Most states require a majority vote by the shareholders, although the MBCA provides that the plan will be approved if more shareholders vote for it than against it. If the plan is approved, the corporation will prepare and file **articles of domestication** with the new state and surrender its articles or charter to the former state of incorporation. Domestication has no effect on the corporation's debts, assets, or liabilities, and after the domestication, the corporation remains the same, except that its state of incorporation has changed.

Domestication
The changing of a corporation's state of incorporation

Plan of domestication
The plan that provides the terms and conditions of a corporation's change of its state of incorporation

Articles of domestication
The document filed with the state to effect a change of a corporation's state of incorporation

2. *Entity Conversion*

MBCA § 9.50 permits corporations to change their structures to unincorporated associations. For example, an Arizona corporation could become a limited liability partnership (LLP) or limited liability company (LLC). Similarly, the reverse could occur: An LLP or LLC may become a corporation. A business corporation may convert to a nonprofit corporation. Such changes are called **entity conversions.**

The process of effecting an entity conversion is nearly identical to that for effecting a domestication. The converting entity must adopt a **plan of entity conversion,** which sets forth the terms and conditions of the conversion and provides how, for example, shares of the corporation will be converted into LLC interests. The plan must be submitted to a shareholder vote. The notice of any meeting must state that the purpose is to consider the plan, and a copy of the governing documents must be included with the plan. Although most states require approval by a majority of shareholders, MBCA § 9.52(5) provides that the plan is approved if more shareholders vote for it than against it. Because some former shareholders may now face personal liability (for example, if a corporation converts to a general partnership), each person who would become subject to such personal liability must sign a separate written consent. Shareholders of a business corporation that is converting to a noncorporate form have appraisal rights. After the conversion has been adopted and approved, **articles of entity conversion** will be prepared and filed with the state. A corporation that converts to an unincorporated form must then surrender its articles or charter.

As is the case with domestication, entity conversion does not affect the company's contracts, liabilities, and so forth.

Entity conversion
A business's change of its structure, for example, converting from a corporation to an LLC

Plan of entity conversion
The plan that provides the terms and conditions of a business's change in its structure

Articles of entity conversion
The document filed with the state to effect a change in a business's structure

G. Role of Paralegal

Due diligence
Careful review of documents and transactions to ensure they are appropriate for a party and in compliance with all pertinent laws

There are numerous tasks for paralegals engaged in changes to corporations or working in the field of mergers and acquisitions. The work is fast-paced, stressful, challenging, and document-intensive. Much of the work is referred to as **due diligence** review, meaning careful review of documents and transactions to ensure a transaction is appropriate, that parties have fulfilled all of their commitments, and that the transaction is in compliance with all applicable federal and state laws. Due diligence work involves investigation of the parties to transactions, review of all documents involved, and evaluation of risks and benefits of the transaction. Paralegals are routinely involved in due diligence work. Additionally, some of the typical tasks paralegals perform include:

- Drafting minutes of directors' meetings or written consent actions authorizing amendment of articles of incorporation, restatement of the articles, or amendment of bylaws;
- Drafting notices of shareholders' meetings called to vote on amendment of the articles of incorporation and preparing minutes of those meetings;
- Preparing and filing articles of amendment (see Figure 12-1) and restated articles and preparing amended bylaws;
- Drafting minutes of directors' meetings or written consent actions to vote on mergers, share exchanges, sales of assets, and acquisitions of stock and preparing notices of meetings called to consider such transactions;
- Preparing various documents needed to complete corporate combinations, such as plans of mergers and asset purchase agreements;
- Preparing and filing articles of merger (see Figure 12-2) or share exchange;
- Preparing HSR premerger notifications; and
- Arranging for the closing of the transaction, preparing and compiling closing binders containing all relevant documents, ensuring all necessary filings have been made, and ordering new corporate supplies, if needed.

Case Illustration
Business Judgment Rule Applies to Directors' Actions in Opposing a Takeover

---

Case: *Panter v. Marshall Field & Co.*, 646 F.2d 271 (7th Cir. 1981)

Facts: Shareholders sued their corporation, alleging that it harmed them by fending off a hostile takeover that would have been profitable for them. Among other complaints, the shareholders alleged that their directors acquired other stores to make the corporation less attractive to the bidder. The district court granted the corporation's motion for a directed verdict.

Holding: The court of appeals affirmed. Not every effort to thwart a takeover can be condemned. The test is whether the board fairly and reasonably exercises its business judgment to protect the corporation and its shareholders. The shareholders' contention that their corporation purchased five other stores to make itself less attractive to the bidder is the type of "Monday-morning quarterbacking" that the business judgment rule is intended to prevent. The shareholders showed no evidence that the defendant directors engaged in manipulative conduct, self-dealing, bad faith, or fraud. Thus, even if the desire to fend off the bidder was among the motives of the board in entering the transactions, because the shareholders did not prove that such a motive was a sole or primary purpose, the business judgment rule will protect the directors' decision.

Key Features
of Corporate Changes and Combinations

- ◆ Significant changes to a corporation typically require shareholder approval.
- ◆ A corporation may amend its articles at any time by resolution by the directors followed by shareholder approval (usually by majority vote). Articles of amendment must be filed with the secretary of state.
- ◆ A corporation may restate its articles to create one composite document superseding prior amendments; shareholder approval is not needed because nothing new is being added to the articles.
- ◆ Amending corporate bylaws is typically handled by directors without shareholder approval because the bylaws regulate only the internal affairs of the corporation.
- ◆ A merger is the combination of two or more corporations into one corporate entity. The survivor acquires all of the business, liabilities, and usually the shareholders of the extinguished corporation. Shareholders of both corporations must approve the transaction.
- ◆ Shareholders who dissent from a merger have the right to have their shares appraised and purchased from them at their fair market value.
- ◆ In a share exchange, the target's shareholders exchange their shares for cash or shares in the acquiring corporation.
- ◆ As an alternative to a merger, one corporation may buy the assets of another. Liabilities are generally not purchased.
- ◆ One corporation may purchase all or a majority of another's stock as a means of gaining control of a corporation. If the acquisition is consensual, all directors vote. In a hostile takeover, the bidder bypasses the target's management and appeals directly to the target's shareholders.

- ◆ Some takeovers are regulated by federal law.
- ◆ Corporations may implement a variety of measures to ward off a takeover.
- ◆ A corporation may change its state of incorporation (domestication) or may convert its business structure to an unincorporated form (such as to an LLC).

Internet Resources

State statutes:	www.law.cornell.edu www.findlaw.com
Text of MBCA:	www.abanet.org/buslaw/committees/ CL270000pub/nosearch/mbca/home. shtml
Securities regulations:	www.sec.gov (site of SEC providing excellent information on securities laws relating to mergers, tender offers, and so forth)
Federal Trade Commission:	www.ftc.gov (information about mergers and HSR reporting requirements)
General information:	www.megalaw.com www.findlaw.com
Secretaries of state:	www.nass.org (for links to secretaries of state and downloadable forms for articles of amendment, articles of merger, articles of domestication and entity conversion, and other documents)
Forms:	www.allaboutforms.com www.lectlaw.com (These sites offer forms for notices of meetings, minutes of meetings, corporate resolutions, and other related forms.)

Key Terms

Articles of amendment
Restated articles
Constituent
√Merger
√Extinguished corporation

Stock purchase
√Tender offer
√Williams Act
Hostile takeover
Foothold

Survivor
Cross-species merger
Consolidation
Letter of intent
Plan of merger
Subsidiary
Short-form merger
Small-scale merger
Dissenting shareholders
Appraisal right
✓Articles of merger
Share exchange
Asset purchase

Proxy contest
Takeover defenses
Golden parachute
Poison pill
✓Hart-Scott-Rodino Act
Due diligence
Domestication
Plan of domestication
✓Articles of domestication
Entity conversion
Plan of entity conversion
Articles of entity conversion

Discussion Questions

Fact Scenario. TelCom Inc. is a telecommunications company incorporated in Delaware in 2000. Its stock is traded on the NYSE and it has 20,000 shareholders and 100,000 shares outstanding. H & A Corp. is a Delaware corporation that has 50,000 shares outstanding. Its stock is not publicly traded. Use the MBCA to answer the following questions.

1. TelCom has decided to change its agent for service of process and to change its name to VisiCom Corp. How will the corporation go about making these changes? Discuss any shareholder approval that may be required.

2. H & A has amended its certificate of incorporation several times, and it is difficult to read. What should H & A do to ensure its certificate is easily readable? Discuss any shareholder approval that may be required.

3. VisiCom has decided to change its fiscal year. How will the corporation go about making this change?

4. VisiCom has decided to acquire H & A. At the conclusion of the transaction, VisiCom will continue to exist but H & A will not. What is this transaction called? Who will vote on it? What will happen to shareholders who disapprove of the transaction? What will happen to a debt that H & A owes to Bank of America?

5. Assume that VisiCom decided to acquire certain assets owned by H & A rather than acquiring the company. What is this transaction called? Who will vote on it? What will happen to shareholders who oppose the transaction?

6. Assume that VisiCom has made a public offer that, if consummated, will result in it owning 8 percent of H & A's stock. What is this called and what requirements, if any, are imposed on VisiCom by making this offer?

7. H & A's contracts with its officers grant them significant amounts of cash and various benefits if they lose their positions as a result of a takeover. What are these provisions called and how do they thwart a takeover?

8. Why might shareholders of H & A dislike a poison pill provision?

9. What government regulations exist to ensure that VisiCom's transaction with H & A does not hinder competition in the communications sector?

10. VisiCom has decided to change its state of incorporation to New York. What is this called and how will VisiCom effect this?

Net Worth

1. What is the fee in Florida for a profit corporation to file articles of amendment?
2. What is the fee in Ohio if a corporation amends its articles by shareholder vote?
3. What is the fee in California if a corporation restates its articles of incorporation?
4. A Florida corporation has decided to change its status to a limited liability company. What fee must be paid to the secretary of state?
5. Access the Web site for the SEC and select "Fast Answers." What is a merger?
6. Access the FTC's Web site and locate information about the Hart-Scott-Rodino Act.
   a. May an HSR filing be submitted electronically?
   b. Assume that the size of a merger is valued at $300 million. What filing fee must be paid?

13

♦ ♦ ♦
___

Qualification of Foreign Corporations
___
♦ ♦ ♦

A. Introduction

Corporations may be formed in one state and yet do business in others. You have seen that many large corporations have elected to incorporate in Delaware due to its moderate fees and taxes, extensive case law, and permissive statutes. Most of these corporations transact business in other states. For a foreign corporation to lawfully conduct business in a state other than its state of incorporation, it must "qualify" or be authorized to do business there. In general, most states require that the foreign corporation file an application to transact business, appoint an agent for service of process, and pay the appropriate filing fees and taxes. Failure to qualify may result in fines being imposed on the corporation or a refusal to allow the corporation to sue another in that state. When the corporation ceases to conduct business in a state, it should formally withdraw from doing business as a foreign corporation.

B. Basis for Qualification

A corporation incorporated in a state is a **domestic corporation** in that state. Because recognition of corporate status is granted only by each state's secretary of state, the corporation has no legal existence beyond the borders of the state in which it was incorporated. To conduct business in other states, the corporation must be granted authority; it must qualify to do business in those states.

Domestic corporation
Corporation doing business in the state in which it was formed

Foreign corporation
Corporation doing business in a state other than the state in which it was formed

A corporation doing business in states other than in its state of incorporation is a **foreign corporation** in those states.

The qualification requirement imposed on foreign corporations provides a way for states to protect their citizens. Requiring qualification ensures that citizens have some basic information about the corporation and are able to sue the corporation and serve its registered agent in the state.

The decision to conduct business in other states begins with the board of directors. Upon seeing a need for expansion into other states, the board will pass a resolution (or act by written consent) authorizing the officers to take needed action so the corporation may transact business elsewhere. One hopes that the decision to expand into other jurisdictions has been carefully considered, and the corporation's name has been registered in the foreign state so it is available to the corporation for use (see Chapter Eight).

Remember also that a corporation can change its state of incorporation by a process called domestication (see Chapter Twelve).

C.   Transacting Business

Transacting business
Generally, statutory list of activities in which a corporation may engage in a foreign state without being required to qualify to do business therein

Generally, most state statutes provide that a foreign corporation may not **transact business** within the state until it obtains a certificate of authority from the secretary of state. The critical question (and one that has resulted in much litigation), is what particular activities are considered "transacting business" such that the qualification is required? What if an Ohio corporation wishes to hold its annual shareholders' meeting in Hawaii? What if an Iowa corporation wishes to open a bank account in Kansas? Must the corporations qualify in the foreign states to engage in these activities?

To reduce litigation over these issues, many states have enacted statutes enumerating certain activities that may be engaged in by a foreign corporation without having to qualify in the state. MBCA § 15.01(b) provides that the following activities do *not* constitute transacting business:

1. Maintaining, defending, or settling any proceeding;
2. Holding meetings of the board of directors or shareholders or carrying on other activities concerning internal corporate affairs;
3. Maintaining bank accounts;
4. Maintaining offices for the transfer, exchange, and registration of the corporation's stocks and bonds;
5. Selling through independent contractors;
6. Soliciting or obtaining orders (whether by mail or through agents or employees) if the orders require acceptance outside the state before they become contracts;
7. Creating or acquiring indebtedness, mortgages, and security interests in real or personal property;
8. Securing or collecting debts or enforcing mortgages and security interests in property securing the debts;
9. Owning, without more, real or personal property;

10.   Conducting an isolated transaction that is completed within 30 days and that is not one in the course of repeated transactions of a like nature; and
11.   Transacting business in interstate commerce.

This list is not exhaustive: Other activities may also be considered as not "transacting business." Most states have similar lists, but others provide little statutory guidance. In such instances, case law within the state will need to be analyzed to determine what sorts of activities have been considered in the past to be "transacting business." Because qualifying is a rather straightforward procedure, any doubts regarding the issue should be resolved in favor of qualification. Qualification will, however, subject the corporation to service of process in that state as well as to various reporting requirements, fees, and taxes.

D.   Procedures in Qualification

All states have statutes setting forth the requirements for foreign corporations for **qualifying to transact business**. Almost all states have forms available from the office of the secretary of state. MBCA § 15.03 requires the following information in the qualification application:

Qualifying to transact business
Process of seeking permission from foreign jurisdiction to do business therein

- **Name.** The name of the foreign corporation must comply with the statutes of the state in which it seeks to qualify. Thus, it may need to include a corporate signal such as "Inc." or "Corp." Moreover, the name cannot be the same as or confusingly similar to that of a domestic corporation in the state or another foreign corporation already authorized to do business in the state. Most states allow a corporation to obtain permission from another corporation to use a similar name.
- **State of Incorporation.** Identification of the state under whose law the foreign corporation is incorporated is necessary so that consumers and potential investors are able to conduct an investigation of the foreign corporation.
- **Date of Incorporation and Duration.** The application must include both the date of incorporation and the period of duration for the corporation.
- **Principal Address and Agent.** The application must provide the street address of the foreign corporation's principal office and its registered office in the state in which it is qualifying as well as identifying a registered agent at that office. A qualified foreign corporation must maintain a registered office in each state in which it transacts business. The registered agent, whose function is to receive service of process, may be an individual who resides in the state or a corporation. Many statutes provide that if there is no registered agent, the secretary of state will receive service of process on behalf of the foreign corporation. Many corporation service companies provide their services to corporations to act as registered agents. For example, CT Corporation acts as the registered agent for more than 200,000 corporations. A list of service companies is provided in Chapter Eight.

- **Identities of Directors and Officers.** The names and usual business addresses of the corporation's current directors and officers must be provided so that potential investors are able to investigate the backgrounds of the managers of the corporation.

Other states may impose additional requirements, such as requiring a description of the business the foreign corporation proposes doing in the state or a description of its stock.

Certificate of good standing
Document issued by state of incorporation verifying corporation is in compliance with state requirements (also called "certificate of existence")

The application must usually be accompanied by a **certificate of good standing** (sometimes called a *certificate of existence*) issued by the secretary of state of the state of incorporation. This is obtained from the state of incorporation upon request and payment of a fee. The secretary of state of the state of incorporation will check various state records to ensure the corporation is in good standing, meaning that it has paid its taxes and has complied with any reporting or other requirements. The certificate is presented to the foreign state as a method of assuring that state that the foreign corporation will comply with the foreign state's laws as well. (See Figure 13-1 for a sample application for certificate of authority to transact business in Delaware.)

Upon its filing with the secretary of state, the application will be reviewed to ensure it complies with the statutory requirements. The secretary of state will then issue a certificate of authority. The foreign corporation may then transact business in the state.

E. Effects of Qualifying

There are four primary effects on foreign corporations that have qualified to do business in another state.

1. The foreign corporation will be subject to any restrictions imposed on domestic corporations. For example, a corporation formed in New Jersey and that operates a gambling casino there may be precluded from operating a casino in Ohio if Ohio does not permit its own domestic corporations to operate for gambling purposes. The internal affairs of the qualifying corporation (such as amending its bylaws, giving notice of meetings, and other similar matters) are governed by its state of incorporation.
2. The foreign corporation will be subject to service of process in the new state. Service of process on the registered agent in the foreign state is as effective as service of process on the corporation's agent in its own state of incorporation.
3. The corporation must pay various fees and taxes to the state that has permitted it to transact business within its borders. These fees and taxes vary from state to state. Some states impose a flat annual tax; other states assess a tax based on the amount of business conducted in the foreign state that year.
4. The corporation must usually file annual reports with the state. The annual report is generally a fairly simple form sent to the corporation each year by the secretary of state. Annual reports are discussed in

STATE *of* DELAWARE
FOREIGN CORPORATION CERTIFICATE

- **The Undersigned,** a corporation duly organized and existing under the laws of the State of _____, in accordance with the provisions of Section 371 of Title 8 of the Delaware Code, does hereby certify:

- **First:** That _____ is a corporation duly organized and existing under the laws of the State of _____ _____ and is filing herewith a certificate evidencing its corporate existence.

- **Second:** That the name and address of its Registered Agent in said State of Delaware upon whom service of process may be had is

- **Third:** That the assets of said corporation are $_____ and the liabilities thereof are $_____. The assets and liabilities indicated are as of a date within six months prior to the filing date of this Certificate.

- **Fourth:** That the business which it proposes to do in the State of Delaware is as follows:

- **Fifth:** That the business which it proposes to do in the state of Delaware is the business it is authorized to do in the jurisdiction of its incorporation.

- **In Witness Whereof,** said corporation has caused this Certificate to be signed on its behalf this _____ day of _____, 20_____.

By:_____
(Authorized Officer)

Name:_____
(Typed or Printed)

Chapter Eight. Most states now require that annual reports be filed electronically with the state.

PRACTICE TIP

For each corporate client, maintain a master list indicating its state of incorporation and then each of the states in which it is qualified to transact business. The list should specify the agent for service of process in each state and each state's requirements and due date for annual reports. Send reminders to clients about 45 to 60 days before each annual report is due. Periodically revisit the list with the client to make sure that the client withdraws its qualification from any state in which it has ceased to do business.

F. Effects of Failure to Qualify

Although they vary from state to state, sanctions are imposed on corporations that have transacted business in a foreign jurisdiction without first having qualified to do so. MBCA § 15.02 provides the following penalties for transacting business in a foreign jurisdiction without authority:

1. The foreign corporation may not maintain a proceeding in any court in the foreign state until it obtains a certificate of authority; and
2. Monetary penalties will be imposed for each day the corporation was not properly qualified (not to exceed a stated amount).

Some states have a harsher approach. A state may provide that any acts performed by the unqualified corporation are void, that its contracts are unenforceable, and that fines may be imposed directly on corporate officers and directors. For example, Alabama provides that the contracts of unauthorized corporations are void.

The more permissive approach and that adopted by the MBCA is to refuse to allow an unqualified corporation to maintain a legal action. The corporation may, however, defend itself in any legal action, and the contracts it entered into are valid. Most states allow a corporation that has failed to qualify to cure the defect by subsequent qualification, even during a lawsuit.

G. Effects of Changes to Domestic Corporation

Just as a domestic corporation must inform the secretary of state of a change of corporate name or merger, so also must a corporation qualified to transact business in a foreign state inform that state of such changes.

Generally, when a corporation amends its articles of incorporation in its state of incorporation it must also file a certified copy of the amended articles (or amend

FIGURE 13-2

Oregon Application for Amendment/Withdrawal of a Foreign Corporation

Phone: (503) 986-2200
Fax: (503) 378-4381

Secretary of State
Corporation Division
255 Capitol St. NE, Suite 151
Salem, OR 97310-1327
FilingInOregon.com

Application for Amendment/Withdrawal—Foreign Corporation

Check the appropriate box below:

☐ AMENDMENT TO APPLICATION FOR AUTHORITY
(Complete only 1, 2, 8, 9)

☐ WITHDRAWAL OF AUTHORITY TO TRANSACT
(Complete only 3, 4, 5, 6, 7, 8, 9)

REGISTRY NUMBER: _____

In accordance with Oregon Revised Statute 192.410-192.490, the information on this application is public record. We must release this information to all parties upon request and it will be posted on our website.

For office use only

Please Type or Print Legibly in **Black** Ink. Attach Additional Sheet if Necessary.

AMENDMENT TO APPLICATION ONLY

1) **ENTITY NAME** _____

2) **AMENDMENT** (The amendment is as follows.)

_____
_____
_____
_____
_____
_____
_____
_____

WITHDRAWAL OF AUTHORITY TO TRANSACT BUSINESS ONLY

3) **NAME** _____

4) **STATE OR COUNTRY OF INCORPORATION** _____

5) **THIS CORPORATION IS NOT TRANSACTING BUSINESS IN OREGON, AND SURRENDERS ITS AUTHORITY TO TRANSACT BUSINESS IN OREGON.**

6) **THIS CORPORATION REVOKES THE AUTHORITY OF ITS REGISTERED AGENT TO ACCEPT SERVICE ON ITS BEHALF AND APPOINTS THE SECRETARY OF STATE AS ITS AGENT FOR SERVICE OF PROCESS IN ANY PROCEEDING BASED ON A CAUSE OF ACTION ARISING DURING THE TIME IT WAS AUTHORIZED TO TRANSACT BUSINESS IN OREGON.**

7) **MAILING ADDRESS** (The address to which the person initiating any proceeding may mail to this Corporation a copy of any process served on the Secretary of State. The Corporation will notify the Corporation Division, Business Registry of any change in this mailing address for a period of five years from the date of this withdrawal.)

_____
_____
_____

8) **EXECUTION**

Signature   Printed Name   Title

_____   _____   _____

9) **CONTACT NAME** (To resolve questions with this filing.)   **DAYTIME PHONE NUMBER** (Include area code.)

_____   _____

FEES	
Required Processing Fee	$50
Confirmation Copy (Optional)	$5
Processing Fees are nonrefundable. Please make check payable to "Corporation Division."	
Note: Fees may be paid with VISA or MasterCard. The card number and expiration date should be submitted on a separate sheet for your protection.	

123 (Rev. 8/07)

its certificate of authority to transact business) in any state in which it transacts business as a foreign corporation (see Figure 13-2). Merely changing a registered agent or registered office is less complicated, and a more simplified form is used.

H.   Withdrawal of Foreign Qualification

Withdrawal
Process of canceling authority to do business in a foreign state

When a corporation ceases doing business in a state in which it previously qualified, it should file an application for **withdrawal**. This will ensure that the corporation is no longer subject to service of process, taxes, or annual reporting requirements in the state.

The application for withdrawal form is usually provided by the secretary of state. (See Figure 13-2 for a sample form for application for withdrawal.) The corporation must provide an address so that the secretary of state can forward any process for any action later filed against the corporation. After examining the application, the secretary of state will issue a certificate of withdrawal. The corporation is then no longer authorized to transact business in the state.

I.   Revocation of Qualification by State

Revocation
Action by a state withdrawing a foreign corporation's authority to do business in that state

In some instances, a state in which a foreign corporation has qualified to transact business may revoke that authority. Typically, **revocation** is triggered by some unlawful act of the corporation or its failure to comply with the state's laws. Common reasons for revocation are failure to file annual reports, failure to pay taxes, or failure to have a registered agent.

Most states provide a delinquency notice to the corporation before revoking its authority to transact business in the state. The corporation is given a period within which to cure its default. If it does not do so, the secretary of state will revoke the corporation's authority to conduct business in the state. In many states, a corporation may apply to be reinstated, especially if the corporation's authority to transact business was revoked for an administrative reason such as failing to file reports or pay taxes. Reinstatement is discussed further in Chapter Fourteen.

J.   Role of Paralegal

Almost all of the activities relating to qualifying a corporation to transact business in a foreign jurisdiction can be performed by paralegals, including the following:

- Applying for name registration;
- Researching state statutes to determine what activities constitute "transacting business" and the procedures for qualifying;
- Making arrangements for someone to serve as an agent for service of process for the corporation in the foreign state (see Chapter Eight for list of agents);

- Obtaining a certificate of good standing from the state of incorporation;
- Preparing and filing the application for authority to transact business in the foreign state (see Figure 13-1);
- Calendaring the dates for annual reports and tax payments; and
- Preparing the application for withdrawal when a corporation ceases to do business in a foreign jurisdiction (see Figure 13-2).

Case Illustration
Effect of Failure to Qualify

Case: *Horton v. Richards*, 594 P.2d 891 (Utah 1979)

Facts: The plaintiff, a Washington corporation, brought suit against a defendant for breach of contract in Utah, although it had not qualified in Utah as a foreign corporation. The trial court dismissed the complaint.

Holding: The court affirmed the lower court. There was ample evidence that the plaintiff was transacting business in Utah. It maintained telephone directory listings, bank accounts, and its president held himself out to be the president of the company's Utah operations. In such a case, the corporation was required to qualify in Utah before transacting business. Because it did not, it was barred from seeking affirmative relief in Utah's courts.

Key Features
of Foreign Qualification

- ◆ Corporations that intend to transact business in other states must "qualify" or be approved by the foreign jurisdiction prior to commencing business in those states.
- ◆ Not all activities are considered to be "transacting business" such that a corporation must qualify in the foreign state. Some activities are considered relatively peripheral or isolated and thus do not require qualification.
- ◆ To qualify, the corporation must complete the foreign state's form and pay a filing fee. The corporation must have an agent for service of process in the foreign state. Qualification will result in the corporation being amenable to service of process in the foreign state and will require the corporation to file annual reports and pay various taxes and fees to the foreign jurisdiction.

- ◆ If a corporation transacts business without qualifying, it is usually forbidden from maintaining an action in that state's courts and may be subject to monetary fines. Other states take a harsher approach and provide that acts engaged in by the unqualified corporation are void.
- ◆ When a corporation makes changes in its state of incorporation or to its articles of incorporation, it should conduct research to determine if foreign jurisdictions in which it operates must be informed of those changes.
- ◆ Once a corporation ceases doing business in the foreign jurisdiction, it should withdraw its qualification.

Internet Resources

State statutes:	www.law.cornell.edu www.findlaw.com
Text of MBCA:	www.abanet.org/buslaw/committees/ CL270000pub/nosearch/mbca/home.shtml
General information:	www.megalaw.com www.findlaw.com
Secretaries of state:	www.nass.org (for links to secretaries of state and downloadable forms for applications to qualify to transact business)
Corporation service companies:	corp.delaware.gov/agents/agts.shtml (Delaware) www.ss.ca.gov/business/bpd_service_companies.htm (California)
Forms:	www.allaboutforms.com www.lectlaw.com (These sites offer forms for notices of meetings, minutes of meetings, corporate resolutions, and other related forms.)

Key Terms

Domestic corporation
Foreign corporation
Transacting business
Qualifying to transact business

Certificate of good standing
Withdrawal
Revocation

Discussion Questions

Fact Scenario. Your Fitness, Inc., is an Oregon corporation engaged in providing fitness classes and related products in Oregon. Use the MBCA to answer the following questions.

1. The corporation would like to sell exercise DVDs over the Internet to locations all around the country. Must the corporation qualify in other states to engage in this activity? Discuss.

2. The corporation has decided to expand into Washington and build several fitness centers there, would like to open various bank accounts in Idaho, and would like to offer one training session to Ted Turner while he is at his ranch in Montana next week. The corporation is also selling various vitamin supplements by taking telephone orders for them and then shipping the vitamins to other states. Must the corporation qualify in these states to engage in these activities? Discuss.

3. Assume that the corporation has qualified to transact business in California. The corporation has amended its articles to change its name to Your Fitness Guru, Corp. What effect does this amendment have, if any, with regard to the corporation's activities in California?

4. If a consumer wishes to sue the corporation in California, who should be served with the summons and complaint?

5. Because its California operations are not profitable, the corporation intends to close its fitness centers in California. What should the corporation do?

6. The corporation has opened a large fitness center in Arizona but has not qualified to transact business there. It has sued its landlord for breach of contract, and he has alleged that he need not pay any damages because the corporation was not properly qualified to transact business in Arizona. Is this a valid defense? What are other possible consequences to the corporation of not qualifying?

Net Worth

1. Access the Web site for Florida's secretary of state. Review the form and cover letter for filing an application to transact business for a for-profit corporation in Florida.
   a. What is the filing fee to file this form?
   b. Is a photocopy of the certificate of existence acceptable?
   c. How long is the certificate of existence valid?
2. Access the Web site for Delaware's secretary of state.
   a. What is the filing fee in Delaware for a foreign corporation to apply to conduct business in Delaware?
   b. Review the information relating to obtaining a corporate certificate of good standing. What is the filing fee to obtain a short-form certificate?
   c. Review the Corporate Certificate Cover Memo. What fee must be paid if one wishes to receive the certificate in one hour?
3. What is the fee in Ohio if a foreign corporation wishes to file a surrender of its application to transact business?

14

♦ ♦ ♦

Termination of Corporate Existence

♦ ♦ ♦

A. Introduction

Just as a corporation can only be created by strict compliance with state statutes, it can only be terminated or dissolved in accordance with state statutes. There are three types of dissolution: voluntary dissolution initiated by the directors or, occasionally, the shareholders; administrative dissolution, initiated by the secretary of state for technical defaults (such as failure to pay taxes); and involuntary dissolution, initiated by the state, shareholders, or creditors. Dissolution ends the corporation's status as a legal "person."

3 Kinds

Once the decision to dissolve has been made, all of the corporation's business must be completed, creditors must be paid, and shareholders must receive any remaining assets. This process of winding up the business affairs of a corporation is called liquidation.

B. Dissolution

Termination of the corporation's existence as a legal entity is referred to as **dissolution**. Dissolution may occur for a variety of reasons: the term of duration specified in the articles of incorporation may expire; the corporation's business may be unprofitable; or the corporation may have merged into another corporation.

Dissolution
Termination of the legal status of an entity

197

1. *Voluntary Dissolution*

A corporation may be dissolved at any time after it is formed. In most cases, a corporation is dissolved only after it has conducted business for some time and has issued shares. Once shares have been issued, shareholders must approve the decision to dissolve because shareholders are the actual owners of the corporation. A dissolution initiated by the corporation itself, namely, its directors or shareholders, is referred to as a **voluntary dissolution**.

Typically, the decision to dissolve is initiated by the directors. As the managers of the corporation, they are in the best position to know whether dissolution is appropriate. The directors will propose dissolution and this will be approved at a directors' meeting by majority vote or by written consent, which must be unanimous.

The directors will then recommend dissolution to the shareholders and must call a special meeting of shareholders to vote on the proposed dissolution, the notice of which must be given to all shareholders, whether or not they are entitled to vote. The notice must specify that the purpose of the meeting is to consider dissolution. Most states require a simple majority vote of shareholders to approve dissolution. Some states, however, require a two-thirds approval. The MBCA approach is similar to its approach on amendments to the articles of incorporation and mergers: The dissolution will be approved if more votes are cast in favor of it than against it. MBCA § 14.02 and § 7.25. Shareholders seldom have appraisal rights because they will share in assets remaining after creditors have been paid.

In some states, such as California, the next step in the dissolution process is for the corporation to file with the secretary of state a **notice of intent to dissolve**, which provides public notice to creditors and others of the corporation's plans to dissolve. The MBCA and many states do not require this public notice; they merely provide that after dissolution is authorized, the corporation may proceed to dissolve by filing articles of dissolution with the secretary of state.

Some states allow shareholders to initiate a voluntary dissolution. Generally, unanimous approval of shareholders is required on the basis that because the shareholders do not manage the corporation they are not likely to be in the best position to evaluate whether dissolution is wise. On the other hand, if *all* of the owners of the corporation agree that it should be dissolved, there is no logical reason it should not be.

2. *Articles of Dissolution*

After dissolution has been approved by both the directors and shareholders, **articles of dissolution** (sometimes called a certificate of dissolution) are prepared and filed with the secretary of state in the state of incorporation. Most states provide forms for the articles of dissolution. Generally, the articles must set forth the following items: the name of the corporation, the date dissolution was authorized, and that the dissolution was approved by the requisite shareholder vote. In some states, including California, the corporation must also state that all of its known debts and liabilities have been paid or assumed and that its remaining assets have been distributed to the persons entitled thereto.

The articles of dissolution are filed in the office of the secretary of state with the appropriate filing fee. The secretary of state will usually require that the corporation submit appropriate documentation showing it does not owe any

---

Voluntary dissolution
Dissolution initiated by a corporation's directors or shareholders

Notice of intent to dissolve
Document filed with state indicating corporation's intent to dissolve

Articles of dissolution
Final document filed with state effecting termination of an entity (also called *certificate of dissolution*)

FIGURE 14-1

Sample Certificate of Dissolution

CERTIFICATE OF DISSOLUTION
STOCK CORPORATION
Office of the Secretary of the State

MAILING ADDRESS:
Commercial Recording Division
Connecticut Secretary of the State
P.O. Box 150470
Hartford, CT 06115-0470
860-509-6003

DELIVERY ADDRESS:
Commercial Recording Division
Connecticut Secretary of the State
30 Trinity Street
Hartford, CT 06106
860-509-6003

Space For Office Use Only	Filing Fee $25.00	Make Checks Payable To "Secretary of the State"

1. NAME OF CORPORATION

2. DATE ON WHICH DISSOLUTION WAS AUTHORIZED _____ / _____ / _____

3. Complete Block (A) if Dissolution was authorized by incorporators or initial directors <u>or</u> block (B) if Dissolution was authorized by directors and shareholders.

(A) Place a check mark next to either 1 <u>or</u> 2 as appropriate:

_____ 1. None of the corporation's shares have been issued   _____ 2. The corporation has not commenced business

The undersigned makes the following assertions in connection with the selection made under section (A) of this form: that no debt of the corporation remains unpaid; that if shares were issued, the net assets of the corporation remaining after winding up have been distributed to the shareholders; and that a majority of the incorporators or initial directors authorized the dissolution.

(B) _____ The proposal to dissolve was duly approved by the shareholders in the manner required by sections 33-600 to 33-998 (inclusive) of the Connecticut General Statutes, and by the Certificate of Incorporation.

4. EXECUTION

Dated this _____ day of _____, 20_____.

Print or type name of signatory	Capacity of signatory	Signature

<u>NOTE: A corporation may only revoke its dissolution within 120 days following the effective date of such dissolution.</u>

Revised 1/2008

outstanding taxes to the state. Most states supply forms for tax clearance. The corporation must also notify the Internal Revenue Service (using Form 966) within 30 days that it is dissolving and make arrangements to pay federal taxes. See Figure 14-1 for a sample certificate of dissolution.

3. Revocation of Dissolution

Almost all states allow corporations to revoke the decision to dissolve by filing articles of revocation of dissolution. Revocation must be approved by the board and then the requisite vote of shareholders. The MBCA allows a corporation to revoke its decision to dissolve within 120 days of the effective date of the dissolution, in which case it is as if dissolution never occurred.

4. Dissolution Under the MBCA

The MBCA requires only one document to effect dissolution, the articles of dissolution, and the corporation is dissolved upon the effective date specified in the articles of dissolution. After the articles of dissolution are filed, the corporation is a "dissolved corporation," but it continues its existence for the purpose of winding up and liquidating its business and affairs and distributing remaining assets to shareholders. Thus, in this approach, dissolution precedes liquidation.

In some states, such as California, liquidation (or winding up the business affairs of the corporation) precedes dissolution, and the articles of dissolution must recite that all known debts have been paid and that assets have been distributed to shareholders. This approach would seem to provide more comfort to creditors because the corporation will not be allowed to dissolve unless its directors state under penalty of perjury that the debts and liabilities have been taken care of and assets have been distributed to those entitled to them.

5. Administrative Dissolution

Nearly all states and the MBCA recognize a type of dissolution that is less serious than involuntary dissolution. In these states, a corporation may be administratively dissolved for one of the following reasons: its failure to pay taxes or file annual reports; failure to have a registered agent for some period of time (often 60 days) or to notify the secretary of state that its registered agent or office have changed; or for continuing to operate after the corporation's period of duration expires. Grounds of this nature are often called *technical*—or *administrative*—*defaults*. Under the MBCA, an action for **administrative dissolution** based on technical defaults is not brought in court; it is handled through the office of the secretary of state, thereby greatly simplifying the process. MBCA § 14.20.

Many states and the MBCA provide for notice to the corporation of technical defaults and give the corporation an opportunity to cure them (often within 60 days). A number of states also allow a corporation to petition to be **reinstated** or revived within a certain period of time (two years under the MBCA) after it has been dissolved on technical grounds if the corporation cures its defaults. If the corporation is reinstated, it is as if the dissolution never occurred. Generally, if the grounds for dissolution were not technical, a corporation may not be reinstated.

Administrative dissolution
A dissolution initiated for technical or administrative defaults, such as failing to file reports or pay taxes

Reinstatement
Process of reviving a corporation dissolved for administrative reasons

PRACTICE TIP

Because a corporation can be dissolved by the state for failure to file annual reports and pay taxes, you should maintain an accurate docket or calendar for all corporate clients. Although many states provide reminder notices to corporations that annual reports are due, clients are often so busy they neglect to file the report on time. Use your docket to remind clients of the critical deadline for filing the annual report.

6. Involuntary Dissolution

Some statutes allow for the dissolution of corporations even when dissolution is not desired by the board of directors. This is referred to as an **involuntary dissolution** or, because the dissolution proceeding is brought before a court, it is also called a **judicial dissolution**. If dissolution is involuntary, a court will enter a decree of dissolution. A corporation may be involuntarily dissolved by the state, its shareholders, or unsatisfied creditors.

Action by the State. Corporations exist only by virtue of the authority of their creator, the state of incorporation. Because a state always has the power and authority to ensure compliance with its laws, a corporation may be dissolved by the state. An action for involuntary dissolution is usually brought by the state attorney general for one of the following reasons. The corporation has:

- Procured the articles of incorporation through fraud; or
- Exceeded or abused the authority given to the corporation by the state.

Action by the Shareholders. If directors act fraudulently or waste corporate assets, it may be nearly impossible for a voluntary dissolution to occur. The negligent directors will not pass a resolution to dissolve a corporation they are in the process of looting. If the directors own stock in the corporation, unanimous shareholder consent is impossible, because acting in their capacity as shareholders, the directors will not vote for dissolution.

In situations such as these, a shareholder may institute a legal action and request that a court dissolve the corporation. To prevail, the shareholder must generally establish one of the following:

- The directors are deadlocked in managing the business of the corporation and irreparable injury is being suffered by or threatened to the corporation;
- Corporate management has acted in an illegal, oppressive, or fraudulent manner;
- The shareholders are deadlocked and have failed to elect directors at two successive annual meetings;
- The corporate assets are being wasted or misapplied; or
- The corporation has failed to conduct business for some statutorily specified period of time.

Involuntary dissolution
Dissolution against the will of a corporation, initiated by state, shareholders, or creditors (also called *judicial dissolution*)

Judicial dissolution
Dissolution brought before court (also called *involuntary dissolution*)

Because dissolution is such a drastic remedy, MBCA § 14.34 and many state statutes provide that if a shareholder alleges one of the grounds specified above, as an alternative to dissolution the corporation or another shareholder may elect to purchase all of the shares owned by the complaining shareholder at their fair market value. This remedy (and the ability of a shareholder to bring an action for judicial dissolution) is not available if the corporation's shares are publicly traded because shareholders of publicly traded corporations can always sell their shares on the open market.

A new provision of the MBCA allows a shareholder to obtain involuntary dissolution in the event the corporation has abandoned its business, but those in control of the corporation have unreasonably delayed in liquidating it and distributing its assets (which may occur if the directors in power wish to continue receiving their salaries). In such an event, a delayed liquidation prejudices creditors and shareholders. MBCA § 14.30(5).

In corporations in which directors hold large amounts of stock, it may be possible for the directors to force a dissolution over the wishes of the minority shareholders. For example, assume a corporation has five directors, three of whom own a total of 52 percent of the corporation's stock. The remaining 48 percent of the stock is held by 100 individuals. Because the three powerful directors constitute a majority of the board, they could pass a resolution recommending dissolution; because they own more than a majority of the outstanding stock, as shareholders their affirmative votes are sufficient to approve a dissolution. If the corporation's business is profitable, they could then dissolve the corporation, pay off the existing shareholders, and form a new company by themselves to do the same business as before and keep all the profits. This type of oppression is known as a *freeze-out* or a *squeeze-out*. Because it is patently inequitable to the minority shareholders, courts will prevent or enjoin dissolutions that have the effect of oppressing minority shareholders and have no legitimate business purpose.

Action by a Creditor.   A creditor of the corporation may institute a proceeding for judicial dissolution of a corporation. Typically, the creditor must establish that the corporation is insolvent and that the creditor has either received a judgment against the corporation for the claim or that the corporation has acknowledged in writing that the claim is owed. Because creditors' claims must be paid before assets are distributed to shareholders upon dissolution, a creditor may believe it is in her best interest to force a dissolution and thereby collect some amount of the claim rather than no amount at all if the corporation is refusing to pay the debt.

C. Liquidation

1. Introduction

Liquidation
Process of collecting assets, paying debts, and distributing remains to business owners (also called *winding up*)

In many states, before a corporation can terminate its legal existence, it must conduct the process of **liquidation**, sometimes called *winding up*. Under MBCA § 14.05, liquidation involves the following activities:

1. Collecting assets;
2. Disposing of properties that will not be distributed to shareholders;

3. Discharging liabilities or making provisions for discharging liabilities; and
4. Distributing the remaining property to the shareholders according to their respective interests.

Additionally, if the corporation is authorized to transact business in other states, the corporation should withdraw its certificate of authority in those states.

2. Nonjudicial Liquidation

When dissolution is voluntary (initiated by the directors or shareholders) or administrative, the officers and directors will liquidate the corporation. Contracts will be completed, creditors will be notified to submit their claims, assets will be collected, creditors will be paid, and the remains will be distributed to shareholders in accordance with their preferences, if any.

Nonjudicial liquidation
Process of winding up by managers of a business entity

3. Judicial Liquidation

A dissolution initiated by the state, shareholders, or creditors is often caused by the directors' failure to manage the corporation properly, oppressive conduct, or by waste of corporate assets. Because a court therefore cannot place confidence in corporate management to conduct liquidation properly, in the event of an involuntary dissolution, the court generally appoints a **receiver** (or *liquidator*) whose function is to receive the assets of the corporation and distribute them to the creditors and then to the shareholders.

Judicial liquidation
Process of winding up by court appointee

Receiver
One appointed by a court to oversee liquidation (also called *liquidator*)

4. Claims Against the Corporation

There are two types of claims that must be resolved by a dissolving corporation: **known claims** (those claims and obligations the corporation knows about) and **unknown claims** (claims that have not yet matured or surfaced against the corporation, for example, claims for injuries that may be sustained in the future due to a defective product the corporation has made). Corporations may not use dissolutions to avoid obligations.

The MBCA provides an orderly process for disposing of claims against the corporation. As for known claims, the corporation may notify the claimants in writing of the dissolution, inform the creditor or claimant where to submit claims, provide at least 120 days for the creditor to make the claim, and inform the creditor that the claim will be barred if not timely submitted to the corporation.

As to unknown claims, the corporation may place a notice of its dissolution in a newspaper of general circulation stating that any claims against the corporation will be barred unless an action to enforce the claim is brought within three years of publication of the newspaper notice. If the corporation's assets have been distributed before the claim is made, shareholders may be liable, but only to the extent of assets distributed to them. The corporation may provide for such unknown claims by purchasing insurance or setting aside some portion of its assets. Alternatively, under MBCA § 14.08, a corporation may initiate a court proceeding to establish an amount that should be set aside for unknown claims.

Known claim
A claim known by an entity

Unknown claim
A claim that has not yet been made against an entity

D. Distributions to Shareholders

Liquidation distribution
Distribution to shareholders in liquidation process

After all debts have been discharged and any expenses of liquidation have been paid, and assuming any assets remain, the shareholders are entitled to receive a distribution, generally called a **liquidation distribution**. Directors are personally liable for distributing assets to shareholders without first paying off claims of creditors, including claims for taxes and employee wages and ordinary debts and obligations, such as rent and insurance owed.

Corporate assets are typically sold and converted to "liquid" form, namely cash, and shareholders will receive cash payments. If preferences exist, they must be honored. Shareholders participate in the distribution according to their ownership interests. For example, if a shareholder owns 9 percent of the common stock of the corporation, the shareholder will be entitled to receive 9 percent of any liquidation distribution made to common shareholders.

E. Role of Paralegal

Paralegals play a direct role in terminating the existence of a corporation and are involved in the following activities:

- Drafting directors' resolutions (or written consent actions) recommending dissolution;
- Preparing notice of the shareholders' meeting to vote on the dissolution and minutes of the meeting;
- Preparing and filing the notice of intent to dissolve with the secretary of state, if required by the state;
- Preparing notices to be sent to known creditors informing them to submit their claims against the corporation and preparing the newspaper notice to be published so that unknown creditors can make claims against the corporation;
- Preparing and filing the articles of dissolution (see Figure 14-1); and
- Assisting in the distribution of assets by preparing deeds, assignments, and other instruments to transfer title from the corporation to the shareholders.

Case Illustration
Dissolution Cannot Be Used to Accomplish a Freeze-Out

Case: *Callier v. Callier*, 378 N.E.2d 405 (Ill. App. Ct. 1978)

Facts: A shareholder brought a suit to liquidate the assets and business of the corporation, and the court ordered such liquidation, based on allegations that the management was deadlocked and irreparable injury was being threatened. The other shareholder (who held an equal interest) was opposed to liquidation.

Holding: The appellate court reversed. There was no evidence of any management deadlock. In fact, the evidence showed that the director-shareholder who petitioned for liquidation was in the process of forming another company to carry on the same kind of business with many of the corporation's employees and customers. Such siphoning off of the value of the corporation is a breach of fiduciary duty and would deprive the other shareholder of his value in the corporation.

Key Features
of Corporate Dissolution and Liquidation

- ◆ Corporations may dissolve voluntarily (usually by action of the directors, which is then approved by shareholders), administratively (for technical defaults such as failure to pay taxes), or involuntarily (by action by the state, shareholders, or creditors).
- ◆ Dissolution usually refers to termination of the corporate entity, whereas liquidation refers to termination of the corporation's business and affairs.
- ◆ If dissolution is voluntary, articles of dissolution will be filed with the state. If dissolution is involuntary, a court will enter a decree of dissolution.
- ◆ An administrative dissolution may be initiated by the state for technical reasons (such as failing to pay taxes). A corporation that is dissolved for such reasons can generally apply to be reinstated.
- ◆ An involuntary dissolution may be initiated by the state if the corporation exceeds state authority or has procured its articles through fraud. Reinstatement is not generally permissible in such an event.
- ◆ Shareholders may initiate a dissolution, often because of director misconduct. In lieu of ordering a dissolution, a court may allow the complaining shareholder's shares to be purchased.
- ◆ Creditors may initiate a dissolution if the corporation is insolvent and their claims are undisputed.
- ◆ If dissolution is voluntary, corporate management will supervise liquidation; if dissolution is involuntary, a court will supervise liquidation.
- ◆ Corporations must generally notify all known claimants and instruct them to submit their claims to the corporation within a certain period of time or be barred thereafter. As to unknown claims, corporations generally publish a notice in a newspaper, and claimants may enforce their claims within three years thereafter.
- ◆ During liquidation, the expenses of liquidation will be paid, creditors will be paid, and then remaining assets will be distributed to shareholders on a pro rata basis in accordance with any preferences.

Internet Resources	
State statutes:	www.law.cornell.edu www.findlaw.com
Text of MBCA:	www.abanet.org/buslaw/committees/ CL270000pub/nosearch/mbca/home.shtml
General information:	www.megalaw.com www.findlaw.com
Secretaries of state:	www.nass.org (for links to secretaries of state and downloadable forms for articles of dissolution)
Forms:	www.allaboutforms.com www.lectlaw.com www.siccode.com/forms.php (These sites offer forms for notices of meetings, minutes of meetings, corporate resolutions, and other related forms.)

Key Terms

Dissolution
Voluntary dissolution
Involuntary dissolution
Notice of intent to dissolve
Judicial dissolution
Articles of dissolution
Administrative dissolution
Reinstatement

Liquidation
Nonjudicial liquidation
Judicial liquidation
Receiver
Known claim
Unknown claim
Liquidation distribution

Discussion Questions

Fact Scenario. KidVid, Inc., a California corporation, was incorporated several years ago but has recently experienced a slowdown, and several creditors are demanding payment for their debts. The corporation has two classes of stock, one of which is nonvoting stock. Use the MBCA to answer these questions.

1. The board of directors has proposed dissolving the corporation and will now submit this proposal for dissolution to the shareholders. Which shareholders are entitled to notice of a meeting to vote on dissolution?

2. The corporation filed its articles of dissolution on March 1 of this year and began to liquidate. On May 1, it received a significant contract that will allow the corporation to make a profit. Is there anything the corporation can do with respect to its dissolution?

3. The corporation sent a notice to one of its creditors, Thad, and stated that Thad's claim would be barred if not received in six months. Thad submitted his claim to the corporation seven months after the corporation sent him notice. Will Thad's claim be paid? Discuss. What result would occur if the corporation's notice stated that the claim would be barred if not received in three months?

4. May Thad initiate an action to dissolve the corporation? Discuss.

5. Assume that the corporation's six directors have not been able to make any decisions regarding the corporation's business and have not been able to make a decision whether the corporation should be dissolved. What might Shareholder A do to resolve such a dilemma? Is there anything Shareholder B can do if Shareholder B is opposed to Shareholder A's action?

6. Assume that the secretary of state dissolved a corporation on June 1 of this year because it did not timely file its annual report. May the corporation be revived? If so, when must the corporation apply for reinstatement? Assume that the corporation entered into a contract after the time it was administratively dissolved and before it was revived. Is the contract valid? Discuss.

7. Assume that a corporation distributed all of its assets in liquidation, and its three shareholders received 50 percent, 40 percent, and 10 percent of the corporation's net assets of $100,000, respectively. If a valid claim is made against the dissolved corporation in the amount of $50,000, how will this be paid?

Net Worth

1. Access the Web site of the South Carolina Secretary of State. What is the fee to file articles of dissolution?

2. Access the Web site of the California Secretary of State and review the Certificate of Election to Wind Up and Dissolve. What "Note" is provided at the top of the form?

3. Access the Web site of the Pennsylvania Secretary of State. What is the fee to file a Statement of Revival for a domestic corporation?

4. Access the Web site of the Ohio Secretary of State and review the form for reinstatement of a corporation. If a corporation has been administratively dissolved, and applies for reinstatement 18 months later, what will happen if its name was taken by another entity last month?

5. Review IRS form 966. Who must file this form?

15

◆ ◆ ◆
_____

Corporate Variations
_____
◆ ◆ ◆

A. Introduction

The major portion of this text has been devoted to the business corporation, the most common type of corporation in the United States. Its distinguishing characteristics are its status as a legal person, which gives rise to double taxation, and the protection of its owners from personal liability. Formed for a profit-making purpose, the business corporation is well suited to the needs of many entrepreneurs. However, other types of corporations are created for specialized purposes, goals, and groups. This chapter briefly examines these other types of corporations and corporations whose shares are publicly traded on the national exchanges.

B. Close Corporations

1. Introduction

A **close corporation** (or _closely held corporation_ or _statutory close corporation_) is a corporation whose stock is not publicly traded. Its stock is generally held by a small group of family members or friends. In most instances, these shareholders are involved in the management of the business of the corporation, and the corporation functions informally. Failure to adhere strictly to some corporate formalities, such as holding meetings and elections, will generally not result in piercing the corporate veil to hold individual shareholders liable for corporate obligations in a close corporation.

Some states have special statutes to address the needs of these smaller owner-managed corporations, which are then referred to as _statutory close corporations_. In other states, close corporations are required to follow all of the statutes relating to corporations in general, except when case law has liberalized those statutes.

Close corporation
Corporation whose shares are held by a small group that is active in managing the corporation (also called _closely held corporation_ or _statutory close corporation_)

209

The increasing popularity of the limited liability partnership (LLP) and limited liability company (LLC), now recognized in all states, will undoubtedly result in fewer close corporations. For example, there are no restrictions on the number of people who may be involved in an LLP or LLC (as there are for close corporations), and both the LLP and the LLC offer pass-through taxation, whereas the close corporation may be subject to double taxation.

2.   Characteristics of Close Corporations

Close corporations share a number of features in common, including the following:

- There is a limitation on the number of shareholders in a close corporation. Some states and the Model Statutory Close Corporation Supplement (MSCCS), a section of special statutes added to the MBCA relating to close corporations, permit up to 50 shareholders, but other states restrict the number of shareholders to 25 or 30.
- The shareholders typically enter into agreements restricting the transfer of shares so that "outsiders" cannot easily enter the entity and upset the working relationships of the family members and friends in the close corporation. Thus, there is no readily available market for the shares of a close corporation. Moreover, the stock is not publicly traded. Under the MSCCS, restrictions on transfers of shares are automatic, and the corporation is given a right of first refusal to purchase any shares a shareholder may wish to sell.
- All or most of the shareholders participate in the management of the corporation.

3.   Formation of Close Corporations

A close corporation is formed in the same way as any other corporation: by filing of articles of incorporation. However, the articles of incorporation for a close corporation must generally recite that the corporation is being formed as a close corporation. Additionally, most states (and the MSCCS) require that the stock certificates for a close corporation contain a conspicuous notice or legend alerting potential purchasers that the corporation is a close corporation and that the rights of shareholders may differ materially from those of shareholders in other corporations.

Status as a close corporation will automatically terminate if the articles are amended to reflect such or if any of the conditions required of a close corporation are breached, for example, the corporation "goes public" and sells its shares to vast numbers of shareholders.

4.   Operation of Close Corporations

Shareholders are almost always active in managing the close corporation and are usually employees of the corporation as well. Management and governance tend to be less formal than in larger corporations. Recognizing the need for flexibility in management of these smaller corporations, many statutes allow close corporations to eliminate a board of directors (with management being vested in the shareholders), omit bylaws, and eliminate annual meetings. In such cases, the close corporation operates much like a general partnership or member-managed LLC.

Because close corporations often lack corporate formality, dissatisfied creditors often consider piercing the veil to hold shareholders liable for corporate obligations. Most statutes anticipate this problem by providing that the failure of a close corporation to observe the usual corporate formalities is not itself a ground for imposing personal liability on the shareholders.

Because the close corporation almost always involves a group of individuals who are well known to each other, the group will be reluctant to allow in "outsiders" who may then change the dynamics of their organization. Thus, shareholders in close corporations enter into agreements, usually called **buy-sell agreements**, whereby they agree to restrict or limit their ability to sell their shares. Most agreements provide that before a shareholder may sell to an outsider, the corporation and other shareholders must have the first opportunity to purchase the shares. Only when they refuse may the shares then be offered for sale to a third party. Under the MSCCS, the restriction on transfers of shares is automatic. These restrictions mean that shareholders will not have a great deal of liquidity because there is no ready market for their shares.

Buy-sell agreement
Agreement among shareholders regarding transfer of shares

C. Nonprofit Corporations

1. Introduction

Nonprofit (or *not-for-profit*) **corporations** are not formed to earn a profit and do not distribute any part of their income or profit to their members. If approved by the Internal Revenue Service (IRS), their income is not subject to federal taxation. Most states have specific statutes governing formation and operation of nonprofit corporations.

Nonprofit corporation
Corporation formed for a purpose other than to earn a profit (also called *not-for-profit corporation*)

Many states recognize three specific types of nonprofit corporations: those formed primarily for charitable purposes, such as those promoting science, health, education, or the arts (called **public benefit corporations**); those formed primarily for **religious** purposes; and those organized for the mutual benefit of their members, such as homeowners' associations, country clubs, or professional associations (called **mutual benefit corporations**).

Public benefit corporation
Corporation formed primarily for charitable purposes

Religious corporation
Corporation formed for religious purposes

2. Formation of Nonprofit Corporations

Nonprofit corporations are formed by the filing of articles of incorporation. The name of the corporation may be subject to various restrictions. For example, some states do not permit a nonprofit corporation's name to include a signal such as "company." Most states require the corporation to identify its specific purposes in its articles. Merely incorporating in a state as a nonprofit corporation does not

Mutual benefit corporation
Corporation formed for the benefit of its members

automatically qualify the corporation for exemption from federal taxes; the corporation must file a separate application with the IRS for tax-exempt status.

3.   Operation and Governance of Nonprofit Corporations

In many ways, nonprofit corporations function similarly to business corporations. A board of directors is elected, bylaws are adopted, and the directors manage the affairs of the corporation. However, stock is not sold and there are no shareholders. Rather, a **membership** is usually what is offered. Generally, an individual or business member is entitled to only one membership.

Membership
What is offered by nonprofit corporations to their "owners" rather than stock

If the corporation is governed wisely, it may earn a profit. The earning of profit will not affect the corporation's nonprofit status. The corporation, however, may not pay a dividend or distribute the profit to its members or managers. Generally, any profits made should be devoted to the purposes of the corporation, such as providing educational assistance to the needy or grants for scientific research. Although salaries may be paid to corporate managers, if these are excessive and the corporation spends little of its income accomplishing its purported purposes, it may be dissolved by the state or lose its tax-exempt status.

4.   Exemption from Taxation for Nonprofit Corporations

After the nonprofit corporation is formed, it should apply for federal tax-exempt status. After the application is filed, the IRS will issue a ruling or determination letter recognizing the corporation's tax-exempt status. Nonprofit corporations generally pay no state income or real property taxes, although they must file the usual annual reports and pay the usual fees charged by the state of incorporation.

Generally, contributions made to a public benefit corporation (such as the American Heart Association, Inc.) are tax-deductible. Similarly, contributions made to religious organizations are usually tax-deductible by the donor. On the other hand, membership fees paid to mutual benefit associations are generally not deductible unless they qualify as valid business expenses. Thus, dues paid to River Oaks Country Club for social purposes are likely not deductible, but membership dues paid by a paralegal to the National Capital Area Paralegal Association may well be tax-deductible.

D.   Parent and Subsidiary Corporations

1.   Introduction

Parent
A corporation that forms another

Subsidiary
A corporation formed by another

One corporation may form another. The creator corporation is called the **parent**, and the corporation it creates is called a **subsidiary**. A corporation may create different subsidiaries for different business divisions or may form a subsidiary to carry out more risky ventures and not subject the parent's assets to possible liability for these activities.

2. *Formation and Characteristics of Subsidiary Corporations*

A subsidiary corporation is formed like any other corporation: by filing articles of incorporation. No special provisions are required in the articles, and the articles need not recite that the corporation being formed is a subsidiary of another.

If a parent creates several different subsidiaries (*A, B,* and *C*), the subsidiaries are sometimes referred to as brother-sister corporations (because they share the same parent) or as **affiliates**.

The distinguishing characteristic of a parent-subsidiary relationship is that the parent owns either all of the subsidiary's stock or the majority of it, such that the parent may elect the directors of the subsidiary and thereby control its business policies. A subsidiary whose stock is owned solely by the parent is called a **wholly owned subsidiary**.

The existence of a subsidiary may subject the constituents to triple taxation: The subsidiary will pay taxes on the money it earns; the subsidiary will then distribute its profit to its sole shareholder, its parent, which must then pay taxes on the money it has received; when the parent distributes cash dividends to its shareholders, they must pay taxes on the money they receive. The same money thus has been taxed three times.

In mid-2003, Congress reduced individual taxes on cash dividends to 15 percent (5 percent for the lowest two brackets) and agreed to eliminate taxes entirely in 2008 for the lowest two brackets. These dividend reductions are scheduled to expire in 2010.

3. *Liability of Parent for Subsidiary's Debts*

In general, the primary issue giving rise to litigation involving parents and subsidiaries is whether the parent is liable for its subsidiary's debts and obligations. Generally, the parent and subsidiary are viewed as separate legal entities with each remaining liable for its own debts. There are, however, a number of instances in which courts have pierced the veil between a parent and subsidiary to impose liability on the parent. If the parent treats the subsidiary's accounts as its own, commingles funds, shares personnel or business departments, files consolidated financial statements or tax returns with the subsidiary, and controls and dominates the subsidiary to the extent that the subsidiary is a mere instrumentality or puppet of the parent, a court may hold the parent liable for the subsidiary's obligations.

E. Professional Corporations

1. *Introduction*

All states allow the incorporation of professional practices (such as law or medical practices). Most states have separate statutes for these **professional corporations** (or *professional associations*). Some states specifically identify the professions that may incorporate. Other states do not; rather, they provide that any individual who must be licensed by the state may incorporate his or her practice or business.

Affiliates
Corporations with common parents (also called *brother-sister corporations*)

Wholly owned subsidiary
A corporation the stock of which is entirely owned by the parent

Professional corporation
The incorporation of the practice of a professional, such as a lawyer or doctor (also called *professional association*)

2. Characteristics of Professional Corporations

There are two distinguishing characteristics of a professional corporation:

1. Share ownership is limited to licensed professionals; and
2. Professionals retain liability for their own acts of malpractice and the acts of others under their supervision.

Thus, perhaps the most important feature of corporate existence, limited liability, is unavailable to the professional. However, there are other advantages. For example, the professional and her staff will be employees of the corporation, and the corporation may then establish various benefit plans for its employees.

The emergence of the new business entities discussed earlier, the LLP and the LLC, may result in a decrease in the number of professional corporations. These new entities protect their partners or members from acts of negligence of their colleagues and yet enjoy pass-through taxation. In all of these entities (the professional corporation, the LLP, and the LLC), professionals remain liable for their own improper acts and for the acts of people they supervise.

3. Formation, Operation, and Liability of Professional Corporations

A professional corporation is formed by filing articles of incorporation. The articles must usually specify the particular service to be provided (for example, accounting services), and the name of the entity (and all of its signage and documents) must include a signal to provide notice to the public that the professional has adopted the corporate form. The most typical signals required are "professional corporation," "professional association," "P.C.," or "P.A."

The articles must specify the number of shares the corporation is authorized to issue. Share ownership is generally restricted to the licensed professionals. Thus, if a law firm is incorporated, shares may be issued to the attorneys but not to the support staff or spouses of the attorneys. Similarly, most states require that the directors and officers of the corporation be licensed as well so that management of the corporation is not conducted by laypersons.

The licensed professional retains liability for her own wrongful acts and those performed under her supervision and control. Thus, attorneys are responsible for the wrongful acts of their secretaries and paralegals.

F. S Corporations

1. Introduction

S corporation
Corporation whose income is not taxed at corporate level but is passed through to its shareholders who pay taxes at their own rates

An **S corporation** is not truly a different form of corporation; rather, it is an existing corporation that qualifies for special tax treatment. Any business corporation that is not an S corporation is simply referred to as a "C corporation." Small corporations will nearly always give serious consideration to electing status as an S corporation.

According to subchapter S of the Internal Revenue Code (26 U.S.C. §§ 1361-1364), a "small business corporation" may elect not to have its income taxed at the corporate level but to have the income passed through to the shareholders, who then pay taxes at their appropriate individual rates. Tax must be paid on income whether or not it is distributed.

The requirement that the corporation be "small" refers to the number of its shareholders (who may not number more than 100), not to the size of its business or to its revenue. Thus, a corporation with a handful of shareholders could elect S status even if its revenue is in the millions of dollars.

Electing S status avoids double taxation by eliminating payment of federal taxes by the corporation. In brief, for tax purposes the S corporation is treated like a sole proprietorship, partnership, LLP, or LLC. "S corps" are the most common form of corporation.

2. Formation, Operation, and Termination of S Corporations

To elect to be treated and exist as an S corporation, a corporation must file certain forms with the IRS (Forms 2553 and 1120S). A corporation may make the election to be treated as an S corporation only if it meets various criteria, including the following:

1. It is a domestic corporation rather than one formed in a foreign country;
2. It has no more than 100 shareholders (a husband and wife are treated as one shareholder, and all members of a family are treated as one shareholder);
3. It has only individuals, estates, or certain trusts (rather than other corporations or partnerships) as shareholders;
4. It has no nonresident alien shareholders; and
5. It has only one class of stock.

The S corporation election is not mentioned or addressed in the corporation's articles, and the state of incorporation has no interest in whether its domestic corporations elect S status. The S election is made with the IRS after incorporation. All shareholders must sign consent statements to make the election, which must be made within a specified time period. S corporation status remains in effect until formally revoked by a majority of the shareholders or until the corporation no longer meets the statutory requirements for S status.

Additionally, to ensure that stock is not transferred to "outsiders," shareholders in most S corporations enter into agreements restricting the transfer of their shares so that shares are not transferred to a 101st shareholder or to another corporation or LLP or LLC, which would result in automatic termination of S status. Because S corporations are relatively small, most shareholders are actively engaged in managing the business.

S status may be particularly helpful in the first few years of a corporation's existence, when it may sustain losses. These losses may be passed through to the individual shareholders, who may then use them to offset other income, thereby decreasing their tax liability.

Although S corporations do not pay federal income tax, they must report their annual income to the IRS (using Form 1120S).

The emergence of the LLC (see Chapter Six), which protects all of its members from liability, can be member-managed, has no limitations on the number of members (who need not be individuals and may be nonresident aliens), all while allowing pass-through of income, may make the S corporation a relic of the past. The LLC avoids the restrictions imposed on S corporations and avoids double taxation. Therefore, it is an increasingly popular investment vehicle.

PRACTICE TIP

Because the corporations discussed in this chapter are subject to special requirements, develop checklists for each type of corporation. For example, for S corporations, questions could include the following:

- How many shareholders will the corporation have?
- Are all shareholders individuals?
- How many classes of stock will the corporation issue?

Such checklists will streamline the process of determining whether clients qualify to be treated as close corporations, professional corporations, and so forth. Additionally, the checklists can be easily modified to use as annual audit forms to ensure clients remain in compliance with all statutory requirements.

G. Publicly Traded Corporations

1. Introduction to Investor Protection

SEC
Securities and Exchange Commission; federal agency charged with regulation of securities

Although public corporations represent a small percentage of all businesses in the United States, their economic impact on the country is significant: Approximately 50 percent of all households in the United States own stock in a public corporation.

1933 Act
Act requiring registration before issuance of securities through interstate commerce

For many years, corporations desiring to sell stock to the public simply distributed their securities by having agents sell stock on commission. The stock market crash of 1929 and the subsequent Great Depression provided the impetus for a public examination of the practices of selling securities. Congress responded by passing the Securities Act of 1933 and then the Securities Exchange Act of 1934, which created the **Securities and Exchange Commission (SEC)**, an independent federal agency charged with regulation of securities. The **1933 Act** focuses on the original issuance of securities to the public; the **1934 Act** is concerned primarily with the buying and selling of securities after their original issuance. Moreover, each state regulates the issuance and sale of securities within its borders.

1934 Act
Act governing resale of securities after their initial issuance

Going public
Sale of shares to the public at large

When a corporation decides to sell its shares to members of the public at large, the decision is referred to as **going public**. The first offering of the corporation's stock to the public is referred to as the **initial public offering** (IPO). The securities to be issued by the corporation are usually in the form of equity securities (*stock* representing ownership interest in the corporation) or debt securities (*bonds* representing money owed by a corporation to a creditor). Securities may, however, take other forms.

Initial public offering
The first offering of stock to the public (an IPO)

2. Securities Act of 1933

If a security is being offered by a corporation, and unless exemptions exist, the issuer must comply with the 1933 Act (15 U.S.C. §§ 77a et seq.). The 1933 Act is often referred to as the "truth in securities" law. The Act has two main objectives:

1. Requiring that investors receive financial and other significant information concerning securities being offered for public sale; and
2. Prohibiting deceit and fraud in the sale of securities.

In general, securities sold in the United States must be registered with the SEC. The registration statement (Form S-1) provides essential information to the public, including the following: a description of the company's business, a description of the security to be offered, information about the management of the company, and financial statements certified by independent accountants. This information enables investors to make informed decisions about whether to purchase a company's securities. The SEC reviews the registration statement, which becomes effective 20 days after registration (unless the SEC requests additional information). Nearly all documents provided to the SEC must be filed electronically using the SEC's system, called **EDGAR** (Electronic Data Gathering, Analysis, and Retrieval). Documents are then available to the public for review through the SEC's Web site at www.sec.gov.

EDGAR
SEC's electronic filing system

Not all offerings of securities must be registered with the SEC. Some exemptions from the registration requirement include the following:

- Private offerings to a limited number of persons (generally, offerings made to more sophisticated investors who are capable of understanding investment risks);
- Offerings of limited size (generally, those that will raise less than $5 million in a 12-month period);
- Intrastate offerings; and
- Securities of municipal, state, and federal governments.

3. Securities Exchange Act of 1934

The 1934 Act (15 U.S.C. §§ 78a et seq.) not only created the SEC, but also regulates brokerage firms and stock exchanges. The 1934 Act focuses on the resale of securities after their original issuance and imposes reporting requirements on companies with more than $10 million in assets whose securities are held by more than 500 owners. These companies, called *Section 12 companies*, must file the following periodic reports with the SEC:

- **Form 8-K.** Form 8-K is called a *current report* and is used to report the occurrence of any material event affecting the company, such as a merger or the resignation of a director.
- **Form 10-Q.** Form 10-Q is a quarterly report that includes unaudited financial statements and provides information about the company's financial position.
- **Form 10-K.** Form 10-K is an annual report that provides audited financial reports and detailed information about the company and its management.

Under Rule 10b-5, the 1934 Act also prohibits **insider trading**, that is, trading of securities based on material information not available to the public at large. For example, if directors know that an upcoming merger will greatly increase the value of the company's stock they may not use this inside information to buy stock prior to public dissemination of the information. Penalties, which range from fines to jail terms, may be imposed on both the tippers and the tippees who receive the inside information.

Finally, § 16(b) of the 1934 Act requires that any profits made by corporate insiders (namely, officers, directors, and shareholders owning 10 percent or more of a class of stock) from the purchase or sale of stock in any six-month period be recaptured by the corporation. It is irrelevant whether the insider has used any inside information or has acted deceptively. Any such profits, called **short-swing profits**, made in such a short time frame must be disgorged even if they have been innocently obtained.

4. State Securities Regulation

A company selling securities must comply with state securities laws as well as with federal laws. Each state has its own statutes regulating the issuance of securities within its borders. These state statutes are called **blue sky laws** (after a statement in a famous case, *Hall v. Geiger-Jones*, 242 U.S. 539, 550 (1917), in which the Court said state regulations were intended to prevent "speculative schemes which have no more basis than so many feet of 'blue sky' "). State blue sky laws vary widely. Generally, however, they are aimed at preventing fraud, regulating the persons involved in the offer and sale of securities, and imposing registration requirements. If a registration statement has been filed previously with the SEC, the process of state registration is relatively straightforward.

5. The Securities Markets

A **stock exchange** is a marketplace where securities are sold. Only those corporations that have met various criteria of the exchanges and are well established list their stock for sale through the exchanges. For example, for a stock to be listed on NYSE Euronext (formed in 2007 by the combination of the New York Stock Exchange and Euronext N.V., and usually called "NYSE"), generally there must be at least 1.1 million shares held by members of the public, with a total

Form 8-K
Form filed with the SEC to report major changes in certain companies

Form 10-Q
Quarterly report filed with the SEC by certain companies

Form 10-K
Annual report filed with the SEC by certain companies

Insider trading
Trading in stock by corporate insiders with information unknown to public at large

Short-swing profits
Profits made by certain corporate insiders within six months that must be disgorged

Blue sky laws
State laws regulating issuance of securities within a state

Stock exchange
Marketplace where securities are traded

market value of $100 million. The company must have earned, pretax, at least $2 million in each of the two most recent years. The NYSE is often said to be an *auction market* where buyers and sellers gather and trade stock, but NYSE refers to itself as a "hybrid market," meaning that it combines the best features of a true auction market with automated trading systems. Note that the American Stock Exchange was acquired by NYSE Euronext in October 2008.

Unlike the NYSE, NASDAQ has no true physical location for trading. Rather, it is a computerized trading system where trading occurs through computers rather than at a specific location. The requirements for listing a stock on NASDAQ are generally more permissive than those for the NYSE. Thus, some companies eventually "graduate" from NASDAQ to the NYSE, which is often called the **big board** to signal that corporations traded on the NYSE are the elite or **blue-chip companies** of the world. For example, the transfer of Krispy Kreme Doughnuts, Inc., from NASDAQ to the NYSE in May 2001 was greeted with great fanfare and the serving of 40,000 doughnuts on the trading floor in New York City.

Companies that do not meet the criteria required to list their stock on the NYSE or on NASDAQ are traded on the **pink sheets**, a reference to the fact that quotes for these stocks historically were shown on pink paper. In January 2002, Enron Corp. was delisted from the NYSE due to its failure to continue to meet NYSE listing requirements.

Over-the-counter markets have no physical place or location; they are computerized trading networks. Thus, in a sense, all stock traded through NASDAQ is over-the-counter.

Big board
Reference to New York Stock Exchange

Blue-chip company
Reference to nationally known and well-established company

Pink sheet stocks
Stocks of companies that are not sold through an exchange

Over-the-counter market
Sale of stock through computerized trading systems, rather than through a securities exchange

Indexes
Averages that track movements of stock

6. Stock Market Indexes

Stock market **indexes** such as Standard & Poor's 500 and the NYSE Composite Index attempt to show the trend of prices of stocks and bonds by reporting on certain selected stocks traded on the various exchanges. The Dow Jones Industrial Average, the best-known of the indexes, reviews the averages of 30 selected blue-chip companies to obtain a snapshot about trends in the market in general.

H. Role of Paralegal

Paralegals play a significant role with regard to the corporate variations discussed in this chapter. Typical tasks include the following:

- Preparing and filing the articles of incorporation to create close corporations, nonprofit corporations, subsidiary corporations, or professional corporations and preparing notices of meetings and minutes of directors' and shareholders' meetings for all corporations;
- Drafting buy-sell agreements for shareholders of close corporations and S corporations;
- Preparing IRS Form 2553 to elect S corporation status and applying for tax-exempt status for nonprofit corporations;
- Conducting research regarding exemptions from registration requirements of the 1933 Act and researching provisions of state blue sky laws;

- Assisting in drafting registration statements for companies desiring to go public; and
- Preparing the periodic reports for publicly traded companies.

Case Illustration
Piercing the Veil Between a Parent and Subsidiary

Case: *Ocala Breeders' Sales Co. v. Hialeah, Inc.*, 735 So. 2d 542 (Fla. Dist. Ct. App. 1999)

Facts: A tenant received a judgment against a subsidiary for breach of a lease. When the tenant learned the subsidiary had no assets, it brought proceedings against the parent to hold it liable for its subsidiary's debts.

Holding: The parent is liable in this case for the act of the subsidiary. To pierce the veil under Florida law, the subsidiary must be a mere instrumentality of the parent and must have been used by the parent to mislead creditors. In this case, the subsidiary had never been capitalized and any funds earned by it went directly to the parent. The two corporations were controlled by the same person and operated out of the same facilities. In such a case, the subsidiary was a mere instrumentality of the parent and was used to mislead creditors. Thus, the tenant may pierce the subsidiary's corporate veil to hold the parent liable.

Key Features
of Other Forms of Corporations

- ◆ A close corporation is a smaller corporation owned and operated by a group of family members and/or friends. There is usually a limit of 25 to 50 shareholders. These shareholders enter into agreements restricting the transfer of their shares. Close corporations are allowed less formality in operation than ordinary C corporations.
- ◆ A nonprofit corporation is one formed not to earn a profit but for some charitable or religious purpose or for the mutual benefit of its members. Stock is not sold. If allowed by the IRS, a nonprofit corporation is exempt from paying federal taxes.
- ◆ A subsidiary corporation is one formed by another, the parent, which will own all or the vast majority of its subsidiary's stock. If the parent dominates and controls the subsidiary such that the two do not operate

as separate corporations, the parent may be liable for the subsidiary's debts.

◆ A professional corporation is formed by a group of professionals, such as doctors. The professionals retain liability for their own negligence and for the negligence of those whom they supervise.

◆ An S corporation is a corporation that has qualified for special tax treatment such that none of its income is taxed at the corporate level but is passed through to the shareholders, who pay at their appropriate rates. An S corporation is limited to 100 or fewer shareholders, who must all be individuals and who may not be nonresident aliens.

◆ Securities (stocks and bonds) may not be offered for sale to the public unless they are either registered with the SEC or exempt from registration.

◆ The Securities Act of 1933 governs the initial issuance of securities, and the Securities Exchange Act of 1934 governs resale of securities and reporting by public companies.

◆ States regulate the sale of securities through their state laws, called blue sky laws.

Internet Resources

Federal and state statutes:	www.law.cornell.edu www.findlaw.com
SEC Web site:	www.sec.gov (site offers excellent information about federal securities laws and access to all documents filed with the SEC)
Tax forms:	www.irs.gov
Secretaries of state:	www.nass.org (for links to secretaries of state and downloadable forms for articles of incorporation for close corporations, nonprofit corporations, and so forth)
NYSE Euronext:	www.nyse.com (excellent information about the NYSE, its listing requirements, and a virtual tour of the trading floor)
NASDAQ:	www.nasdaq.com (for information about NASDAQ, its history, listing requirements, and general trading information)
Forms:	www.allaboutforms.com www.lectlaw.com www.siccode.com/forms.php (for forms for notices of meetings, minutes of meetings, corporate resolutions, and so forth)

Key Terms

Close corporation
Buy-sell agreement
Nonprofit corporation
Religious corporation
Public benefit corporation
Mutual benefit corporation
Membership
Parent
Subsidiary
Affiliates
Wholly owned subsidiary
Professional corporation
S corporation
SEC
Going public
Initial public offering

1933 Act
1934 Act
EDGAR
Form 8-K
Form 10-Q
Form 10-K
Insider trading
Short-swing profits
Blue sky laws
Stock exchange
Big board
Blue-chip company
Over-the-counter market
Pink sheet stocks
Indexes

Discussion Questions

1. ABC, Inc. is a close corporation with 25 shareholders. The corporation has no board of directors and no bylaws. A creditor of the corporation is owed money, and the corporation cannot pay all of the debt. Discuss whether the creditor would be successful in attempting to pierce the veil to hold the individual shareholders liable because the corporation is not observing formalities.

2. Why do close corporations usually have agreements among the shareholders restricting their transfer of stock?

3. Discuss whether your contributions to the following organizations would be tax-deductible to you: American Red Cross, United Methodist Church, and River Oaks Country Club.

4. P Corp. has formed a subsidiary, Sub Corp. P owns all of Sub's outstanding shares. The two corporations use separate offices, have different bank accounts, and have different boards and officers. Discuss whether a creditor would be able to pierce the veil between the two corporations to hold P liable for Sub's debt to the creditor.

5. Dana Powers, M.D., has incorporated her medical practice. Is Dr. Powers liable for malpractice committed by her nurse? May Dr. Powers issue stock to her insurance clerk? Discuss.

6. XYZ Corp. is a corporation with 90 shareholders. What advantage does electing S status afford the corporation or its shareholders? What if one of the shareholders objects to the proposal to elect S status and will not consent to the election? Assume the corporation elects S status. What is the result if one of its shareholders transfers his shares to 12 of his book group members? How could such a transfer be prevented?

7. Assume that Director O'Malley purchased stock in his publicly traded company on March 1 of this year for $50 per share. Two months later, O'Malley

sold the stock for $70 per share to obtain money to put his twins through college. On October 1, O'Malley sold more stock for $80 per share. Have any securities laws been violated? Discuss fully.

Net Worth

1. Access the Web site for the Delaware Secretary of State. What is the basic fee to form a close corporation?
2. Access the Web site for the California Secretary of State and review the articles of incorporation for a professional association. What does Article II provide?
3. Access the New York Secretary of State Web site. Search the New York Corporations and Business Database. What "type" of corporation is each of the following?
   a. Cancer Action, Inc.
   b. Alpha Delta Gamma, Inc.
   c. Medical Associates of Manhattan, P.C.
4. Access www.hoovers.com. What type of corporation is The Iams Company?
5. Use either the Web site of the NYSE or NASDAQ. Identify whether the following companies are listed on the NYSE or NASDAQ: Dell Incorporated, Intel Corporation, Gannett Co., Inc., and General Motors Corp.
6. Use the Web site of NYSE and determine what companies trade under the ticker symbols "C" and "V."

A

◆ ◆ ◆

Secretaries of State and State Corporations Statutes

◆ ◆ ◆

The following are the references to each state's business corporations statutes and the addresses of each state's secretary of state. Web sites for each secretary of state are also given. All states have Web sites for their secretaries of state, and all sites offer basic information about corporations. All Web sites provide forms for downloading; all Web sites provide fee schedules; and nearly all states offer searching for corporate and UCC data through their Web sites. An easy way to locate individual state Web sites is to access the home page of the National Association of Secretaries of State at www.nass.org. Go to "About NASS," then "Our Members," and then "Contact Roster" and you will be presented with a link to each state's secretary of state. When you access the Secretary of State's Web site, select "Corporations," "Business Services," and so forth.

ALABAMA

Ala. Code §§ 10-2B-1.01, et seq.

Secretary of State
P.O. Box 5616
Montgomery, AL 36103-5616
(334) 242-5324
www.sos.state.al.us

ALASKA

Alaska Stat. §§ 10.06.005, et seq.

Division of Corporations, Business, and
Professional Licensing
P.O. Box 110808
Juneau, AK 99811-0808
(907) 465-2530
www.commerce.state.ak.us/occ/home.htm

ARIZONA

Ariz. Rev. Stat. Ann. §§ 10-120, et seq.

Secretary of State
Corporations Division
1300 West Washington
Phoenix, AZ 85007-2929
(602) 542-3026 or (800) 345-5819
www.azsos.gov

ARKANSAS

Ark. Code Ann. §§ 4-27-101, et seq.

Secretary of State
State Capitol
Little Rock, AR 72201-1094
(501) 682-3409 or (888) 233-0325
www.sosweb.state.ar.us

CALIFORNIA

Cal. Corp. Code §§ 1, et seq.

Secretary of State
1500 11th Street, Third Floor
Sacramento, CA 95814-5701
(916) 657-5448
www.ss.ca.gov

COLORADO

Colo. Rev. Stat. §§ 7-101-101, et seq.

Secretary of State
1700 Broadway, Suite 200
Denver, CO 80290
(303) 894-2200
www.sos.state.co.us

CONNECTICUT

Conn. Gen. Stat. §§ 33-600, et seq.

Secretary of State
210 Capitol Avenue
Suite 104
Hartford, CT 06106
(860) 509-6200
www.sots.state.ct.us

DELAWARE

Del. Code Ann. tit. 8, §§ 101, et seq.

Secretary of State
P.O. Box 898
Dover, DE 19903
(302) 739-3073
http://corp.delaware.gov/default.shtml

DISTRICT OF COLUMBIA

D.C. Code Ann. §§ 29-101.01, et seq.

Department of Consumer and Regulatory Affairs
(Corporate Division)
941 N. Capitol Street, N.E.
Washington, D.C. 20002
(202) 442-4400
http://dcra.dc.gov/dcra/site/default.asp

FLORIDA

Fla. Stat. Ann. §§ 607.0101, et seq.

Department of State
Division of Corporations
P.O. Box 6327
Tallahassee, FL 32314
(850) 245-6000
www.dos.state.fl.us

GEORGIA

Ga. Code Ann. §§ 14-2-101, et seq.

Secretary of State
315 West Tower
2 Martin Luther King, Jr. Drive
Atlanta, GA 30334-1530
(404) 656-2817
www.sos.state.ga.us

HAWAII

Haw. Rev. Stat. §§ 414-1, et seq.

Department of Commerce and Consumer Affairs
Business Registration Division
220 South King Street
Suite 2190
Honolulu, HI 96810
(808) 586-2744
www.state.hi.us

IDAHO

Idaho Code Ann. §§ 30-1-101, et seq.

Secretary of State
700 West Jefferson, Room 203
P.O. Box 83720
Boise, ID 83720-0080
(208) 334-2300
www.idsos.state.id.us

ILLINOIS

805 Ill. Comp. Stat. 5/1.01, et seq.

Secretary of State
Michael J. Howlett Bldg.
501 S. 2nd St., Room 328
Springfield, IL 62756
(217) 782-6961
www.sos.state.il.us

INDIANA

Ind. Code §§ 23-1-17-1, et seq.

Secretary of State
Business Services
302 W. Washington
Room E-018
Indianapolis, IN 46204
(317) 232-6531
www.in.gov/sos

IOWA

Iowa Code §§ 490.101, et seq.

Business Services Division
Office of the Secretary of State
Lucas Building, 1st Floor
321 E. 12th Street
Des Moines, IA 50319
(515) 281-5204
www.sos.state.ia.us

KANSAS

Kan. Stat. Ann. §§ 17-6001, et seq.

Secretary of State
Corporation Division
First Floor, Memorial Hall
120 S.W. 10th Avenue
Topeka, KS 66612-1594
(785) 296-4564
www.kssos.org

KENTUCKY

Ky. Rev. Stat. Ann. §§ 271B.1-010, et seq.

Secretary of State
Filings Branch
700 Capitol Avenue
Suite 154
Frankfort, KY 40601-3493
(502) 564-2848
www.sos.state.ky.gov

LOUISIANA

La. Rev. Stat. Ann. §§ 12:1, et seq.

Secretary of State
Corporations Section
P.O. Box 94125
Baton Rouge, LA 70804-9125
(225) 925-4704
www.sos.louisiana.gov

MAINE

Me. Rev. Stat. Ann. tit. 13C, §§ 101, et seq.

Secretary of State
Bureau of Corporations, Elections and Commissions
101 State House Station
Augusta, ME 04333-0101
(207) 624-7752
www.state.me.us

MARYLAND

Md. Code Ann., Corps. & Ass'ns §§ 1-101, et seq.

Assessments and Taxation Department
301 West Preston Street, Room 809
Baltimore, MD 21201-2395
(410) 767-1340
www.dat.state.md.us

MASSACHUSETTS

Mass. Gen. Laws. ch. 155, §§ 1, et seq.

Secretary of the Commonwealth
Corporations Division
One Ashburton Place, 17th Floor
Boston, MA 02108
(617) 727-9640
www.sec.state.ma.us

MICHIGAN

Mich. Comp. Laws. §§ 450.1101, et seq.

Department of Labor and Economic Growth,
    Corporation Division
Bureau of Commercial Services, Corporation Division
P.O. Box 30054
Lansing, MI 48909-7554
(517) 241-6470
www.michigan.gov/sos

MINNESOTA

Minn. Stat. §§ 302A.001, et seq.

Secretary of State
Business Services
Retirement Systems of Minnesota Building
60 Empire Drive
Suite 100
St. Paul, MN 55103
(651) 296-2803
www.sos/state/mn.us/home/index.asp

MISSISSIPPI

Miss. Code Ann. §§ 79-4-1.01, et seq.

Secretary of State
P.O. Box 136
Jackson, MS 39205-0136
(601) 359-1633
www.sos.state.ms.us

MISSOURI

Mo. Rev. Stat. §§ 351.010, et seq.

Business Services
P.O. Box 778
Jefferson City, MO 65102-0778
(573) 751-4153
www.sos.mo.gov

MONTANA

Mont. Code Ann. §§ 35-1-112, et seq.

Secretary of State
P.O. Box 202801
Helena, MT 59620-2801
(406) 444-2034
www.sos.mt.gov

NEBRASKA

Neb. Rev. Stat. §§ 21-2001, et seq.

Secretary of State
State Capitol, Room 1301
P.O. Box 94608
Lincoln, NE 68509-4608
(402) 471-4079
www.sos.state.ne.us

NEVADA

Nev. Rev. Stat. §§ 78.010, et seq.

Secretary of State
Capitol Complex
202 N. Carson Street
Carson City, NV 89701-4201
(775) 684-5708
http://sos.state.nv.us

NEW HAMPSHIRE

N.H. Rev. Stat. Ann. §§ 293-A:1.01, et seq.

Secretary of State Corporation Division
107 N. Main Street
Concord, NH 03301
(603) 271-3246
www.state.nh.us/sos

NEW JERSEY

N.J. Stat. Ann. §§ 14A:1-1, et seq.

New Jersey Division of Revenue
Business Services
P.O. Box 308
Trenton, NJ 08646
(609) 292-9292
www.state.nj.us/njbgs

NEW MEXICO

N.M. Stat. Ann. §§ 53-11-1, et seq.

Office of the New Mexico Secretary of State
Public Regulation Commission
P.O. Box 1269
Santa Fe, NM 87504
(505) 827-4502 or (800) 947-4722
www.nmprc.state.nm.us/cb.htm

NEW YORK

N.Y. Bus. Corp. Law §§ 101, et seq.

Secretary of State
Division of Corporations, State Records and
    Uniform Commercial Code
One Commerce Plaza
99 Washington Avenue
Suite 600
Albany, NY 12231-0001
(518) 473-2492
www.dos.state.ny.us

NORTH CAROLINA

N.C. Gen. Stat. §§ 55-1-01, et seq.

Secretary of State
P.O. Box 29622
Raleigh, NC 27626-0622
(919) 807-2225
www.secstate.state.nc.us

NORTH DAKOTA

N.D. Cent. Code §§ 10-19.1-01, et seq.

Secretary of State
State Capitol
600 East Boulevard Avenue, Dept. 108, 1st Floor
Bismarck, ND 58505-0500
(701) 328-2900
www.nd.gov/sos

OHIO

Ohio Rev. Code Ann. §§ 1701.01, et seq.

Secretary of State
P.O. Box 1390
Columbus, OH 43216
1-877-SOS-FILE
www.sos.state.oh.us

OKLAHOMA

Okla. Stat. Ann. tit. 18, §§ 1001, et seq.

Secretary of State
2300 North Lincoln Boulevard, Suite 101
Oklahoma City, OK 73105-4897
(405) 521-3912
www.sos.state.ok.us

OREGON

Or. Rev. Stat. §§ 60.001, et seq.

Secretary of State
Corporations Division
Public Service Building, Suite 151
255 Capitol Street, NE
Salem, OR 97310
(503) 986-2200
www.sos.state.or.us

PENNSYLVANIA

Pa. Stat. Ann. §§ 1101, et seq.

Secretary of State
Corporations Bureau
206 North Office Building
Harrisburg, PA 17120
(717) 787-1057
www.dos.state.pa.us

RHODE ISLAND

R.I. Gen. Laws §§ 7-1.2-101, et seq.

Secretary of State
Corporations Division
148 W. River St.
Providence, RI 02904-2615
(401) 222-3040
www.sec.state.ri.us

SOUTH CAROLINA

S.C. Code Ann. §§ 33-1-101, et seq.

Secretary of State
P.O. Box 11350
Columbia, SC 29211
(803) 734-2158
www.scsos.com

SOUTH DAKOTA

S.D. Codified Laws §§ 47-1A, et seq.

Secretary of State
Capitol Building
500 East Capitol Avenue, Suite 204
Pierre, SD 57501-5070
(605) 773-4845
www.sdsos.gov

TENNESSEE

Tenn. Code Ann. §§ 48-11-101, et seq.

Secretary of State
312 Eighth Avenue North, 6th Floor
William R. Snodgrass Tower
Nashville, TN 37243
(615) 741-2286
www.state.tn.us/sos

TEXAS

Tex. Bus. Orgs. Code Ann. §§ 1.001, et seq.

Secretary of State
Corporations Section
P.O. Box 13697
Austin, TX 78711
(512) 463-5555
www.sos.state.tx.us

UTAH

Utah Code Ann. §§ 16-10a-101, et seq.

Division of Corporations and Commercial Code
160 East 300 South
2nd Floor
Salt Lake City, UT 84111
(801) 530-4849
www.commerce.utah.gov

VERMONT

Vt. Stat. Ann. tit. 11A, §§ 1.01, et seq.

Secretary of State
81 River Street, Drawer 09
Montpelier, VT 05609
(802) 828-2386
www.sec.state.vt.us

VIRGINIA

Va. Code Ann. §§ 13.1-601, et seq.

State Corporation Commission
1111 East Broad Street
4th Floor
Richmond, VA 23219
(804) 786-2441
www.soc.state.va.us

WASHINGTON

Wash. Rev. Code Ann. §§ 23B.01.010, et seq.

Secretary of State
Corporations Division
801 Capitol Way South
Olympia, WA 98504-0234
(360) 725-0377
www.secstate.wa.gov

WEST VIRGINIA

W. Va. Code §§ 31D-1-101, et seq.

Secretary of State
1900 Kanawha Boulevard East
Charleston, WV 25305-0770
(304) 558-8000
www.wvsos.com

WISCONSIN

Wis. Stat. Ann. §§ 180.0101, et seq.

Department of Financial Institutions
Corporations Bureau, 3rd Floor
P.O. Box 7846
Madison, WI 53707-7846
(608) 261-7577
www.wdfi.org

WYOMING

Wyo. Stat. Ann. §§ 17-16-101, et seq.

Secretary of State
214 West 15th Street
Cheyenne, WY 82002
(307) 777-2843
http://soswy.state.wy.us

B

◆ ◆ ◆

General Partnership Agreement

◆ ◆ ◆

GENERAL PARTNERSHIP AGREEMENT

THIS AGREEMENT is entered into this _____ day of _____, 20 _____, by and among Christopher Walter (Walter), an individual residing at _____, Timothy Mislock (Mislock), an individual residing at _____, and Erin Murphy (Murphy), an individual residing at _____. Walter, Mislock, and Murphy are hereinafter sometimes referred to individually as "Partner" and collectively as "Partners."

RECITALS

WHEREAS the Partners desire to form a partnership for the purpose of _____ and have decided that it is in their best commercial interests to do so. NOW, THEREFORE, for good and valuable consideration, the receipt and sufficiency of which are hereby acknowledged, the parties hereto agree as follows:

1. *Formation and Purpose of the Partnership.* The Partners hereby form a general partnership (the Partnership) under the laws of the State of _____ for the purpose of _____, and the carrying on of any and all activities necessary and incident thereto.

2. *Partnership Name and Address.* The name of the Partnership is "WMM Enterprises" and its principal place of business shall be located at _____, in the City of _____, State of _____, and at such other places as may be mutually agreed upon by the Partners.

3. *Term.* The Partnership shall commence on _____ and shall continue until dissolved by mutual agreement of the Partners or as provided in Paragraph 13 below.

4. *Capital Contributions.*

(a) Initial Capital Contributions. Each Partner shall contribute the following amounts:

Name	*Amount*
Walter	$_____
Mislock	$_____
Murphy	$_____

The contributions shall be made to the Partnership on or before _____, 20_____, or this Agreement shall be void and of no effect.

(b) Additional Capital Contributions. At such time or times as the Partners mutually agree that additional capital is necessary to operate the business of the Partnership, the Partners shall contribute additional capital in accordance with their respective partnership interests at the relevant time and in accordance with the agreed amount of the additional capital contribution and the method of payment thereof determined by the Partners. In the event that a Partner fails to make an additional capital contribution required to be made under this Agreement within the time period prescribed, such Partner shall be deemed to be a "Defaulting Partner" and a non-defaulting Partner shall be entitled to make the contribution on behalf of the Defaulting Partner, and such contribution shall be a personal debt due and owing to the non-defaulting Partner from the Defaulting Partner(s) with interest at the rate of _____ percent (_____%) per annum until paid. No money or assets may be distributed by the Partnership to a Defaulting Partner unless and until the Defaulting Partner shall have paid in full the amount owed to the non-defaulting Partner(s), together with interest. Accordingly, all distributions from the Partnership which would have been made to the Defaulting Partner shall instead be made to the non-defaulting Partner(s) until the personal debt of the Defaulting Partner to the non-defaulting Partner(s) is paid in full.

(c) Return of Capital Contribution. No interest shall be paid on any Partner's capital contribution. No Partner has a right to receive a return of all or any part of his or her capital contribution except as expressly provided in this Agreement or in the event of liquidation or dissolution of the Partnership, and then only to the extent of the net assets of the Partnership available for distribution.

5. *Interests of Partners in Partnership*. Each Partner shall own the following interest in the Partnership:

Name	Partnership Interest
Walter	_____%
Mislock	_____%
Murphy	_____%

Any change in the partnership interest of any Partner shall be reflected in writing and signed by all Partners.

6. *Profits and Losses*. Partners shall share in the profits and losses of the Partnership in accordance with his or her respective partnership interests.

7. *Voting*. The Partners shall be vested with voting rights in the Partnership equal to their respective partnership interests. Except as otherwise agreed by the Partners, actions of the Partnership shall require majority action of the outstanding partnership interests.

8. *Management*. The management and operation of the business and affairs of the Partnership shall be conducted by the Partners or by such person or persons as are designated by the Partners to perform such functions on behalf of the Partnership. Walter shall be the Managing Partner and shall be entitled to enter into contracts and agreements on behalf of the Partnership for the conduct of partnership operations in the ordinary course of business. Persons dealing with the Partnership shall be entitled to rely on the power and authority of Walter.

Notwithstanding the foregoing, nothing herein is intended to grant Walter the authority to make all decisions regarding the business of the Partnership. The authority vested in Walter pertains only to the right to bind the Partnership, without the consent or approval of any other Partner, for contracts or obligations in the ordinary course of business which are necessary, appropriate, or incidental to the performance of the Partnership's business.

Walter shall not undertake any of the following business activities without the majority vote of the Partners:

(a) borrow money in excess of _____ Dollars ($_____);

(b) purchase or sell any real estate;

(c) enter into any agreement which requires the Partnership to make any payment of more than $_____ per year;

(d) compromise any claim or institute any litigation or other proceeding on behalf of the Partnership; or

(e) sell all or substantially all of the Partnership's assets.

9. *Duties of Partners*. Each of the Partners shall give his or her undivided time and attention to the business and affairs of the Partnership and shall use his or her best efforts to promote the interests of the Partnership. Partners shall have fiduciary duties to each other and to the Partnership.

10. *Books of Account*. Books of account of the transactions of the Partnership shall be kept at the principal place of business of the Partnership and shall be available at all reasonable times for inspection by any Partner. Financial statements shall be prepared on a quarterly basis and shall include a statement of cash flow. The financial statements shall be prepared by independent certified public accountants selected by the Partners. The tax and accounting year of the partnership shall be the calendar year. Any Partner, at his or her sole expense, may cause the books of the Partnership to be audited at any time. No later than thirty (30) days after the close of the fiscal year, an annual accounting shall be prepared by the Partnership's independent certified public accountants.

11. *Bank Accounts*. The funds of the Partnership shall be kept in such bank accounts or in such manner designated by the Partners. Checks drawn on partnership funds in any account shall be signed by Walter or such person or persons as the Partnership shall designate from time to time.

12. *Withdrawals, Distributions, and Expenses*.

(a) Withdrawal. Each Partner shall be permitted to draw from the funds of the Partnership _____ Dollars ($_____) per _____ for the Partner's living expenses. The sums so drawn shall be charged to the Partner and at the annual accounting shall be charged against that Partner's share of the profits. If the Partner's share of the profits is insufficient to equal the sum drawn, the Partner must pay the amount of the deficiency within ten (10) days notice from the Partnership and said deficiency shall draw interest at the rate _____ of percent (_____%) per year until paid.

(b) Distributions. So far as is practicable, the net cash flow, if any, of the Partnership (after allocation of an amount agreed upon by the Partners for working capital obligations and contingencies) shall be distributed among the Partners in accordance with their respective partnership interests at least annually or on a more frequent basis as decided by the Partners.

(c) Expenses. Partners who have incurred expenses on behalf of the Partnership in the ordinary course of Partnership business shall be reimbursed therefor upon submission to the Partnership of appropriate evidence of such expenses, as determined in the sole discretion of the Partners.

13. *Dissolution*. The Partnership shall be dissolved upon the agreement of all Partners or the sale or other disposition of all or substantially all of its assets. Upon dissolution of the Partnership, the Partners shall proceed with reasonable promptness to

liquidate the assets of the Partnership. Thereafter, the assets of the Partnership shall be used and distributed in the following order: first, to pay or provide for the payment of all Partnership liabilities and liquidating expenses; and second, to distribute to the Partners, in accordance with their respective partnership interests, the remaining assets of the Partnership.

14. *Change of Partners.* Any change of Partners shall be done only in the manner set forth in this Paragraph and any attempt to transfer otherwise shall be null and void.

(a) <u>Withdrawal of Partner.</u> Any Partner may withdraw from the Partnership by giving to each of the other Partners and the Partnership at least thirty (30) days' prior written notice of the Partner's intent to withdraw. On withdrawal of a Partner, that Partner's partnership interest shall be determined by appraisal of the value of the Partnership, and the withdrawing Partner shall be repaid his or her capital contributions within _____ days of the appraisal of the Partnership's value. After deduction for any draw or indebtedness, the withdrawing Partner shall receive cash payments in _____ equal installments, commencing immediately after the end of the fiscal year for the Partner's interest in the Partnership's profits.

(b) <u>Bankruptcy, Death, or Permanent Disability.</u> The bankruptcy, death, or permanent disability of a Partner shall not result in the dissolution of the Partnership unless required by law. The death of a Partner, the filing of any petition by any Partner under the federal Bankruptcy Act, or the permanent disability of a Partner due to sickness or injury shall immediately terminate all right, title, and interest of that Partner in the Partnership. The deceased, bankrupt, or permanently disabled Partner's share of the Partnership shall be established based on the Partner's date of death or permanent disability or date of filing of any petition under the federal Bankruptcy Act, and, after deduction for any draw or any indebtedness of the Partner, the Partner's estate, trustee in bankruptcy, or the permanently disabled Partner shall be paid a cash payment representing the Partner's capital contribution to the Partnership, the Partner's share of the net profits or losses for the current fiscal year to the date of death or permanent disability or of such filing of such petition, and the Partner's share of the current Partnership business as of the date of death or permanent disability or the date of filing of such petition

(c) <u>New Partner.</u> New partners may be added to the Partnership by invitation from the then-existing Partners or by purchase of a withdrawing, deceased, bankrupt, or permanently disabled Partner's interest.

An invitation to a new Partner may be extended on a vote of existing Partners representing _____ percent (_____%) of the outstanding interests in the Partnership. When a Partner's interest is to be sold to a third party by a Partner leaving the Partnership, a vote on the acceptability of the proposed new partner shall be made by a vote of existing Partners representing _____ percent (_____%) of the outstanding interests of the Partnership. A new partner must execute an Amendment to this Agreement agreeing to the terms and conditions of this Agreement. In the event a proposed new partner is not found acceptable as herein provided, the Partnership shall purchase the departing Partner's interest at the price and upon the terms offered by the third party and the Partnership may resell the interest to a candidate acceptable to the Partners.

15. *Miscellaneous Provisions.*

(a) <u>Valuation.</u> Any valuation or appraisal of the Partnership or any Partner's interest therein shall be conducted by an independent appraiser selected by Partners representing a majority of the outstanding interests of the Partnership.

(b) <u>Notices.</u> All notices required by law or this Agreement shall be in writing and may be delivered to the Partners personally or may be deposited in the United States mail, postage prepaid, addressed to the Partners at their addresses identified in this Agreement.

(c) <u>Disputes.</u> Any dispute arising under the terms of this Agreement that cannot be resolved amicably by the parties shall be submitted to binding arbitration in accordance with the rules of the American Arbitration Association.

(d) <u>Amendments to Agreement.</u> No change or modification of this Agreement shall be valid or binding upon the Partners, nor shall any waiver of any term or provision hereof be deemed a waiver of such term or provision unless such change, modification, or waiver shall be in writing and signed by all of the Partners.

(e) <u>Time of Performance.</u> Whenever performance by a Partner or the Partnership is required under this Agreement, time shall be of the essence.

(f) <u>Counterparts.</u> This Agreement may be executed in one or more counterparts, but all such counterparts shall constitute one and the same Agreement.

(g) <u>Severability.</u> In the event any provision of this Agreement is invalid or unenforceable, then such provision shall be deemed severable from this Agreement.

(h) <u>Applicable law.</u> This Agreement shall be governed under the laws of the State of _____.

IN WITNESS WHEREOF, the Partners have executed this Agreement at _____ as of the day and year given herein.

Name: _____   Address: _____

Name: _____   Address: _____

Name: _____   Address: _____

C

◆ ◆ ◆

Corporate Bylaws

◆ ◆ ◆

BYLAWS OF _____

ARTICLE I—OFFICES

Section 1. *Registered Office:* The registered office of _____ ("the Corporation") in the State of _____ shall be _____, County of _____, _____. The registered agent of the Corporation at such address shall be _____.

Section 2. *Other Offices:* The Corporation may also have offices at such other places, both within and without the State of _____, as the Board of Directors may from time to time determine or the business of the Corporation may require.

ARTICLE II—MEETINGS OF SHAREHOLDERS

Section 1. *Place of Meetings:* Meetings of shareholders shall be held at the principal office of the Corporation or at such place as may be determined from time to time by the Board of Directors.

Section 2. *Annual Meetings:* The Corporation shall hold annual meetings of shareholders commencing with the year _____, on such date and at such time as shall be determined from time to time by the Board of Directors, at which meeting shareholders shall elect a Board of Directors and transact such other business as may properly be brought before the meeting.

Section 3. *Special Meetings:* Special meetings of the shareholders, for any purpose or purposes, may be called at any time by the President of the Corporation, or the Board of Directors, or shareholders holding at least _____ percent (_____%) of the issued and outstanding voting stock of the Corporation.

Business transacted at any special meeting shall be confined to the purpose or purposes set forth in the notice of the special meeting.

Section 4. *Notice of Meetings:* Whenever shareholders are required or permitted to take any action at a meeting, a written notice of the meeting shall be provided to each shareholder of record entitled to vote at or entitled to notice of the meeting, which shall state the place, date, and hour of the meeting, and, in the case of a special meeting, the purpose or purposes for which the meeting is called.

Unless otherwise provided by law, written notice of any meeting shall be given not less than ten (10) nor more than sixty (60) days before the date of the meeting to each shareholder entitled to vote at such meeting.

Section 5. *Quorum at Meetings:* Shareholders may take action on a matter at a meeting only if a quorum exists with respect to that matter. Except as otherwise provided by law, a majority of the outstanding shares of the Corporation entitled to vote, represented in person or by proxy, shall constitute a quorum at a meeting of shareholders. Once a share is represented for any purpose at a meeting (other than solely to object to the holding of the meeting), it is deemed present for quorum purposes for the remainder of the meeting, and the shareholders present at a duly organized meeting may continue to transact business until adjournment, notwithstanding the withdrawal of sufficient shareholders to leave less than a quorum.

The holders of a majority of the outstanding shares represented at a meeting, whether or not a quorum is present, may adjourn the meeting from time to time.

Section 6. *Proxies:* Each shareholder entitled to vote at a meeting of shareholders or to express consent or dissent to corporate action in writing without a meeting may authorize another person or persons to vote for him or her by proxy, but no such proxy shall be voted or acted upon after one year from its date, unless the proxy provides for a longer period.

A duly executed proxy shall be irrevocable if it states that it is irrevocable and if, and only so long as, it is coupled with an interest sufficient in law to support an irrevocable power.

Except as otherwise provided herein or by law, every proxy is revocable at the pleasure of the shareholder executing it by communicating such revocation, in writing, to the Secretary of the Corporation.

Section 7. *Voting at Meetings:* If a quorum exists, action on a matter (other than the election of directors) is approved if the votes cast favoring the action exceed the votes cast opposing the action. Directors shall be elected by a plurality of the votes cast by the shares entitled to vote in the election (provided a quorum exists).

Unless otherwise provided by law or in the Corporation's Articles of Incorporation, and subject to the other provisions of these Bylaws, each shareholder shall be entitled to one vote on each matter, in person or by proxy, for each share of the Corporation's capital stock that has voting power and that is held by such shareholder. Voting need not be by written ballot.

Section 8. *List of Shareholders:* The officer of the Corporation who has charge of the stock ledger of the Corporation shall prepare and make, at least ten days before any meeting of shareholders, a complete list of the shareholders entitled to vote at the meeting, arranged alphabetically, and showing the address of each shareholder and the number of shares and class of shares held by each shareholder. The list shall be open to the examination of any shareholder for any purpose germane to the meeting, during ordinary business hours, for a period of at least ten days before the meeting, either at a place in the city where the meeting is to be held, which place must be specified in the notice of the meeting, or at the place where the meeting is to be held. The list shall also be produced and kept available at the time and place of the meeting, for the entire duration of the meeting, and may be inspected by any shareholder present at the meeting.

Section 9.   *Consent in Lieu of Meetings:*   Any action required to be taken or which may be taken at any meeting of shareholders, whether annual or special, may be taken without a meeting, without prior notice, and without a vote, if a consent in writing, setting forth the action so taken, shall be signed by the holders of all outstanding shares.

The action must be evidenced by one or more written consents, describing the action taken, signed and dated by the shareholders entitled to take action without a meeting, and delivered to the Corporation at its registered office or to the officer having charge of the Corporation's minute book.

No consent shall be effective to take the corporate action referred to in the consent unless the number of consents required to take action are delivered to the Corporation or to the officer having charge of its minute book within sixty days of the delivery of the earliest-dated consent.

Prompt notice of the taking of the corporate action without a meeting by less than unanimous vote shall be given to those shareholders who have not consented in writing.

Section 10.   *Conference Call:*   One or more shareholders may participate in a meeting of shareholders by means of conference telephone, videoconferencing, or similar communications equipment by means of which all persons participating in the meeting can hear each other. Participation in this manner shall constitute presence in person at such meeting.

Section 11.   *Annual Statement:*   The President and the Board of Directors shall present at each annual meeting a full and complete statement of the business and affairs of the corporation for the preceding year.

ARTICLE III — DIRECTORS

Section 1.   *Powers of Directors:*   The business and affairs of the Corporation shall be managed by or under the direction of the Board of Directors, which may exercise all such powers of the Corporation and do all lawful acts and things, subject to any limitations set forth in these Bylaws or the Articles of Incorporation for the Corporation.

Section 2.   *Number, Qualification, and Election:*   The number of directors which shall constitute the whole board shall be not fewer than _____ nor more than _____. Each director shall be at least 18 years of age. The directors need not be residents of the state of incorporation. Directors need not be shareholders in the Corporation. The directors shall be elected by the shareholders at the annual meeting of shareholders by the vote of shareholders holding of record in the aggregate at least a plurality of the shares of stock of the Corporation present in person or by proxy and entitled to vote at the annual meeting of shareholders. Each director shall be elected for a term of _____year[s], and until his or her successor shall be elected and shall qualify or until his or her earlier resignation or removal.

Section 3. *Nomination of Directors:* The Board of Directors shall nominate candidates to stand for election as directors; and other candidates may also be nominated by any shareholder of the Corporation, provided such nomination[s] is submitted in writing to the Corporation's Secretary no later than _____ days prior to the meeting of shareholders at which such directors are to be elected, together with the identity of the nominator and the number of shares of the stock of the Corporation owned by the nominator.

Section 4. *Vacancies:* Except as otherwise provided by law, any vacancy in the Board of Directors occurring by reason of an increase in the authorized number of directors or by reason of the death, withdrawal, removal, disqualification, inability to act, or resignation of a director shall be filled by the majority of directors then in office. The successor shall serve the unexpired portion of the term of his or her predecessor. Any director may resign at any time by giving written notice to the Board or the Secretary.

Section 5. *Meetings:*

    a. <u>Regular Meetings</u>: Regular meetings of the Board of Directors shall be held without notice and at such time and at such place as determined by the Board.

    b. <u>Special Meetings</u>: Special meetings of the Board may be called by the Chairperson or the President on _____ days' notice to each director, either personally or by telephone, express delivery service, telegram, or facsimile transmission, and on _____ days' notice by mail (effective upon deposit of such notice in the mail). The notice need not specify the purpose of a special meeting.

Section 6. *Quorum and Voting at Meetings:* A majority of the total number of authorized directors shall constitute a quorum for transaction of business. The act of a majority of directors present at any meeting at which a quorum is present shall be the act of the Board of Directors, except as provided by law, the Articles of Incorporation, or these Bylaws. Each director present shall have one vote, irrespective of the number of shares of stock, if any, he or she may hold.

Section 7. *Committees of Directors:* The Board of Directors, by resolution, may create one or more committees, each consisting of one or more Directors. Each such committee shall serve at the pleasure of the Board. All provisions of the law of the State of _____ and these Bylaws relating to meetings, action without meetings, notice, and waiver of notice, quorum, and voting requirements of the Board of Directors shall apply to such committees and their members.

Section 8. *Consent in Lieu of Meetings:* Any action required or permitted to be taken at any meeting of the Board of Directors or of any committee thereof, may be taken without a meeting if all members of the Board or committee, as the case may be, consent thereto in writing, such writing or writings to be filed with the minutes of proceedings of the Board or committee.

Section 9. *Conference Call:* One or more directors may participate in meetings of the Board or a committee of the Board by any communication, including videoconference, by means of which all participating directors can simultaneously hear each other during the meeting. Participation in this manner shall constitute presence in person at such meeting.

Section 10. *Compensation:* The Board of Directors shall have the authority to fix the compensation of Directors. A fixed sum and expenses of attendance may be allowed for attendance at each regular or special meeting of the Board. No such payment shall preclude any director from serving the Corporation in any other capacity and receiving compensation therefor.

Section 11. *Removal of Directors:* Any director or the entire Board of Directors may be removed, with or without cause, by the holders of a majority of the shares then entitled to vote at an election of directors.

ARTICLE IV — OFFICERS

Section 1. *Positions:* The officers of the Corporation shall be a Chairperson, a President, a Secretary, and a Treasurer, and such other officers as the Board may from time to time appoint, including one or more Vice Presidents and such other officers as it deems advisable. Any number of offices may be held by the same person, except that the President and the Secretary may not be the same person. Each such officer shall exercise such powers and perform such duties as shall be set forth herein and such other powers and duties as may be specified from time to time by the Board of Directors. The officers of the Corporation shall be elected by the Board of Directors. Each of the Chairperson, President, and/or any Vice Presidents may execute bonds, mortgages, and other documents under the seal of the Corporation, except where required or permitted by law to be otherwise executed and except where execution thereof shall be expressly delegated by the Board to some other officer or agent of the Corporation.

Section 2. *Chairperson:* The Chairperson shall have overall responsibility and authority for management and operations of the Corporation, shall preside at all meetings of the Board of Directors and shareholders, and shall ensure that all orders and resolutions of the Board of Directors and shareholders are effected.

Section 3. *President:* The President shall be the chief operating officer of the Corporation and shall have full responsibility and authority for management of the day-to-day operations of the Corporation. The President shall be an ex-officio member of all committees and shall have the general powers and duties of management and supervision usually vested in the office of president of a corporation.

Section 4. *Secretary:* The Secretary shall attend all meetings of the Board and all meetings of the shareholders and shall act as clerk thereof, and record all the votes of the Corporation and the minutes of all its transactions in a book to be kept for that purpose, and shall perform like duties for all committees of the Board of Directors when required. The Secretary shall give, or cause to be given, notice of all meetings of the shareholders and special meetings of the Board of Directors, and shall perform such other duties as may be prescribed by the Board of Directors or President, and under whose supervision the Secretary shall be. The Secretary shall maintain the records, minutes, and seal of the Corporation and may attest any instruments signed by any other officer of the Corporation.

Section 5. *Treasurer:* The Treasurer shall be the chief financial officer of the Corporation, shall have responsibility for the custody of the corporate funds and securities, shall keep full and accurate records and accounts of receipts and disbursements in books belonging to the Corporation, and shall keep the monies of the Corporation in a separate account in the name of the Corporation. The Treasurer shall provide to the President and directors, at the regular meetings of the Board, or whenever requested by the Board, an account of all financial transactions and of the financial condition of the Corporation.

Section 6. *Term of Office:* The officers of the Corporation shall hold office until their successors are chosen and have qualified or until their earlier resignation or removal.

Unless an officer or agent serves pursuant to a valid employment agreement, any officer or agent elected or appointed by the Board may be removed at any time, with or without cause, by the affirmative vote of a majority of the Board of Directors. Any vacancy occurring in any office as a result of death, resignation, removal, or otherwise, shall be filled for the unexpired portion of the term by a majority vote of the Board of Directors.

Section 7. *Compensation:* The compensation of officers of the Corporation shall be fixed by the Board of Directors.

ARTICLE V — CAPITAL STOCK

Section 1. *Stock Certificates:* The shares of the Corporation shall be represented by certificates, provided that the Board of Directors may provide by resolution that some or all of any or all classes or series of the stock of the Corporation shall be uncertificated shares. Notwithstanding the adoption of such a resolution by the Board of Directors, every holder of stock represented by certificates and, upon request, every holder of uncertificated shares, shall be entitled to have a certificate signed in the name of the Corporation, by the Chairperson, President or any Vice President, and by the Treasurer or Secretary. Any or all of the signatures on the certificate may be by facsimile. The stock certificates of the Corporation shall be numbered and registered in the share ledger and transfer books of the Corporation as they are issued and shall bear the corporate seal.

Section 2. *Lost Certificates:* The Corporation may issue a new certificate of stock in place of any certificate previously issued and alleged to have been lost, stolen, or destroyed, and the Corporation may require the owner of the lost, stolen, or destroyed certificate, or his or her legal representative, to make an affidavit of that fact, and the Corporation may require indemnity against any claim that may be made against the Corporation on account of the alleged loss, theft, or destruction of any such certificate or the issuance of such new certificate.

Section 3. *Transfers:* Transfers of shares shall be made on the books of the Corporation upon surrender and cancellation of the certificates therefor, endorsed by the person named in the certificate or by his or her legal representative. No transfer shall be made which is inconsistent with any provision of law, the Articles of Incorporation for the Corporation, or these Bylaws.

Section 4. *Record Date:* In order that the Corporation may determine the shareholders entitled to notice of or to vote at any meeting of shareholders, or any adjournment thereof, or to take action without a meeting, or to receive payment of any dividend or other distribution, or to exercise any rights in respect of any change, conversion, or exchange of stock, or for the purpose of any other lawful action, the Board of Directors may fix a record date, which record date shall not precede the date upon which the resolution fixing the record date is adopted by the Board of Directors and shall not be less than ten nor more than fifty days before the meeting or action requiring a determination of shareholders.

If no record date is fixed by the Board of Directors:

a. for determining shareholders entitled to notice of or to vote at a meeting, the record date shall be at the close of business on the day next preceding the day on which notice is given, or, if notice is waived, at the close of business on the day next preceding the day on which the meeting is held or other action taken;

b. for determining shareholders entitled to consent to corporate action without a meeting, the record date shall be the day on which the first written consent is delivered to the Corporation in accordance with these Bylaws; and

c. for determining shareholders for any other purpose, the record date shall be at the close of business on the day on which the Board of Directors adopts the resolution relating thereto.

ARTICLE VI—DIVIDENDS

Section 1. *Dividends:* The Board of Directors may declare and pay dividends upon the outstanding shares of the Corporation, from time to time and to such extent as the Board deems advisable, in the manner and upon the terms and conditions provided by law and the Articles of Incorporation of the Corporation.

Section 2. *Reserves:* The Board of Directors may set apart, out of the funds of the Corporation available for dividends, said sum as the directors, from time to time, in their absolute discretion, think proper as a reserve fund for any proper purpose. The Board of Directors may abolish any such reserve in the manner it was created.

ARTICLE VII—GENERAL PROVISIONS

Section 1. *Insurance and Indemnity:* The Corporation shall purchase and maintain insurance in a reasonable amount on behalf of any person who is or was a director, officer, agent, or employee of the Corporation against liability asserted against or incurred by such person in such capacity or arising from such person's status as such.

Subject to applicable statute, any person made or threatened to be made a party to any action, suit, or proceeding, by reason of the fact that he or she, his or her testator or intestate representative, is or was a director, officer, agent, or employee of the Corporation, shall be indemnified by the Corporation against the reasonable expenses, including attorneys' fees, actually and necessarily incurred by him or her in connection with such an action, suit, or proceeding.

Notwithstanding the foregoing, no indemnification shall be made by the Corporation if judgment or other final determination establishes that the potential indemnitee's acts were committed in bad faith or were the result of active or deliberate fraud or dishonesty or clear and gross negligence.

Section 2. *Inspection of Corporate Records:* Any shareholder of record, in person or by attorney or other agent, shall, upon written demand under oath stating the purpose thereof, have the right during the usual hours for business to inspect for any proper purpose the Corporation's stock ledger, a list of its shareholders, and its other books and records, and to make copies or extracts therefrom. A proper purpose shall mean a purpose reasonably related to such person's interest as a shareholder. In every instance in which an attorney or other agent shall be the person seeking the right to inspection, the demand under oath shall be accompanied by a power of attorney or such other writing authorizing the attorney or other agent to so act on behalf of the shareholder. The demand under oath shall be directed to the Corporation at its registered office or its principal place of business.

Section 3. *Fiscal Year:* The fiscal year of the Corporation shall be the calendar year.

Section 4.   *Seal:*   The corporate seal shall be in such form as the Board of Directors shall approve. The seal may be used by causing it or a facsimile thereof to be impressed, affixed, or otherwise reproduced.

Section 5.   *Execution of Instruments:*   All contracts, checks, drafts, or demands for money and notes and other instruments or rights of any nature of the Corporation shall be signed by such officer or officers as the Board of Directors may from time to time designate.

Section 6.   *Notice:*   Whenever written notice is required to be given to any person, it may be given to such person, either personally or by sending a copy thereof through the United States mail, or by telegram, facsimile, or electronic transmission, charges prepaid, to his or her address appearing on the books of the Corporation, or supplied by him or her to the Corporation for the purpose of notice. If the notice is sent by mail or by telegraph, it shall be deemed to have been given to the person entitled thereto when deposited in the United States mail or with a telegraph office for transmission to such person. If the notice is sent by facsimile, it shall be deemed to have been given at the date and time shown on a written confirmation of the transmission of such facsimile communication. If the notice is sent by electronic transmission, it shall be deemed to have been given at the close of business on the day transmitted. Such notice shall specify the place, day, and hour of the meeting, and, in the case of a special meeting of shareholders, the purpose of and general nature of the business to be transacted at such special meeting.

Section 7.   *Waiver of Notice:*   Whenever any written notice is required by law, or by the Articles of Incorporation or by these Bylaws, a waiver thereof in writing, signed by the person or persons entitled to such notice, whether before or after the time stated therein, shall be deemed equivalent to the giving of such notice. Except in the case of a special meeting of shareholders, neither the business to be conducted at nor the purpose of the meeting need be specified in the waiver of notice of the meeting. Attendance of a person either in person or by proxy, at any meeting, shall constitute a waiver of notice of such meeting, except where a person attends a meeting for the express purpose of objecting to the transaction of any business because the meeting was not lawfully convened or called.

Section 8.   *Amendments:*   The Board of Directors shall have the power to make, adopt, alter, amend, and repeal from time to time the Bylaws of the Corporation except that the adoption, amendment, or repeal of any Bylaw regulating the election of directors shall be subject to the vote of shareholders entitled to cast at least a majority of the votes which all shareholders are entitled to cast at any regular or special meeting of the shareholders, duly convened after notice to the shareholders of that purpose.

The foregoing Bylaws were adopted by the Board of Directors on _____.

_____
Secretary

Glossary

Accredited investor: An investor with a certain net work or otherwise sufficiently sophisticated that he or she does not require the registration protections afforded by the Securities Act of 1933.

Accumulated earnings tax: Tax penalty imposed on corporations that retain earnings beyond reasonable business needs.

Actual authority: The grant of authority, either express or implied, by a principal to an agent.

Administrative dissolution: A dissolution initiated for technical or administrative defaults, such as a corporation's failure to file reports or pay taxes.

Affiliates: Subsidiaries formed by a common parent corporation.

Agency: Relationship between parties whereby one agrees to act on behalf of another.

Agency by estoppel: Agency arising from acts that lead others to believe an agency relationship exists.

Agent: One who acts for or represents another, called a principal.

Agent for service: *See* Registered agent.

Aggressor: Corporation (or individual) attacking or wishing to acquire control over another corporation, typically called the target.

Alien corporation: Corporation formed in a country other than the United States.

Alter ego: When corporate shareholders fail to respect the fact that the corporation is an entity separate and apart from them, they are said to view the corporation as their "alter ego," namely, a mere extension of themselves. Shareholders who treat the corporation as their alter ego may have personal liability imposed on them for the corporation's debts.

Annual meeting: Yearly meeting of shareholders of a corporation to elect directors and conduct other business.

Annual report: Form required to be filed, yearly by business entities in most states, providing information about the entity.

Apparent authority: Conduct of a principal causing a third party to believe an agent had authority to act for the principal.

Appraisal rights: Authority given to dissenting shareholders to have their shares appraised, or valued, and bought out.

Articles of amendment: Document filed with secretary of state that amends articles of incorporation.

Articles of dissolution: Document filed with the secretary of state to effect a dissolution or termination of a corporation as a legal entity. Sometimes called a certificate of dissolution.

Articles of domestication: The document filed with the state to effect a change of a corporation's state of incorporation.

Articles of entity conversion: The document filed with the state to effect a change in a business's structure.

Articles of incorporation: Document that creates a corporation. Sometimes called a certificate of incorporation.

Articles of merger: Document filed with the secretary of state to effect a merger or other combination of two or more corporations.

Articles of organization: Document filed with the appropriate state official creating a limited liability company.

Asset purchase: Acquisition by one corporation of some or all of another's properties.

Assignment: Transfer of one's interest in certain property.

Assumed name: *See* Fictitious business name.

Authorized share: Share identified in the articles of incorporation as being capable of and subject to issuance by a corporation.

Blue-chip stock: Stock of elite and nationally known corporations.

Blue sky law: State law regulating the issuance, purchase, and sale of securities.

Board of directors: *See* Director.

Bond: Instrument issued for the purpose of raising capital for an entity.

Bondholder: One to whom a debt is owed by a corporation.

Broad purpose clause: Clause in corporate articles that states the corporation may engage in any legal activity (also called full purpose clause).

Bulletproof state: A state offering full protection from liability (whether arising in tort or contract) in a limited liability partnership (also called full shield state).

Business corporation: *See* Corporation.

Business judgment rule: Court-made rule immunizing directors and officers from liability for their decisions so long as the decision was reasonable and made in good faith.

Buy-sell agreement: Agreement entered into by shareholders or owners of a business restricting the transfer or sale of their stock or interest in the business.

Bylaws: Rules governing the management and operation of a corporation.

C corporation: Corporation for profit that is subject to double taxation; one other than an "S" corporation.

Call: Right of a corporation to reacquire stock it has issued to a shareholder (generally, a preferred shareholder).

Cancellation: Elimination of shares reacquired by a corporation.

Capital: Generally, money used to form and operate a business.

Cash dividend: Distribution of cash by a corporation to its shareholders.

Certificate of good standing: Document issued by a secretary of state showing that a corporation is in compliance with that state's laws (also called certificate of existence).

Chair: Individual who presides at corporate meetings.

Charter: Name used by some states to refer to a corporation's articles of incorporation.

Check-the-box: Method by which businesses select how they wish to be taxed, namely, whether as partnerships or corporations.

Chief executive officer: Individual who supervises other officers.

Chief financial officer: Individual with primary responsibility for all financial matters.

Class action: Action brought by one or a few shareholders on behalf of numerous other shareholders who are similarly situated.

Class voting: Voting rights given to a class of stock.

Close (closely held) corporation: Corporation whose shares are held by a few people, usually friends or relatives active in managing the business. Some flexibility is permitted with regard to observing corporate formalities.

Commingling: Combining shareholders' personal funds improperly with those of the corporation; liability may be imposed on shareholders who fail to respect the corporate entity by commingling funds.

Common stock: Stock in a corporation that has no special features, as does preferred stock; usually has the right to vote and share in liquidation distributions.

Consolidation: Combination of two or more corporations into a new corporate entity (example: A + B = X).

Constituent corporations: Corporations that are parties to a merger, consolidation, or other combination.

Conversion right: 1. Right of preferred shareholders to convert preferred stock into some other security of the corporation, usually common stock.
2. Right of creditors to convert debt security (often a bond) into equity security (shares).

Corporation: Legal entity existing by authority of state law, owned by its shareholders and managed by its elected directors and appointed officers.

Creeping tender offer: *See* Toehold.

Cross-species merger: Merger between corporation and some other business entity.

Crown jewel defense: Sale by a target of its valuable assets, usually to make itself unattractive to an aggressor.

Cumulative dividend: Distribution that "adds up" over time and must be paid to a preferred shareholder when the corporation has funds to do so, before any distribution can be made to other shareholders (also called cumulative distribution).

Cumulative voting: In an election for directors, a type of voting whereby each share carries as many votes as there are directors' vacancies to be filled; assists minority shareholders in electing representatives to the board of directors.

D & O insurance: Insurance procured to protect directors and officers from claims and lawsuits.

DBA: "Doing business as"; another name for a fictitious business name statement.

Debt financing: Borrowing money to raise capital.

Debt security: Instrument evidencing a corporation's debt to another.

De facto corporation: Literally, "in fact"; a corporation with a defect in its incorporation process such that it may not have de jure status; it may not be attacked by a third party, although the state may invalidate it.

De jure corporation: Literally, "of right"; a corporation formed in substantial compliance with the laws of the state of incorporation, the validity of which cannot be attacked by any party or the state.

Derivative action: Action brought by a limited partner or shareholder not to enforce his or her own cause of action but to enforce an obligation due the business entity; the action "derives" from the claimant's ownership interest in the business entity.

Direct action: Action brought by a limited partner or shareholder of a corporation for direct injury sustained by the claimant, for example, being refused the right to examine books and records.

Director: One who directs or manages a corporation. When more than one director exists, they function as a board.

Dissenter's rights: *See* Appraisal rights.

Dissenting shareholder: Shareholder opposing some corporate action, such as amendment of the articles of incorporation, merger, or consolidation.

Dissociation: Departure by a partner from a partnership.

Dissolution: Termination of a business organization as a legal entity, such as dissolution of a partnership or corporation; may be voluntary or involuntary for corporation.

Distribution: Direct or indirect transfer by a corporation of money or other property (other than its own shares) to or for the benefit of its shareholders, whether a distribution of corporate profits or a distribution at the time of liquidation. The older view used this term to refer to distribution to shareholders *other than* distributions of the corporation's own profits.

Dividend: Corporation's distribution of its profits to its shareholders by way of cash, property, or shares. The modern approach is to refer to any distribution as a dividend, whether a distribution of corporate profits or a distribution at the time of liquidation.

Dividend reinvestment plan: Plan allowing shareholders to immediately use cash dividends to purchase more stock; usually called DRIPs.

Domestication: The changing of a corporation's state of incorporation.

Domestic corporation: A corporation created or incorporated in the state in which it is conducting business.

Double taxation: Taxation of corporate income at two levels: once when the corporation earns money and then again when shareholders receive distributions from the corporation.

Draw: Advance payment to an employee against anticipated compensation.

Due diligence: Careful review of documents and transactions to ensure they are appropriate for a party and in compliance with all pertinent laws.

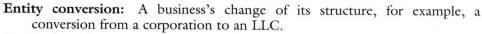

Entity conversion: A business's change of its structure, for example, a conversion from a corporation to an LLC.

Equity financing: Issuance of shares to raise capital.

Equity insolvency test: Test to determine if dividends may be paid in which corporation must be solvent (meaning it must be able to pay its debts as they come due).

Equity security: Security demonstrating a person's ownership interest in a corporation.

Estoppel: Prohibition imposed on a party to preclude a challenge to some fact or event because such a challenge would be inequitable based on party's conduct.

Excess assets test: Test to determine if dividends may be paid in which equity exceeds liability (also called balance sheet test).

Exchange: *See* stock exchange.

Ex-dividend: The status of a shareholder or share that has no right to receive a declared dividend.

Exempt security: Security that is exempt from compliance with the registration requirements of the Securities Act of 1933.

Exempt transaction: Transaction exempt from compliance with the registration requirements of the Securities Act of 1933.

Express agency: Agency created by agreement, whether oral or written.

Express authority: Acts specifically directed or authorized by a principal.

Extinguished corporation: Corporation that does not survive a merger or some other combination. Sometimes called a merged corporation.

Fictitious business name: Name adopted for use by a person, partnership, corporation, or other business that is other than its true or legal name; sometimes called an assumed name or "dba" for "doing business as."

Fiduciary relationship: Relationship in which a party owes the utmost duties of good faith and candor to another or others.

Financing statement: Document recorded with the secretary of state or county recorder to provide notice of a security interest claimed in personal property (also called UCC-1 form).

Fiscal year: Twelve-month reporting period adopted by a business for accounting purposes; it need not be the calendar year.

Foothold: *See* Toehold.

Foreign corporation: Corporation conducting business in a state other than the one in which it is incorporated. Occasionally, corporations formed outside the United States are called foreign corporations, though they are more properly termed alien corporations.

Foreign partnership: Partnership conducting business in a state other than the one in which it is organized.

Franchise tax: Fee or tax imposed by a state for the privilege of conducting business in the state.

Freeze-out: Impermissible tactic by directors to compel a corporate dissolution or merger to dispose of minority shareholders; sometimes called a *squeeze-out*.

Full shield state: State offering full protection from liability (whether arising in tort or contract) for partners in limited liability partnership.

GAAP: Generally accepted accounting principles.

General agency: Act of a partner in carrying out the usual business of the firm that will bind the partnership unless the person with whom the partner is dealing knows the partner has no authority to perform that act.

General partner: Individual or entity managing or controlling a general partnership or a limited partnership.

General partnership: Entity affording full ability to manage and control to all of its partners and in which all partners have unlimited personal and joint and several liability.

General proxy: A proxy authorizing the proxy holder to vote a shareholder's shares in the proxy holder's discretion.

Going public: Offering securities to members of the public at large. *See* Initial public offering.

Golden parachute: Lucrative compensation package given to key corporate managers who leave or are let go by a corporation.

Governance guidelines: Formal written policies relating to management of corporations and often sought by shareholders.

Hart-Scott-Rodino Antitrust Improvements Act: A federal statute requiring premerger notification to the government so it can determine if the proposed transaction would have an anticompetitive effect.

Holder of record: Owner of stock as of a particular date. *See* Record date.

Hostile takeover: Transaction pursued by bidder without support of target's management.

Householding: Practice of sending only one report and proxy statement to shareholders with same surname at same address.

Illegal dividend: Dividend paid out of an unauthorized account or made while a corporation is insolvent.

Implied agency: Agency relationship in which there is no express agreement, but parties' words or conduct show existence of the agency relationship.

Implied authority: Authority to perform acts customarily performed by agents, even if not expressly so directed by a principal.

Incorporator: Person who prepares and signs the articles of incorporation to form a corporation.

Indemnify: Compensating or reimbursing one who has incurred a debt or obligation on another's behalf.

Independent director: Director with no family or business ties to a corporation other than board membership.

Information returns: Documents filed with the Internal Revenue Service reporting income earned by or distributed to partners, members of an LLC, or shareholders.

Inherent authority: Authority that naturally flows from one's position.

Initial public offering: First offering of securities to the public; usually the offering by a corporation of its securities to the public as a means of raising capital; often referred to as "going public."

Inside director: A director who is also an employee or officer of the corporation.

Insider trading: Transaction by corporate insiders, such as directors and officers, to achieve some benefit from the purchase or sale of securities based on inside information, namely information that is not available to the public at large. Prohibited by SEC Rule 10b-5.

Insolvency: Generally, inability to pay one's debts as they become due in the usual course of business or condition created by excess of liabilities over assets.

Interest in partnership: A partner's right to profits (or share of losses).

Involuntary dissolution: Dissolution forced upon an entity, such as a partnership or corporation, through a judicial proceeding initiated by either the state or owners of the entity, or perhaps by creditors. Sometimes called judicial dissolution.

Issuance: Process of selling corporate securities.

Joint and several liability: When each member of an association is liable to pay all of a debt or obligation; when a creditor may sue all individuals in an association or pick among them to satisfy a debt.

Joint venture: Type of partnership formed to carry out a particular enterprise rather than an ongoing business.

Judicial dissolution: *See* Involuntary dissolution.

Judicial liquidation: Liquidation of a corporation that has been involuntarily dissolved by a court; often performed by a court-appointed receiver or trustee.

Known claim: A claim against an entity that is known by an entity.

Legend: Generally, a notation on a stock certificate stating that it is subject to some restriction, typically as to transfer of stock represented by the certificate.

Letter of intent: Initial document setting forth basic understanding of parties to a transaction.

Limited liability: Liability that is confined to that amount contributed by an investor to an enterprise; when personal assets of an investor cannot be used to satisfy business debts or obligations.

Limited liability company: New form of business enterprise, recognized in all states, offering the pass-through tax status of a partnership and the limited liability of a corporation.

Limited liability limited partnership: A limited partnership that files with the secretary of state so its general partner has no liability for partnership obligations; recognized fully only in some states.

Limited liability partnership: *See* Registered limited liability partnership.

Limited partner: Individual or entity having membership in a limited partnership, but who does not manage or control the enterprise, and whose liability is limited to the amount contributed to the limited partnership.

Limited partnership: Partnership formed under statutory requirements that has as members one or more general partners and one or more limited partners.

Limited partnership agreement: Agreement among partners in a limited partnership, usually written, regarding the affairs of the limited partnership, the duties of the general partner, rights of limited partners, and the conduct of the business.

Limited partnership certificate: Document filed with a state agency to create a limited partnership.

Limited proxy: A proxy directing a proxy holder to vote as specified by the shareholder giving the proxy.

Liquidation: Process of completing the affairs of a business; for corporations, the process of collecting corporate assets, discharging debts, and distributing any remains to the shareholders; may be judicial or nonjudicial. Sometimes called winding up.

Liquidation distribution: Distribution made to business owners after creditors have been paid upon dissolution of a business entity (also called liquidation dividend).

Liquidator: *See* Receiver.

Marshaling of assets: Requirement that partnership creditors must first exhaust partnership assets before attacking a partner's personal assets to satisfy a debt or obligation.

Member: Owner or investor in a limited liability company.

Membership: What is offered by a nonprofit corporation rather than offering shares and what is offered by a limited liability company.

Merger: Combinations of two or more corporations into one corporate entity (example: A + B = A).

Mini-tender offer: A tender offer to purchase less than 5 percent of a target's outstanding shares; not subject to SEC rules relating to tender offers.

Minute book: Binder or book used to maintain minutes of corporate meetings and other records.

Minutes: Written summary of the proceedings at directors' or shareholders' meetings.

Mortgage bond or note: Debt security in which a corporation pledges real estate as security for its promise to repay money borrowed from a creditor.

Name registration: Reservation of a corporate name in foreign states in which the corporation intends to do business in the future.

Name reservation: Reservation of proposed corporate name prior to filing of articles of incorporation; generally effective for some specified period.

Name saver: Subsidiary incorporated in a state expressly to ensure name is available for corporate parent in that state.

Nonaccredited investor: Investor who is not sophisticated or "accredited"; *see* Accredited investor.

Noncompetition agreements: Agreements whereby an individual, usually an employee or senior manager, agrees not to compete with employer after employment ends (also called noncompete clauses).

Noncumulative distribution: A distribution that does not accumulate and is lost if it cannot be paid.

Nonjudicial liquidation: Liquidation of an entity that has been voluntarily dissolved (without court involvement); in a corporation, such liquidation is performed by corporate directors and officers.

Nonprofit corporation: Corporation formed for some charitable, religious, educational, or scientific purpose or for the mutual benefit of its members, rather than for the purpose of making a profit.

No par value stock: Stock having no stated minimum value; the price may be determined by a corporation's board of directors.

Notice of intent to dissolve: Document filed with state indicating corporation's intent to dissolve.

NYSE Euronext: Largest auction market for trading of securities, which also uses automated trading; located in New York City and usually referred to as NYSE.

Officer: One appointed by corporation's board of directors to carry out management functions as delegated by the board.

Operating agreement: Agreement governing the operation of a limited liability company.

Organizational meeting: First meeting of a corporation held after incorporation to finalize the incorporation process by electing directors, appointing officers, adopting bylaws, and so forth.

Outside director: Director who is not an employee or officer of the corporation.

Outstanding shares: Shares issued by a corporation and held by a shareholder.

Over-the-counter market: Computerized securities trading network with no physical trading location.

Parent corporation: Corporation that creates another corporation (called a subsidiary) and which holds all or a majority of its shares.

Partial shield state: A state offering full protection from liability to partners in a limited liability partnership for acts arising out of wrongful conduct of co-partners but no protection for acts arising out of contractual obligations.

Partnership: An association of two or more persons to carry on a business as co-owners for profit; often called a general partnership to distinguish it from a limited partnership.

Partnership at will: Partnership with no specific term of duration.

Par value: Minimum consideration for which share of stock may be issued; usually set forth in a corporation's articles of incorporation.

Pass-through taxation: Tax status of an entity in which all income is passed through to individuals, who pay taxes on that income at their individual rates; entity itself does not pay taxes.

Person: According to most statutes, a "person" is a natural individual or a business organization, such as a partnership or corporation.

Personal liability: Liability for debts and obligations in excess of that originally invested, namely, liability extending to one's personal assets (also called unlimited personal liability).

Piercing the veil: Holding individual investors liable for a business's obligations to prevent fraud or injustice.

Plan of domestication: The plan that provides the terms and conditions of a corporation's change of its state of incorporation.

Plan of entity conversion: The plan that provides the terms and conditions of a business's change in its structure.

Plan of merger: Blueprint for a merger containing all of the terms and conditions relating to a merger.

Plurality: The number of votes received by a successful candidate who receives less than 51 percent of the votes cast in an election; counting only votes "for" a nominee and not counting votes "against" or withheld.

Poison pill: Privileges and rights of a target's shareholders triggered by a tender offer; designed to thwart a takeover (also called shareholder rights plan).

Preemptive right: Rights given to shareholders in articles of incorporation allowing shareholders to purchase newly issued stock in an amount proportionate to their current share ownership.

Preferred stock: Corporate stock that has some right, privilege, or preference over another type of stock.

Preincorporation agreement: Agreement entered into between promoters of corporation and some third party prior to creation of the corporation; promoter is bound by the agreement until expressly released.

Preincorporation share subscription: Offer by a party to purchase stock in a corporation made before the corporation is formed.

Principal: One who appoints another, called an agent, to act for or represent him or her.

Priority: Process of making one debt senior, or prior, to another (which is referred to as subordinate).

Privately held corporation: Corporation whose shares are not sold to the public but are held by a small group of investors, often family and friends.

Process: Complaint filed in court by a plaintiff and the summons issued thereafter by the court to the party named as defendant requiring an appearance or response.

Professional corporation: Corporation formed by a person or persons practicing a certain profession, such as law, medicine, or accounting, who retain liability for their own misconduct and those acting under their control.

Promissory note: Document evidencing one's debt to another.

Promoter: One who plans and organizes a corporation.

Property dividend: Distribution that is not cash or shares in the issuing corporation but is generally some physical or tangible item.

Proxy: Written authorization by a shareholder directing another to vote his or her shares.

Proxy fight: Solicitation of a target's shareholders by management of the aggressor and management of the target to vote for each party's management slate (also called a proxy contest).

Public corporation: Corporation whose shares may be purchased and sold by members of the general public.

Public offering: Issuance of securities to the general public that generally must first be registered according to the Securities Act of 1933.

Put: Right of a shareholder (usually, a preferred shareholder) to compel a corporation to reacquire stock issued to the shareholder.

Qualification: Process by which a corporation formed in one state is authorized to transact business in another.

Qualified small business stock: Stock in certain small businesses (C corporations with less than $50 million) that qualifies for tax advantages by excluding from taxable income one-half of any gain on the sale of the stock.

Quorum: Minimum number of shareholders or directors required to be present at a meeting to conduct business; usually a majority.

Ratification: Acceptance or approval of a certain act; may be express or implied from conduct.

Receiver: Individual or firm appointed by a court to oversee a judicial or involuntary dissolution. Sometimes called a liquidator.

Recitals: Preliminary clauses in agreements, often identifying the parties to agreement and the intent or purpose of the agreement.

Record date: Date selected in advance of a meeting or action used to determine who will be entitled to notice of a meeting and who will be entitled to vote at a meeting or who will be entitled to the benefits of some action.

Redemption right: 1. Right given to corporation to repurchase the stock of preferred shareholders (call) or the right given to a preferred shareholder to compel the corporation to repurchase preferred stock (put).
2. Right of a debtor to pay off, or redeem, debt owed to a creditor before the stated maturity date.

Registered agent: Individual or company designated by a business to receive notices, litigation pleadings, documents, and service of process on the business's behalf.

Registered limited liability partnership: Newly recognized form of partnership in which a partner has no personal liability for the misconduct of another partner (and, in some states, no personal liability for contractual obligations of the partnership); formed by filing an application with the appropriate state official (also called limited liability partnership).

Registered office: Principal location of a business organization identified in various state forms or filings so that third parties may contact the business.

Registrar: Bank or other institution that maintains a corporation's list of shareholders.

Registration: 1. Process of reserving a corporate name in another state.
2. Process of complying with the Securities Act of 1933, when securities are first offered to the public.

Registration statement: Form or document filed with the Securities and Exchange Commission pursuant to the Securities Act of 1933, when securities are first offered to the public.

Regular meeting: Routinely scheduled meeting of corporate directors.

Reinstatement: Process of reviving a corporation after it has been dissolved for a technical violation of state law, such as failure to file annual report.

Relation back: Doctrine that certain actions are viewed as having occurred on an earlier date.

Reservation: *See* Name reservation.

Respondeat superior: Latin phrase meaning "let the master answer"; legal theory by which liability is imposed on an employer-principal for an employee-agent's acts committed in the course and scope of the employment or agency.

Restated articles of incorporation: Document filed with the secretary of state to combine previously amended articles into a more comprehensible document.

Reverse stock split: Reduction by a corporation in the number of its outstanding shares; often done to eliminate smaller shareholders.

S corporation: Corporation in which all income is passed through to shareholders who pay taxes at appropriate individual rates. Certain eligibility requirements must be met to elect S status.

Safe harbor: Generally, list in statute identifying permitted or "safe" activities.

Scrip: Certificate evidencing a fractional share; scrip does not typically possess voting, dividend, or liquidation rights.

Seal: Instrument used to emboss documents to verify authenticity.

Section 12 company: Company required to register its securities pursuant to Section 12 of the Securities Exchange Act of 1934 (namely, a company traded on a national securities exchange or one having assets of $10 million or more and 500 or more shareholders).

Section 1244 stock: Stock that when sold at a loss provides certain tax advantages; the loss is treated as an ordinary rather than as a capital loss. Certain requirements must be met to issue Section 1244 stock.

Secured debt or transaction: Debt secured by some asset that can be seized upon the borrower's default in repayment of its loan obligation.

Securities Act of 1933: Federal law imposing requirements on a company's original issuance of securities to the public.

Securities and Exchange Commission (SEC): Independent federal agency charged with the regulation of securities.

Securities Exchange Act of 1934: Federal law imposing requirements on the trading of stock, primarily the purchase and sale of securities after their original issuance.

Securities Litigation Reform Act: Federal law intended to reduce frivolous shareholder suits for securities fraud.

Security: Share or ownership interest in a corporation (equity security) or obligation of the corporation to an investor (debt security).

Security agreement: Agreement between a debtor and a lender in which debtor pledges personal property (rather than real estate) as collateral to secure repayment of the debtor's loan to the creditor.

Service of process: Delivery of a summons and complaint (i.e., process) upon a defendant or its agent.

Share: A unit into which the proprietary interests of a corporation are divided.

Share dividend: Distribution to shareholders of the corporation's own shares.

Share exchange: Process by which the shareholders of a target exchange their shares for those of another corporation or for cash.

Shareholder: One who owns an interest in a corporation; synonymous with stockholder.

Share purchase: *See* Stock purchase.

Share subscription: Agreement whereby a party offers to purchase stock in a corporation.

Short-form merger: Merger between a parent and its subsidiary in which the parent owns at least 90 percent of the subsidiary's stock.

Short-swing profits: Profits made by a Section 12 company's officers, directors, or principal shareholders within a six-month period that must be disgorged to the corporation, even without a showing of insider trading or bad faith.

Small business corporation: Domestic corporation, with no more than 75 shareholders, all of whom are individuals, which may elect to be treated as an S corporation and thereby avoid double taxation.

Small-scale merger: Merger not dramatically affecting the survivor corporation's shareholders that is therefore not subject to approval by the survivor's shareholders.

Sole proprietor: Individual who owns a business (also called individual proprietor).

Sole proprietorship: Business managed and owned by one person, the sole proprietor, who has sole authority for all decision-making and faces unlimited personal liability for business debts and obligations.

Solvency: Generally, ability to pay debts as they come due.

Special meeting: Any meeting held between the annual meetings of shareholders or regular meetings of directors.

Squeeze-out: *See* Freeze-out.

Stagger system: Process of varying election dates for board members so they are not all elected at the same time.

Statement of Authority: Document filed with state providing notice of partners who have authority to do certain acts for partnership.

Statement of Denial: Document filed with state denying information in a Statement of Authority.

Stock: *See* Share.

Stock certificate: Document evidencing an ownership interest in a corporation.

Stock certificate book: Book containing stock certificates to be issued to shareholders.

Stock exchange: Marketplace where securities are traded.

Stockholder: *See* Shareholder.

Stock purchase: Acquisition of stock in a corporation.

Stock split: Division by a corporation of its outstanding shares, often done to encourage trading.

Straight voting: The right carried by each outstanding share of record to one vote.

Subordination: Process of making one debt junior, or subordinate, to another (which is said to have priority over it).

Subsidiary: Corporation formed by another corporation, called the parent; all or the majority of the subsidiary's stock is owned by the parent.

Survivor: Corporation that continues in existence after a merger.

2001 Act: Revised version of uniform limited partnership act, adopted in fully six states, providing significant protection from liability for all partners.

Takeover: *See* Hostile takeover.

Takeover defenses: Strategies implemented by a target to thwart a takeover.

Target: Corporation being attacked or subject to takeover by another corporation or some third party.

Tax year: An annual accounting period for keeping records and reporting income and expenses.

Tender offer: Public offer by an aggressor to shareholders of a target corporation seeking to acquire their shares.

Thin incorporation: Condition of a corporation's debt being disproportionately higher than its equity.

Tippee: One who receives tips or information about a corporation's finances or operations from a corporate insider.

Tipper: Corporate insider who gives tips or information to others about the corporation's finances or operations.

Toehold: Stock of a target purchased by an aggressor wishing to take over the target; usually less than 5 percent. Sometimes called a foothold or creeping tender offer.

Transacting business: Activities engaged in by an entity doing business in a state other than its state of formation that will require it to formally qualify with that host state to conduct business.

Transfer agent: Bank or other institution that physically issues or cancels stock certificates for large corporations.

Treasury stock: Stock reacquired by a corporation and that is considered issued but not outstanding.

Triple taxation: Taxation of income when received by a subsidiary, then when received by the parent as a distribution, and finally when received by the parent's shareholders as a distribution.

Ultra vires **act:** Act beyond the purposes and powers of a corporation. The doctrine of *ultra vires* is limited by modern statutes that allow a corporation to perform any lawful act and that prohibit the corporation or a third party from disaffirming a contract.

Uncertificated share: Share issued without a formal share certificate.

Uniform Commercial Code (UCC): Statute drafted by National Conference of Commissioners on Uniform State Laws and adopted by every state but Louisiana; governing the sale of goods, leases, bulk transfers, secured transactions, and so forth; state variations exist.

Unknown claim: Claim that has not yet been made against an entity.

Unlimited liability: Liability not limited to a party's investment in an enterprise but which rather may be satisfied from the investor's other, personal assets, savings, and property (also called personal liability).

Unsecured debt: Debt for which no property is pledged as collateral to secure repayment of the loan; in the event of default, a creditor must sue the debtor to recover money loaned to the debtor.

Vicarious liability: Liability imposed on another for an act that is not his or her fault; typically it is liability imposed on an employer for an employee's torts.

Voluntary dissolution: Dissolution of an entity initiated by the entity itself; with regard to a corporation, a dissolution initiated by corporate directors or shareholders.

Voting agreement: Agreement among shareholders specifying the manner in which they will vote. Sometimes called a pooling agreement.

Waiver of notice: Giving up the right to receive notice of some action or event, usually a meeting of directors or shareholders.

Watered stock: Stock issued for less than its par value (or for property or service worth less than its par value).

Williams Act: Federal law regulating tender offers and takeovers.

Winding up: *See* Liquidation.

Withdrawal: Request by an entity wishing to cease being qualified in a state in which it has transacted business.

Written consent: Action taken by board of directors or shareholders without necessity of meeting in person; most states require written consent to be unanimous.

Wrongful dissolution: Departure from a partnership in breach of partnership agreement.

Index